To Valerie, with Love, Jenny

DEBBIE PARKER

Copyright © 2020 by Debbie Parker.

ISBN   Softcover   978-1-950596-49-2

All rights reserved. No part of this book may be reproduced or transmitted in any form or by any means, electronic or mechanical, including photocopying, recording, or by any information storage and retrieval system without express written permission from the author, except in the case of brief quotations embodied in critical reviews and certain other non-commercial uses permitted by copyright law.

Printed in the United States of America.

To order additional copies of this book, contact:
Bookwhip
1-855-339-3589
https://www.bookwhip.com

This book is dedicated to my mother. I miss you and wish we could have had more time.

To my sister, Valerie, I will always wonder what goes on in your mind and how much you really understand.

To my sister, Dela, thank you for always helping me take care of Valerie. I'm still waiting for you to return my fur coat.

To my niece, Anna, you've been a tremendous help to me, more than you'll ever realize.

Lastly, to anyone who has ever had a dream, it's never too late for dreams to come true.

CONTENTS

Chapter 1. Beginnings 1
Chapter 2. Ooo Baby Baby 10
Chapter 3. Don't Pull Your Love 13
Chapter 4. Oh Girl 19
Chapter 5. No Matter What 30
Chapter 6. I Think I Love You 40
Chapter 7. Burning Love 47
Chapter 8. A Beautiful Morning 60
Chapter 9. Seasons In The Sun 72
Chapter 10. All I Have To Do Is Dream 84
Chapter 11. I Heard It Through The Grapevine 94
Chapter 12. Because 101
Chapter 13. Two Out Of Three Ain't Bad 108
Chapter 14. Everything I Own 118
Chapter 15. The Long And Winding Road 126
Chapter 16. Sooner Or Later 133
Chapter 17. Don't Give Up On Us 141
Chapter 18. Hello, It's Me 150
Chapter 19. The Rain, The Park, And Other Things 161
Chapter 20. Cherish 175
Chapter 21. Undercover Angel 184
Chapter 22. Yesterday Once More 193
Chapter 23. I Got a Name 198

Chapter 24. This Diamond Ring 206
Chapter 25. Ma Belle Amie 212
Chapter 26. Reflections Of My Life 221
Chapter 27. Traces Of Love 233
Chapter 28. The Letter... 246

About the Author...251

CHAPTER ONE

Beginnings

It was May, 1972, the last day of junior high for Valerie. She sat at her desk with her head down, and her forehead resting on her left arm. She ignored the paper airplanes descending on her head, but she could no longer ignore being shot by rubber bands. She knew who the shooter was, and he quickly buried his face in a book when she lifted her head. If Jason were a little taller, with a little more meat on his bones, she might return the affection he's had for her since elementary school.

There were still twenty-five minutes left until the bell rang. Since Mr. Duncan, the science teacher, stepped out of the room, many of her classmates took the opportunity to get an early start on their summer vacation. Valerie decided that she would do the same. She gathered her belongings, and sneaked out of the classroom; down the hall, down the stairs, and finally, exited the building.

Once the heavy door closed behind her, making a loud banging sound, she knew she was on borrowed time; in a few minutes she might encounter a teacher whose curiosity of the loud noise would lead them to find her sneaking away. It was too close to the end of her time in junior high for her to get into trouble over a few minutes' worth of truancy. She ran two blocks to the corner convenience store, hoping that her friends, Karen and Debra, would be along soon. They often stopped by this store after school to get a bottle of soda, and snacks for the walk home. The idea of drinking a cold beverage was especially inviting on this day, as the temperature rose to 98 degrees. This was sweltering weather for May, even in the town of Crystal Springs, Texas.

Minutes after the bell rang, Karen and Debra caught up with Valerie. After the girls made their snack purchases, they started for home. Valerie's house was the first stop on their way. She lived there with her parents, Frank and Anna Negron. Frank was eleven years older than Anna. They had three daughters, the youngest being Valerie, who was the last still living at home. Each of Anna's pregnancies had been unplanned, but cherished.

Every house in the neighborhood which Valerie lived had a nice big yard, with at least half an acre. Both one and two-story homes lined the blocks; most had long driveways leading to the back, where there might also be a garage. Parked in Valerie's garage was a blue, 1964 Ford Mustang. It belonged to Frank, but since he bought a pickup truck, the mustang was rarely used. The house also had a front porch, which wrapped around to one side. An assortment of trees provided pecans, shade, and a place to hang a tire swing.

As the girls approached Valerie's house, they noticed an unfamiliar black sports car parked on the front lawn.

"Get a load of that, whose car is it, Valerie?" asked Debra.

"One of Didi's boyfriends must have bought a new car, or maybe Didi got a new boyfriend," Valerie said, affectionately referring to her sister, Delores, as Didi.

"Your sister sure does have a lot of boyfriends, and look at her washing that car; she makes everything look sexy," said Debra. "She's my hero."

"Mine too," said Karen.

Six years older than Valerie, Delores is tall, like their father. Her hourglass figure empowered her to, effortlessly, draw attention from men. Her hair was blond, a medium shade of amber, and it was long. She usually complemented her blue eyes by wearing blue or turquoise eyeshadow. She wore white hot pants, which had a red and blue peace sign patch sewn on the rear, and a yellow happy face patch sewn on the front, below the zipper. Her red t-shirt was very tight fitting, perhaps it was a size too small. It was cut at the torso, something Delores frequently did to alter her t-shirts, allowing her to reveal her toned abs. She also removed the sleeves, and the collar, giving it a whole new look.

Most of Delores' boyfriends were guys she met in college, but she also enjoyed the advantages that went along with dating older men; such as romantic weekend getaways, using their credit cards, and driving around in their expensive sports cars.

As she dunked the sponge into a bucket of water, then onto the car, she carelessly spilled a generous amount of water on her t-shirt. She seemed to enjoy turning the mundane task of washing a car into an erotic performance. As cars drove by the house, some drivers slowed down to get a better look at her. An alluring glance from Delores prompted a few guys to pull over, maybe in hopes of a private show at a later time.

"Hey, Val, do you think Delores would give us a ride in the cool sports car?" Debra asked.

"We can ask, but I'll have to be nice to her. I was nice to her yesterday, this will make two days in a row," Valerie grumbled.

Walking up to the driveway, their greetings to Delores were ignored. Valerie had learned, over time, that the best way to get her sister's attention was to pay her a compliment. Flattery, albeit insincere, was powerful rhetoric when properly used.

"Hi, Didi," said Valerie. "You look foxy! These guys must think so too, look how slow they're driving by to get a better look at you."

"Yeah, they are," said Delores.

"But they could also be checking out this groovy car. It's bad-ass! Whose is it?"

"Grow up, Valerie. You have a lot to learn about men. If you were washing this car, you can bet these guys would be slowing down to look at the car."

"Well, excuse me! Whose car is it, anyway?"

"It belongs to a friend of mine, he's letting me use it while he's out of town. I promised him that I would take care of it while he was gone."

"Well, how about a ride? I've never been in a sports car."

"Dream on, Dipwad," Delores said, while looking at her audience, which has now grown by a few more cars.

She made eye contact with a guy in an El Camino, who parked in front of the house. He was good looking, enough so that Delores smiled at him, and gave him the peace sign. Their enchanted stares came to a halt when Priscilla, Frank and Anna's oldest daughter, drove up in her gold Plymouth Duster. Not quite proficient at driving a four-speed transmission, her abrupt stop caused her passengers' shopping bags to ricochet off the back seat. She and her parents just returned from the hourlong drive to San Antonio.

Priscilla, like Valerie, resembled their mother. They had long, dark hair, and brown eyes. While Delores had a fair complexion; Priscilla and Valerie had a medium skin tone, like that of Anna, who had a mixed heritage of German and Mexican. Priscilla was intelligent, and gifted; she was able to graduate from high school at the age of fifteen.

After moving to Austin to attend college, she graduated summa cum laude from the University of Texas. Then at the age of eighteen, she became the youngest person to enroll in law school. Now at twenty-two, she was married to Michael; an established attorney practicing law at his family's firm in San Antonio. Just about every attorney who worked at the firm was a family member, either by blood or marriage. Priscilla looked forward to joining the firm after she passed the bar exam, which she was prepared to take.

It took Frank a few minutes after exiting the car to recover from the effects of whiplash. He kept his pain to himself, not wanting to complain for the sake of his oldest daughter's feelings.

"Thank you for taking your mother and me to the city, Princess."

"You're welcome, Dad. Anytime," said Priscilla.

Frank became annoyed seeing a car parked on his lawn.

"Whose car is this?" he asked.

"Sorry, Dad," Delores answered. "I'll move it in a few minutes."

"Well, whose car is it? Where's your Pinto?" asked Anna.

"It belongs to a friend, Mom. The Pinto is parked at Jennifer's house. You know Jennifer."

"Delores, you didn't pay almost $1700 for a brand-new car just to have it parked at Jennifer's house. Are you able to keep up with the payments? The repo man isn't looking for it, is he?"

"I'm making the payments, Mom. It's just parked there while I'm driving this car."

"Who is this guy parked in front of the house, and why are these other cars driving by so slow?" asked Frank.

When he didn't get an answer to his question, he yelled at the driver of the El Camino.

"What are doing in front of my house? Huh? What are you looking at? How would you like a knuckle sandwich?"

The driver of the El Camino immediately drove off, which prompted the others to follow suit, abandoning their lustful hopes of a later encounter with Delores.

"Dad, you wouldn't hit him, would you?" asked Delores.

"No, of course not. I'm just having fun."

Frank shook his head in dismay when he noticed the revealing outfit Delores was wearing. He was not happy with her style of clothing; he wanted her to dress modestly, like Priscilla. He blamed her provocative style of dress on Anna; when Delores was a little girl, Anna took her to see a Marilyn Monroe movie. Since then, Delores developed a flair for tight fitting, low plunging blouses, and very short skirts.

"Where did you get this car, Delores?"

"It belongs to a friend, Dad."

"What friend?"

"You don't know him."

"That's not what I asked you. What's his name?"

"It doesn't matter, you don't know him."

Sensing trouble brewing, as it usually did with Delores and her father, Karen and Debra decided that it would be best if they went home. Though they had never actually been present during the shouting matches between Delores and her father, Valerie had always given them the play by play on her sister's antics, and they knew it would be best to leave.

"Delores, I wish you wouldn't borrow expensive cars from your friends. You never know what could happen. You don't want that responsibility," Anna said.

"It's not a big deal, Mom."

"You need to change your clothes," said Frank. "Your shorts are too short, and your blouse is … is that a blouse?"

"It's a t-shirt, Dad. I designed it myself. Do you like it?"

Frank's deep-seated aversion to Delores' wardrobe translated to a look of unsettledness on his face.

"Dad, can Didi take me for a ride in her sports car?"

"And another thing," said Frank, "I want you to return this car. Like your mother said, we don't like you accepting this sort of thing from people. You have too many boyfriends. You need to focus on school, not boys. Now give your sister a ride around the block before you return this car."

"I'm not giving Valerie a ride, she's a dork."

"Honey, there's no reason for you to be so rude to Valerie," Anna said. "She just wants to ride in the fancy sports car. After all, you're the one who's showing it off."

"That's not all she's showing off," Valerie said, sarcastically.

"Valerie, don't start with your sister," Frank said. "Delores, I've already told you to change your clothes, and take Valerie for a ride."

"That's alright, Dad," said Valerie. "I don't want to ride in the dumb car, anyway. It probably stinks." Valerie opened the car door, and waved her hand in front of her nose. "Whew! It smells like someone was getting it on right there on the leather seat. Didi, is that where he popped your cherry?"

"Valerie! That's enough!" Frank shouted.

"Sorry, Dad. I forgot, Didi got her cherry popped a long time ago; way before she got this car."

"Valerie Lynne Negron," Frank said, sharply, "you get in the house, right now."

"Okay, Dad, I'm sorry."

"This is why I won't take you for a ride, Valerie. You're a little dipwad," Delores said.

"Girls, that's enough. Valerie, what did I tell you about getting in the house? Delores, what have I told you about your clothes?"

"I don't live here, Dad, so you can't tell me what to do."

In no time flat, a flaming blaze of crimson replaced the natural hues in Frank's face. His clenched fists caused his knuckles to turn white as he slowly walked towards Delores. Standing face to face with his middle daughter, he slowly began to count to ten, reaching as far as the number five, before she interrupted him.

"Dad, I'm sorry. Don't be mad. I'll take Valerie for a ride in the car," she said, with regret. She hugged her father, who stood rigid, and unyielding. Pulling away from her, he took her hands into his, and gave them a tight squeeze.

"Delores, my lovely girl. Don't ever come to my house, and speak to me that way. And don't ever come to my house dressed like a two-bit party girl, have some self-respect. You need to take this car back to whatever playboy, going through a midlife crisis, you got it from; then you need to stay away from him. I'm sure that his wife would appreciate it."

Without catching sight of anyone else, Frank turned to make his way to the house.

"Why do you always have to start trouble?" asked Priscilla. "You've upset Dad. You know that he wanted to take us out to dinner tonight so that he and Mom could make their special announcement to Valerie. Now you've ruined it."

"Announcement? What announcement? About what?" asked Valerie.

Priscilla and Delores looked at their mother, while she looked at her manicured hands to avoid eye contact with her youngest daughter.

"Mom, what's this announcement?" asked Valerie.

Anna remained silent for a moment, before reminding Valerie that her father told her to go into the house.

"Alright, I'll go inside. I'll ask Dad, he'll tell me."

"Dad is really ticked off, Valerie. He's not going to tell you anything," Delores said.

"He's not mad at me, he's mad at you," Valerie said, before running into the house.

"He's mad at you too!" Delores shouted at her sister. She turned to her mother and asked, "Mom, how mad do you think that Dad is? Should I still go to dinner with y'all tonight?"

"Delores, honey, I haven't seen your father this angry since ... well, I've never seen him this angry. You know your father, he's easy going. You shouldn't have talked to him that way. As it is, he's still a little high strung about my condition. It came as a surprise to him, really to both of us. I guess sometimes the Rhythm Method isn't the most effective way. Maybe I should try something else. I've heard something about a pill, I wonder if it works. What do you girls use?"

"Mom, please," said Priscilla.

"I'll tell you what I use, Mom," said Delores. "Because I don't think the Rhythm Method works very well if you have a little too much to drink, and Dad usually has a little too much to drink when he's celebrating."

"Ain't that the truth? Your father did a little too much celebrating the night of your uncle Jim's wedding. I lost track of how many beers he had. But that's alright, I like when he's a little tipsy. Do you know why? I'll tell you why; because when your father drinks, he really turns me on. Well, he turns me on anyway, even when he's sober, so I guess it doesn't matter if he drinks. But we did have a lot of fun that night of Jimmy's wedding. And all night long he told me how gorgeous, and sexy I looked. 'Annie,' he said to me, 'you look gorgeous in that dress.' And then he said, 'Annie, that dress really accentuates your curves. You're driving me wild.' I'm telling you, girls, your father couldn't keep his hands off of me; even more than usual."

"Mom, I don't want to know," Priscilla said, prudishly.

"Well, your father bought that dress for me. It was a little more low-cut than I usually wear, but he really liked it. When we were slow dancing, he said to me, 'Annie, you look very sexy in that dress. I love the way it hugs your body, and I can't wait till we get home, so I can …"

"Mom!" Priscilla interrupted. "Please don't start again with that story. We already know where babies come from, and how much you and Dad enjoy each other. Believe me, Didi and I have heard the sounds of love come from your bedroom, more times that we can count. We were the only kids at school to learn about the birds and the bees from the sounds we heard our parents make while they were in their bedroom. We could hear you all the way downstairs! Another thing, what's uncle Jim on, his third or fourth wife? He needs to settle down already."

"Jim's on his fourth wife, and I didn't know it was a crime for a husband to show his wife affection," Anna said.

"I'm sorry, Mom. I shouldn't have snapped at you. I just meant that the details of what you and Dad do in the bedroom should be kept to yourself. Don't you think? But I am happy about the outcome. A baby is always a happy occasion."

"That's alright, dear. I know that your father and I tend to get a bit loud. I mean, your father is quite a lover."

"Okay, Mom. This is what I mean when I say that you should keep the details to yourself."

"I'm happy for you too, Mom," Delores said, "and I don't mind hearing the details. I'm grateful for how I learned about sex. That's how my friend, Jennifer, learned about it too."

"Jennifer's parents are pretty active? Good for them!" said Anna.

"No, Jennifer learned all about it the same as I did; by overhearing you and Dad in the bedroom. Mom, what should I do about Dad?"

"Delores, you have to return that car. If your father sees it again, he's not going to be happy with you. And neither will I. It's wrong, dear."

"Alright, Mom. I'm sorry."

"Goodbye, sweetheart," Anna said, as she kissed Delores' cheek. "Don't cry. I want you to come over tomorrow, I'm making spaghetti. Mike's coming too, isn't he, Priscilla?"

"Yes, he'll be here," said Priscilla. "Bye, Didi. See ya tomorrow. Go get your car from Jennifer, and give this one back. He's not the guy for you, but another will be along soon. I promise. You'll be alright." She hugged her sister before walking into the house with their mother.

CHAPTER TWO

Ooo Baby Baby

Valerie could hardly contain her excitement as she sat in the living room, waiting for her father to come downstairs to reveal the big announcement. She wondered about the big news; could it be that they were getting new furniture? Probably not, Frank just bought the orange and white floral living room set a few months before. He got the sofa and loveseat, but didn't get the matching chair. He didn't want to spend the money on a new chair when there was nothing wrong with the chair they already had; it was comfortable enough for him. It was a green velvet, Victorian style accent chair with an ottoman that didn't match. Valerie hated the chair; the color didn't go with the new set, and she thought it was ugly. Maybe the announcement was about summer vacation. She had always wanted to go to Disneyland, though they usually went camping. With the exception of Delores, the family looked forward to their camping trips.

As Valerie anxiously waited for her father, she noticed that the pendulum on the grandfather clock was not swinging; so, she had no idea how long she had been waiting. She felt as if she had been waiting for an eternity, when it had actually been only a few minutes. Just as Anna and Priscilla walked into the house, Frank joined the family in the living room. Valerie jumped up from the sofa to greet her father.

"So? Dad? What's going on?" Valerie asked. "I can't wait another minute! Not even another second! I'm dying to know what's going on, I'm literally dying."

"Valerie, you're not literally dying," Priscilla said.

"Come here, Cupcake," Frank said. "I've always called you my Cupcake because you're so sweet, and I love cupcakes." He took her hand into his, "Your mother and I have some great news, it's pretty exciting."

"What, Dad? What's going on? This seems heavy, man."

"Valerie, do you know what it means when someone says, the rabbit died?"

"A rabbit died? Oh no, poor rabbit. Dad, that makes me sad. Whose rabbit was it? Why haven't you ever got me a rabbit before?"

"Valerie, it's not a real rabbit, it's an expression. What I mean is, we're going to have an addition to our family."

"An addition? Are we getting a dog? Yay! We're getting a dog! Finally, do you know how long I've wanted a dog? I've wanted a dog since forever; that's a long time, Dad."

"We're not getting a dog, it's better than a dog. Valerie, you're going to have a baby brother or baby sister."

"What? Get out! Jeepers creepers, is this true? That's gross, Dad!" Valerie had a repulsive look on her face as she withdrew her hand from her father's, and took a few steps back.

"Valerie," her mother said, as she took her by the arm, "your father and I are excited that we're going to have another baby."

"What's to be excited about? It's a bummer. It's embarrassing to the max!"

"Valerie!" Frank snapped. "Don't speak to your mother that way."

"I'm sorry, Dad. It's just that … you're both old. Mom's too old to be having a baby, and you're like a dinosaur. I thought that when people get old, then they couldn't do *it* anymore. But if Mom's going to have a baby, that means that you and her still do *it*. Eew! What a nightmare! I can't believe that you two still do *it*. Do you do *it* in this house? The house that I live in? Is that why the door to your room is always closed? Is that when y'all are doing *it*? Oh, please! How freaky-deaky is that? That's it! We have to move! We'll have to buy another house! I can't live here anymore! Every time I walk through this house, I'm going to wonder, 'Did Mom and Dad do *it* in this room? Did Mom and Dad do *it* in that room?' I'm always going to wonder!"

"Valerie, you need to settle down. Just because your mother and I may be a little older than a lot of parents are when they have children, doesn't mean that we're too old."

"Yeah, it does, Dad. I'm fourteen years old, and Priscilla and Didi are already old too. We're too old to have a baby brother or baby sister, and you and Mom are too old to still be doing *it*."

"Hey, I'm not that old," Priscilla said.

"Valerie," Anna chimed in, "lots of people have children when they are older."

"Not people that I know. If old people have babies, then the babies will be born deformed. Didn't you know that? I thought everybody knew that. Mom, do you know what you need to do? You need to get an abortion. And then after that, you and Dad shouldn't ever do *it* again. Ever."

"That's enough, Valerie. I won't have another daughter disrespecting me, or your mother."

"Dad, I'm not disrespecting you, but I don't want you and Mom to have another baby. Can't you see that you're both too old? And even if it's not deformed, who's going to change the diapers? Not me! I don't know how to use those big ole safety pins. What if I poked myself? I can't stand the sight of blood!"

"Valerie, go to your room," Anna said, trying to hold back her tears.

"Okay, fine! I'll go to my room, but you don't need to have another baby! I'd rather have a dog!" she screamed, as she stormed off.

Priscilla put her arms around her mother's shoulders. "She didn't mean it, Mom. She's just a kid, she doesn't know what she's saying."

"Come on, Annie. Come on, Princess. We're still going out to celebrate. I've had this evening planned for days. I'm not going to let Delores or Valerie ruin it," Frank said.

Valerie looked out the window; she watched as her parents, and sister drove away. "How could they do this to me?" she asked herself. "I'd rather have a dog."

She cried, as she envisioned a life with a deformed baby brother or sister. Though she could not begin to imagine the impact her new sibling would have on her life. How, in the course of time, a freakish circumstance would bring about a friendship that she could never imagine.

CHAPTER THREE

Don't Pull Your Love

Christmas was Valerie's favorite time of the year, and it was fast approaching. However, since she was a little bummed out about the impending arrival of her new sibling, she wasn't as festive as she usually would be. Since there was nothing she could do about the situation, she decided to make the best of it. Expressing her anguish in the form of writing in her diary proved to be therapeutic.

A week before Christmas, Frank asked Valerie to help him with some shopping. She was anxious to get out of the house, so she followed her father outside, and jumped in the front seat of the pickup truck. Most of the time, she rode in the truck bed, but it was cold that morning.

"Your mother usually does all the shopping, and I sign my name to the tag. But she's tired, she needs her rest."

"I don't mind, Daddy. I'll close my eyes when you get to my gift. But will Mom be alright? I mean, what if the baby comes while we're out?"

"She'll be fine. Delores will be over soon, and besides, we won't be gone long. Maybe an hour."

"An hour? Dad, that's not enough time to shop for everyone. This could take hours, maybe all day. I hope you're not going to use the green stamps for your shopping. We almost have enough books filled up to get a color TV. I really need one for my room because I want Karen and Debra to come over so we can watch our favorite show in color; we're tired of watching it in black and white. Neither one of them has a color TV. Debra's mom just bought new dishes with their stamps, and Karen's mom is saving for new drapes for their living room. That means that I have to be the one to get a color TV, Dad."

"Your favorite show? Is that the one with the guy that sings, and his mother drives a psychedelic school bus. What do you call him? A fox?"

"Dad, I'm going to marry him, someday. He'll be your son-in-law."

"First, he'll have to get a haircut; then we'll see. But don't worry, Cupcake. I'm not going to use your stamps. Your mother has already taken care of most of the shopping, but there is one special gift that I still have to get. It's for someone very special."

"Do you mean Mom?"

"No, not for your mother. I give your mother something special every night, when we go to bed."

"Daddy! Please! There are some things that I just don't want to know."

"You don't want to know that I read the Bible to mother every night when we go to bed? It's a beautiful thing, Valerie. Last night I read her Proverbs; it talks about a virtuous woman. Your mother is a virtuous woman."

"Sorry, Dad. I thought you were talking about something else."

"I know what you thought, that's alright. We do that too, after we read the Bible."

"Dad!"

"What? It's okay, we're married. Anyway, that's in the Bible too. Don't you pay attention in Sunday school? Or to Pastor Craig's sermons?"

"Yes, Dad. Most of the time, I do. But sometimes I fall asleep."

"You're not supposed to sleep in church, Cupcake."

"I know, but sometimes Pastor Craig's sermons make me sleepy. Where are we going, anyway? Downtown is the other way. It looks like we're going out to the country."

"Well, the special gift that I want to give you is not something that I can get from the stamp redemption center or a department store. I have to come all the way out here to pick it up."

"Me? The special gift is for me?"

"Of course, Cupcake. You're my youngest child; for now, anyway."

"Thanks, Dad. But why are we driving out to the country? What could my special gift possibly be? There are no stores out here. Not even very many houses; it looks like a bunch of farms. Look at that house; it's pretty. So is that one. Dad, some of these houses are beautiful. I wish we lived here. But look at this one coming up. It looks rundown. It could be haunted. Dad, why are you turning into this driveway? This house could be haunted."

"It's not haunted, Valerie."

"Well, the driveway is not even paved, what a nightmare! Why are we coming here? Who lives here in this rickety old house?"

"Come on, Valerie. Let's get out."

"Dad, what about my gift?"

"Let's see my rickety old friend who lives in this rickety old house."

The enthusiasm Valerie had for shopping, minutes before, rapidly soured as she trailed her father on the path leading to the house.

"Dad, this house doesn't even have a sidewalk. My shoes will get dirty."

"Quit being so dramatic, Valerie. See this tree?"

"I see a tree branch sticking out of the ground pretending to be a tree."

"Well, it's a little puny right now, but in a few years this will be a big, and tall pecan tree. I cut this from the tree we have in our yard. Max has always wanted a pecan tree so I helped him out. Come on, let's see Max. He's probably out back."

"Dad, my shoes!"

"Use the stepping stones, Valerie."

Frank walked ahead of Valerie, around to the back of the house.

"This is a load of bull," she said to herself.

She had to hurry to catch up with her father, who was now out of sight. The backyard was fenced; it had a wire fence with a gate that her father left partially opened for her. She carefully squeezed through, trying not to let any part of her body touch the gate. She walked towards her father, who was talking to an old man wearing dingy overalls. The old man wasn't wearing a winter coat, but he didn't seem to be bothered by the cold weather.

As Valerie approached her father, she began to feel annoyed at being there. Frank offered a quick introduction before walking away, leaving Valerie to fend for herself with the old man. Reluctantly, she took his hand, which he extended to her for a handshake. His grip was firm, leaving her hand feeling a bit crushed. The whole ordeal lasted a little longer than a usual handshake, forcing Valerie to escape by wiggling her hand to break his hold.

"Ya must be Valrie," said the old man.

"No duh," Valerie said, under her breath. Out loud, she said, "Yes, sir. I'm Valerie, it's nice to meet you."

"Valrie, last time I seen ya was when yur daddy take us all ta San Antone, back in '68. Ya 'member? He take us all ta the big fair o'er at the tall buildin'. I never seen a buildin' so tall before, almost touched the sky."

"Do you mean the Hemisfair Tower in San Antonio? Yes, sir, I remember."

"That sur was fun. Look at ya now, Valrie, all grown up an just 'bout as purdy as yur mama."

"Thank you, sir."

"Ya like animals? I hear ya like animals. In particulars, I hear ya like dogs. Do ya like dogs, Valrie?"

"I've always wanted a dog, sir. Well, I've wanted a rabbit, too. Either a dog or a rabbit."

"Naw, ya don't want no rabbit. Ya never know when yur daddy might not gitter paycheck an yur mama hafta do what she needs ta do ta git food on the table. Ya know what I mean? Cain't tell ya how many pets me an my brother got when we was kids. Ya know, dogs, cats, birds, rabbits, squirrels; once we even got a possum, an some of 'em ended up as Sunday supper. Not the dogs or cats, but 'em other critters. I din't know mama cooked Peter til I was eatin' on my second plate. He sure turn out ta be tasty grub."

"Was Peter your possum, or squirrel?"

He gave her a quick wink along with a semi-toothless smile.

"Neither. Peter was a rabbit. I got him 'bout couple er weeks before mama got hold a him. A dog's better, don't ya think? People don't never wanna eat a dog. At least not people 'round here. I don't know 'bout 'em people in 'em other countries, but people here in this country, Texas, we don't do that."

"No, sir, we don't. Not the people here, in this country of Texas," she said, with a bit of sarcasm. She had to come up with a quick plan to ditch the old man. "Oh, darn it! I just remembered that I… um… uh… well … uh … I forgot to flush the toilet this morning. Me and my dad should be getting home so that I could do that. My mother will be very upset if she finds out." Valerie called out to her father, "Dad? Where are you? We need to get going."

"Awe, that ain't nothin' ya gotta worry 'bout," said the old man. "I flusher once a day 'round here. But I use the dang toilet all day long. It waste lot a water e'ry time ya flush. Did ya know that?"

"No, sir. I didn't know that. I'll bet my father doesn't know that either. I should tell him, he'd want to know."

Again, Valerie called out to her father, "Dad?"

"Valerie, I know about that. It's good advice, a good money-saving tip. Come here, I want to show you something."

"Okay, Dad. I'll be right there," she said. "Sir, I have to go see what my dad wants. But I've enjoyed our conversation."

"Ya did? Well, c'mon o'er ta the house sometime, anytime ya want."

"Okay, thank you, sir," Valerie said, before turning to her father. "Dad! I'm coming."

When Valerie was about ten feet away from her father, he walked up a little further, towards the barn. He called out to her to follow him.

"Dad, what are we doing here? Let's blow this taco stand. Come on, let's book it on out of here so we can get my gift."

"Valerie, your gift is here. Max was nice enough to help me out with that."

"Here? Where? We're on a stinky old farm. Dad, I remember that old man. He broke Mrs. Beasley's string. She hasn't been able to talk since. Do you remember?"

"He's not that old, Valerie. And yes, I remember that you hadn't played with Mrs. Beasley for a long time, and Max accidently pulled the string too hard, and it broke. But he gave you jewelry to make up for it."

"Jewelry? He gave me a candy necklace that was half eaten. Why are you hanging around an old man, anyway?"

"He's my friend, and he's only a few years older than me. He looks a lot older because he's had a rough life. He's been working this farm since he was a kid. Your uncles and I grew up on a farm too, but all we raised were chickens. Max used to sell us milk, bacon, and beef. Sometimes my dad didn't have enough money to pay for it, Max used to let us slide. He wasn't able to go to school, so he has no education. But he sure is a heck of a farmer, and he's helped plenty of us folks around here. His wife died last year, she had cancer. She was a very sweet woman, very good to you and your mother."

"I'm sorry to hear that, Dad. Did they have any kids? I don't remember any."

"He has a daughter, about Delores' age. His sons were both killed in Vietnam."

"Dad, I'm sorry. I'm very sorry for being rude about coming here. You made me so mad for bringing me to this stinky old farm."

"Cupcake, don't pull your love out on me."

"No, Daddy, I would never do that. I'm a little ashamed of myself."

"Don't be. Maybe this will make you feel better."

Frank opened the door to the barn, and led Valerie inside.

"Valerie, I'd like you to meet the latest addition to our family."

"Dad! It's a baby dog!"

"A baby dog is called a puppy, Valerie."

"I know that, I just forgot. I'm excited! Is this for me? Is this my gift?"

"She's all yours, Valerie. Do you like her?"

"I love her. Thank you, Daddy. Thank you so much."

"Are you still mad at me?"

"No, Daddy, I could never stay mad at you."

"I'm glad that you like your gift, Valerie. This is the last gift that I give to you, as my youngest child. These next few days will be the last days that you will be my youngest child."

"But I'll always be your Cupcake. Right, Dad?"

"Yes, you will. You will always be my Cupcake."

"Thank you, Daddy. This is the best gift that you've ever given me."

"You're welcome, Cupcake."

CHAPTER FOUR

Oh Girl

Valerie played with her puppy on the living room floor. Her mother rested on the couch, with her feet up. Her weight had steadily climbed during her last trimester. As her mother watched her play with her puppy, Valerie hoped that she hadn't noticed the stains in the carpet from the earlier instances when her puppy peed and pooped on the floor. The spots were hardly noticeable; she cleaned up what she could, and what she couldn't get clean, blended seamlessly into the orange shag carpet.

"What are you going to name your puppy?" asked her mother. "You've had her for two days now. She needs a name."

"I know, I'm still thinking about it. I kind of like the name, Trixie, like the baby from the Sunday comics. But it's a people name. Do you think it's alright to name her a people name?"

"I think it's fine. You can name her what you want to name her."

"What are you going to name the baby, Mom? Have you and Dad thought about the name?"

"Well, if it's a boy, your father wants to name him Anthony, after his father; and we would call him Tony. But I want to name him after your father, Francis Robert."

"What? Dad's name is Frances? You gotta be joshin'. That's a girls' name."

"Frances with an E, is a girl's name; Francis with an I, is a boys' name. Just like Frank Sinatra."

"Really? That's looney. What about if it's a girl?"

"We can't decide. Your father wants to name her Sandra Irene, after my mother, but I want to name her Myrtle, after my grandmother."

"Myrtle? Mom, nobody names their baby Myrtle. That's old-fashioned, like from the 1800's. Why not Sandra Irene, like grandma?"

"I was close to my grandma, Myrtle. She died shortly after Delores was born. She was sweet, and kind, and she loved my growing family. I loved my mother, but I don't want my daughter's initials to be S.I.N."

"Well, you should have named Didi, Sandra Irene. Those initials are perfect for her."

"Valerie, that's not nice."

"Okay, Mom."

"Hello, everyone."

"Michael, where's Priscilla?" Valerie asked.

"Hi, Dollface. She's talking to your dad, outside. Hi, Anna. How are you feeling? Is it almost time?"

"Almost," said Anna.

"Is Didi here yet? I hear that she has a new boyfriend, and he may be the *one*," Michael said.

Delores was to arrive soon, with Jeff, her new boyfriend. Though she had always managed to nab men who were attractive, and charming, Jeff was unlike the slew of users and losers that made their way through the turnstile of Delores' bedroom. Valerie took an instant liking to him, and he took an interest in her, asking her about school, and about her hobbies.

A short time after Priscilla and Michael arrived, Delores arrived with Jeff. Valerie introduced the newest member of the family, Trixie, to her sisters. Priscilla thought the name, Trixie, was cute; while Delores expressed her disapproval.

"Oh, Doll, she's adorable. Come here, Trixie, let me pet you. You are so cute. Yes, you are. Yes, you are," Priscilla said, in a high-pitched, exaggerated tone; similar to the tone one uses when talking to babies.

"What kind of dog is she?" asked Delores. "She looks like a mutt."

"She's a mixed breed. Who cares what kind of dog she is? She's beautiful, and I love her."

"Valerie, Trixie is not a dog's name, it's a human name. There's a girl in my sorority named Trixie," said Delores.

"Really? Did you steal her boyfriend when she had her back turned?"

Delores gave Valerie the evil eye, before walking away. After the coast was clear, Jeff divulged a secret to Valerie, by whispering in her ear; "That was Jennifer."

Frank turned on the TV in the living room, so that he and the men could catch a football game. He stretched out on the couch, Michael sat on the loveseat with his legs up, while Jeff sat on the ugly chair. Valerie helped Priscilla fix sandwiches for lunch. Delores and Anna sat at the kitchen table, where Delores fascinated Anna with the details of her whirlwind romance with her new, ruggedly handsome boyfriend. For the most part, their conversation was at a normal sound level. Every now and then, voices were reduced to whispers. Valerie imagined that was when the discussion took a spin to the topic of sex. The look of exhilaration on her mother's face confirmed it. After a while of stimulating conversation between Anna and Delores, Delores jumped up from the chair, and shouted at Frank.

"Dad! Get over here! Now! It's Mom! It's time!"

"Are you sure?" Frank asked, running to Anna. "Aren't you supposed to time it or something? Didn't we time it when Valerie was born? We were just about to eat in a few minutes."

"Dad, look at her face," Delores said. "You need to take her to the hospital, right now."

"Annie, do I need to take you to the hospital right now? Could it be false labor?" Frank asked.

"Frank, WHOA... take me. I've been having contractions for a while now."

"Why didn't you say anything, Mom?" asked Delores.

"Because, Delores, I love to hear you talk about your boyfriends. But I need to get to the hospital now. Frank, we need to go," Anna moaned.

"Alright, let's go," Frank said.

Before doing anything, he grabbed a couple of sandwiches which were already cut into triangles. He quickly gulped them down. Then he took Anna by the arm, and grabbed her overnight bag; which was already packed, and near the doorway. He walked her outside to the pickup truck, and helped her in. Within a few minutes, they were off to the hospital.

Delores put the food away in the refrigerator while Priscilla called Gina, to let her know what was going on. Gina was Frank's sister-in-law, married to Danny, Frank's younger brother. Jim was the youngest of the Negron brothers, and the best looking of the three. He was on his fourth marriage, which, after only a few months, had hit the rocks. Since childhood, the brothers have shared a close bond, so naturally, they'd want to be at the hospital for the birth of their brother's last child. Danny and Gina had a son, Mario, about the same age as Delores. He recently moved to Lubbock to attend Texas Tech University. Jim was childless, by choice.

"Valerie, you can ride with us to the hospital," Jeff said.

"Okay," Valerie replied, "I'll ride with you and Didi."

Michael and Jeff stayed with Valerie in the lobby of the hospital as she napped. Upon waking up, they took her to Anna's room. She didn't know what to expect when she met her new sibling. To some extent, she was still apprehensive about her parents having another baby, and the uncertainty her new sibling would bring. At the same time, the notion of being someone's big sister ignited an unexpected thrill. Several hours after arriving at the hospital, Anna gave birth to a bouncing baby girl. Unbeknownst to Valerie, her new baby sister was born with Down syndrome. Other than that diagnosis, she appeared to be in good health.

Frank paid the hospital extra cash for a private room, so that his family could share the joy with Anna and him. Gina was crocheting a baby blanket while sitting in a chair next to Anna, who was sleeping. Frank and his brothers sat in a corner, on the floor, eating pizza; which Frank sneaked into the room under a blanket. Priscilla was sitting on a chair as she held the baby. Delores was next to her, sitting on the arm of the chair.

"Look at big sister, Valerie," Priscilla said to the baby. "Come here, Doll. Come and meet your baby sister."

Michael gently pushed Valerie in the direction of the baby. Then he and Jeff joined the men for some pizza.

"Hi, baby, I'm Valerie."

"Do you want to hold her, Valerie?" asked Priscilla.

"No, not right now. I just want to look at her. Is she alright? Is anything wrong with her?"

"Is anything wrong with you?" Delores asked Valerie. "Why would you ask that? I hope Mom didn't hear you."

"Didi, she didn't mean anything by it. Valerie, when Mom wakes up, we'll talk about things," Priscilla said.

"About what things?" Valerie asked.

Frank got up from the floor, and pulled up a chair next to Priscilla. He instructed Valerie to sit close by. Looking adoringly at his four daughters, he gently caressed the baby's cheek as Priscilla held her.

"Girls, I love you so much. Your mother and I are truly blessed to have you as our daughters. Priscilla, my oldest girl, you're my Princess. I remember the day you were born; your mother was so young. Her mother, and your aunt Teresa were with her when she had you; her grandma Myrtle delivered you at home."

"I wasn't born in a hospital?"

"Nope. Valerie was the first baby on your mother's side of the family to be born in a hospital. Your great-grandma Myrtle delivered every single baby in the family. Rumor has it, she even gave birth to her own children without help from anyone. When the time came, she squat, and voila; there was your grandma Sandra. I don't know if that's true, but that's the rumor."

"That's crazy, Dad," said Priscilla.

"Yeah, your mother's family was crazy. Especially your grandpa. He liked to smoke that wacky tobacky. He was always getting high. Sometimes your uncle Jim would join him."

"That was some good stuff. I sure do miss that guy," said Jim. "You know your grandma Sandra used to beat him with a shoe? She beat me a couple of times too."

"I'm sure you deserved it, Jim," said Gina.

"Anyway," said Frank, "I wanted to name you Anna, after your mother. But she chose the name Priscilla, because she wanted to make her grandma happy. Your mother's aunt Priscilla died before your mother was born. Grandma Myrtle was so happy that we named you Priscilla. Then, years later, when Elvis Presley got married to a woman named Priscilla, your mother was beyond excited that her daughter, and Elvis' wife shared the same name. That's how much your mother loves Elvis."

"I know Mom loves Elvis. I think it's pretty cool that his wife and I have the same name. But, Dad, they're getting a divorce, did you know that?"

"No. They are not getting a divorce. Don't let your mother hear you talk that way."

"Yes, they are, Dad. They're separated right now. I read about it in a magazine. I have the magazine, if you want to read it."

"It's a lie," Frank said. "It's fake news. Don't believe everything you read in a gossip magazine. That's how they sell magazines, they make up lies."

"It's true, Dad. I read a magazine too," Delores said.

"It's not true, it's a bunch of malarkey," said Gina.

"See, Gina knows."

"Dad," Priscilla said.

"Not another word about it. It took your mother years to get over Lucy and Desi getting divorced. But Elvis and Priscilla getting a divorce? This will devastate her. She really loves him, and she loves when I impersonate him."

"Dad," said Priscilla, "you can't impersonate Elvis, no one can."

"My brother makes a good Elvis."

"See, Danny knows. Well, maybe I'm not that great. I mean, I know that no one can really impersonate Elvis, but sometimes, I put your mother's black cake mascara on my sideburns to exaggerate them, and I'll sing to her. She loves when I do that. My favorite is that song about the three wise men rushing in."

"No, Frank. Fools rush in, wise men said it. And there weren't three of them, no one really knows how many," said Gina.

"Well, I don't know all the words, but you know which song I mean. Your mother's favorite is Jailhouse Rock; she loves it! And I can really get into it. I shake my pelvis, I got the moves just like him. Your mother likes it when I make her quiver. Even just the other night, we were in the bedroom, and ..."

"Dad, please stop. I'm sure it was wonderful, but we really don't care."

Delores giggled, while Valerie looked squeamish.

Turning to Delores, Frank said, "Delores, you're my lovely girl. You were named Delores because your uncle Jimmy asked your mother if she would name you Delores, and your mother never says no to Jim."

"Really? Mom never says no to you, Uncle Jim?" asked Delores.

"Your mother and I are the same age; we were classmates. I asked her to go with me to the Spring Dance; she was thinking it over. She came over to the house to tell me her answer in person. Your father answered the door, and it was love at first sight for both of them. I think her answer would have been yes."

"Daddy, I never knew that you stole Mom away from Uncle Jim," said Delores.

"So why does Mom never say no to you, Uncle Jim?" asked Priscilla.

"Because she feels a little guilty," said Frank.

"Your mother has no reason to feel guilty; your father didn't steal her away from me. We never dated. If we had, she would have picked me," said Jim. "Look at me, then look at your father. You can't tell me that he's better looking."

"That's true," said Frank.

"So why did you name me Delores?"

"When I turned 18, Danny took me across the border for my birthday. We met some girls; we each had two girls, one for each arm. Remember, Danny?"

"Vaguely," said Danny, as he avoided eye contact with his wife, who was staring him down.

"One of the girls I was with, her name was Delores. I have never been able to get her out of my mind. She was this beautiful Mexican girl with long, dark hair. She wore a red dress, and it went off her shoulders. She had nice legs; they were long, and soft. She had a beauty mark on her upper thigh, it almost looked like a heart. I think she was 36-24-36."

"Uncle Jim!" said Priscilla. "Dad, will you hit him?"

Frank got up from the chair, and smacked Jim across the head.

"What's that for? Delores asked me why I chose her name."

"Uncle Jim, did you name me after a prostitute?"

"Jim! How could you?" asked Gina.

"Jimmy! You named my daughter after a prostitute?"

A laughing Valerie said, "Well, that makes sense."

"I'm sorry, Delores. She seemed like a nice girl. She was very giving."

"Yeah, Uncle Jim, the more she gave, the more she charged," said Valerie.

"I'm named after a prostitute?"

"I'm sorry, honey. But you do have a beautiful name. Delores is a beautiful name," said Jim.

"And if you can't find a job after you graduate from college, you can always be a prostitute," laughed Valerie.

"Valerie! Don't you start with your sister."

"Okay, Dad. Well, Didi, it is the world's oldest profession; at least you'll always have a job."

"Valerie, do you want me to take you over my knee?"

"Would you really do that, Daddy?"

"Do you want to find out?"

"No sir. Didi, I'm sorry."

"What are you sorry for?" asked Delores.

"I'm sorry that you were named after a prostitute."

"Dad!"

"Valerie!" Frank said, sternly.

"That's not very nice, Dollface."

"Okay, I'm sorry. Didi, I am sorry. Delores is a beautiful name."

"Alright," said Delores. "Uncle Jim, when you die, I want all of your money."

"That's fair, honey," said Jim.

"You can have all of our money too, dear," said Gina. "Valerie, you get nothing."

"Thank you, Aunt Gina," said Delores.

"Daddy, who am I named after?"

"You weren't named after anyone. Your mother and I just like the name Valerie."

Valerie smiled at her father, it was a tender moment that wouldn't last much longer.

"Girls, help me up out of this chair."

Frank put his right arm out so that Delores and Valerie could grab it to pull him up, while using his left arm to push up off the chair. Simultaneously, a thundering sound emitted from the area between Frank's rear end, and the seat of the chair; which was immediately followed by a rotten stench.

"Frankie, what are you trying to do? Kill us?" asked Danny.

"Frank, you're going to gas us to death," said Gina.

"Dad, this can't be good for the baby," Priscilla said.

"Dad, you cut the cheese." Valerie laughed until she almost peed.

Anna was awoken by the foul smell. It didn't bother her as much as it bothered the others, as she was used to it. Valerie took her newborn sister from Priscilla's arms, then sat in the chair, and held her. She looked adoringly at the baby. She seemed to be getting used to the idea of being a big sister. Now there was someone who would look to her for advice on boys, make-up, life in general, and other subjects which she knew nothing about.

"Mom, what are you going to name the baby?" Valerie asked.

"I'll let your father tell you what we've decided."

"Dad?"

"Valerie," Frank said, "your mother and I have decided that we're going to let you choose the name of your baby sister."

"As long as you don't pick a silly or crazy name, we'll go with what you choose," Anna added.

"You're going to let Valerie make an important decision like this? Really?" asked Delores. "She can't even pick out a good name for the dog. Why don't you let me do it?"

"I can always rename the dog, Delores," Valerie said.

"Don't you dare!" Delores said, harshly.

"Don't worry, I won't. We can't have two bitches with the same name."

"Oh my!" exclaimed Gina.

"Dad! Did you hear what she said to me?"

"Valerie, don't speak that way to Delores. What kind of example are you setting for your baby sister? Apologize, now!" Frank said.

"Dad, she's just a newborn. She can't understand what I'm saying. Besides, bitch is not a bad word."

"First of all, you don't know what the baby can understand. Secondly, you meant that to be derogatory towards Delores. You'd better apologize to your sister, right now."

"But, Dad…"

"Right now."

"Didi, I'm sorry for saying that you're a…. you know… a bitch."

"Dad!" an irked Delores called out.

"Someone had better cool it!" said Jim.

"I hope your father takes you over his knee," said Gina.

"Frankie, do you want my belt? It's got a big buckle," Danny said.

"Valerie," Frank said, sternly.

"I'm sorry, Dad. Please don't take off your belt, Uncle Danny. I still remember the last time I got it with your belt, I couldn't sit down for a week. I'm sorry that I said a bad word. And I really am sorry to you, Didi. Honest. But you always treat me like a dumb kid, and I hate it."

"That's true, Didi. You do that," Priscilla said.

"Alright, Valerie. I'm sorry too," Delores said.

"See," Anna said, "you girls can get along. Now, Valerie, what should we name the baby?"

"Mom! You're still going to let her pick the baby's name?"

"Well, yes, Delores. She apologized to you. Valerie, like we said before; don't try to be silly or crazy. Choose a name wisely. Take the afternoon to think about it."

"I won't have to do that, I have a great name," Valerie said. She turned to look at Jeff, then to Delores, and finally, her parents, "I like the name Jenny."

The suggestion of Jenny was met with mixed reaction. Jeff's uneasiness was cause for a stare-down between him, and a furious Delores. Priscilla, while aware of the situation, appeared nonchalant. Everyone else remained in the dark about Jeff's earlier involvement with a girl named Jennifer, while Valerie's spiteful selection of the name amused her.

Jeff was still dating Jennifer when he met Delores. He broke up with her to be with Delores. Jennifer and Delores had known each other since junior high, and were once the best of friends. It was Jennifer who consoled Delores when Delores thought she might not have enough credits to graduate from high school. It was Jennifer who offered her support, and understanding to Delores, when Delores thought she might be pregnant. It was Jennifer who Frank forbade Delores from hanging out with, after believing the cigarettes he found in Delores' bedroom belonged to Jennifer. And it was Jennifer who got kicked to the curb, after introducing her boyfriend, Jeff, to her best friend, Delores. Although it went unspoken, Jeff and Delores were guilt-ridden over how they treated someone who once played a significant role in their lives.

"Dad, Mom, please don't let her name the baby," Delores said, as she looked down at the floor.

"I like the name," said Anna, "Jennifer."

"No, Mom," said Valerie. "Not Jennifer, just Jenny. My baby sister is going to be named Jenny."

"I like Jenny. How about it, Didi? Her name will be Jenny, not Jennifer," Priscilla said.

"I like it too," Frank said.

"Me too," said Anna. "She'll need a middle name, but her first name will be Jenny."

As far as Delores was concerned, Jenny was the same as Jennifer. If she and Jeff went their separate ways someday, for the rest of her life, every time she spoke Jenny's name, she would be reminded of what she did to her best friend.

CHAPTER FIVE

No Matter What

With the 1975-1976 school year only a few weeks away, Valerie and her friends anxiously waited for school to begin. After all, now they would be high school seniors, facing new endeavors, and challenges. Debra had a boyfriend whom she met several months earlier at the skating rink during spring break, his name was Brando. They met after he fell, while taking the curve a little too fast, landing on top of Valerie. She didn't exit the floor quick enough when the DJ announced that it was a boys' fast skate. After picking himself up off of her, he helped her get up, and made sure that she was alright.

When Debra and Karen skated over to check on Valerie, Debra caught Brando's eye. Unable to take his eyes off of her, he fell head over heels in love. He had a friend with him, Cory, who seemed to take a liking to Karen. With her friends having boyfriends, Valerie remained hopeful for the chance to meet her Prince Charming.

She wondered if her prince could be the guy who worked the counter at Andy's Handy Pharmacy. She had seen him there for the first time while with her mother, who stopped by to pick up diaper rash cream for Jenny. As well as getting the cream, Anna suggested that the three of them stop by the counter for a bite to eat. That was when a handsome guy with dark hair, asked Valerie, and her mother, if he could take their lunch order. Valerie was instantly smitten, but shied away as soon as her eyes met his.

Thereafter, each time Valerie saw him while with her mother, he went out of his way to greet her with a big 'Hello', or 'Hi there'. Valerie was never able to return the greeting. She was mesmerized by the sight of his magnificent form, which rendered her speechless.

"So, do you like the boy?" Anna asked, while driving home one Saturday afternoon. "He really seems to like you."

"I don't know what you're talking about, Mom. Can I roll the window down? Jenny wants to stick her head out."

"Sure, stick her head out the window, but just a little; I don't want her to fall out of the car if I have to stop suddenly. And yes, you do know what I am talking about. But if you'd rather not tell me, that's alright. Hopefully, I'll get invited to the wedding."

"Mom, I'm just about to start my senior year of high school, I won't be getting married to him for a very long time. Besides, I don't even know his name. And I don't know what you are talking about, anyway."

"Of course, you don't."

"Do you think that I should take Karen and Debra with me the next time, so that they could check him out? You know, to see what their opinion is about whether or not he likes me."

"Take Karen and Debra with you where, Valerie? To see if who likes you? I don't know what you're talking about," said her mother.

The following week, the girls paid a visit to Andy's Handy Pharmacy. Debra went to the cosmetic counter, while Valerie and Karen made a mad dash for the lunch counter in the back.

"Should we sit at the counter or a booth? Maybe a table?" Valerie asked.

It wasn't a big dining area; the counter had six bar stools, three tables, and three booths.

"Let's sit at the counter," said Karen. "Isn't that where you and your mom were sitting when you first saw him?"

"I want to sit at a table," Valerie said.

"Okay, we can sit at a table."

"No, let's sit at the counter."

"Valerie, can we just sit down anywhere? This table is fine."

"Where's Debra?"

"She'll be here in a few minutes. Valerie, don't be nervous. He's just a guy; there's no reason to be nervous. You don't see me acting nervous when I'm around Cory."

"That's because you're both squares. And I'm not nervous."

"Hey, backatcha."

"I'm sorry, Karen."

"What are you sorry for?" asked Debra, as she rejoined the group.

"She's nervous about seeing that guy," Karen said.

"Hang loose, Val."

"I'm not nervous. Why would I be nervous? Are you kidding? I'm cool, in fact, I'm super cool. Everything's groovy. But he doesn't seem to be around, I'll bet it's his day off. No big deal. Anyway, I told my mom that I would help her with Jenny, so I'll catch you girls on the flipside."

As Valerie stood up to leave, she pushed her chair out much further than necessary. In doing so, she bumped into the person standing behind her, causing him to drop the tray he was holding. The tray fell to the floor. The plates and mugs went crashing down, smashing loudly as they made contact with the hard tile. The accumulation of root beer and Nehi Orange, created a small pool on the floor, which Valerie was now standing in. Shattered pieces of glass and ceramic made its way across the flooring. Hamburgers, french fries, and onion rings went flying, before settling in the puddle of soft drinks.

"Hi, are you alright? You're not leaving, are you?" asked the waiter, whom she bumped into. He was handsome; tall, with dark hair. Coincidentally, he happened to be the reason for her visit to the drug store.

"Um..." Valerie stammered.

"I hope I didn't splash you when I dropped the tray."

"Uh..." said Valerie.

"Are you sure that you're alright? You look like you want to say something. Do you want to say something?" asked the handsome guy.

"Uh.... I like your apron."

"Thank you, they make us wear these."

"You're welcome," said Valerie.

"Sit down, let me get this cleaned up. I'll be right back," he said.

"Is that him, Valerie?" asked Debra.

"Yeah," answered Valerie. She spoke barely loud enough to be heard.

"Wow, he's dreamy. I think he likes you. He probably thinks that you're cool, no, super cool. If you like the apron, they sell them here. They're in aisle four, between the rubbers and the K-Y Jelly," Debra said, while trying to contain her laughter.

"Oh, Debra, get lost!" said Karen. "She feels bad enough that he thinks she's a spaz. Don't you think that she probably just wants to die? Look at her, she's humiliated. How will she ever face him when he comes back? How can she ever face anyone, ever again? If I were you, Valerie, I'd lock myself in my room, and never come out."

Valerie knew that she had to make a quick getaway before the tears gushed down her face. Casting aside goodbyes, she bolted out of Andy's Handy Pharmacy, as fast as she could. As she hightailed it out of there, she looked straight ahead, ignoring her friends as they called out to her.

"Hey, Valerie! Are you still going to the drive-inn later?" Karen called out.

"Be there or be square!" cried out Debra. "Later days, chick!"

Her Saturday was ruined. There was no way that she would keep her plans to go to the drive-inn later with her friends. She wasn't about to take the chance of running into the mysterious, handsome guy, whom she had secretly admired for some time. She thought she might save what little dignity she had remaining by staying home.

Valerie decided that she would spend some time with Jenny. She hadn't spent very much time with her, and for that, she felt guilty. She also felt guilty, where Jenny was concerned, for another reason. A personal feeling, which she had not shared with anyone. Valerie had a little resentment towards her baby sister. Because Jenny was born with Down syndrome, consequently, she was not the quality of sister that Valerie had hoped for.

By no means was her disappointment of Jenny's disability, a reflection of her feelings for her; Valerie loved Jenny. But she felt robbed of her role as a big sister. She wanted to be the kind of big sister that her little sister would turn to; much like she turned to Delores for advice on things such as boys, makeup, and questions about life in general.

Not in a thousand years, would it be possible to have a bond with Jenny, like that of the bond she shared with Priscilla. In no way, would there be a possibility for them to have a personal relationship, even if it was combative at times, such as what she had with Delores. The thought of such a kinship was unlikely, and the reality was non-existent. Valerie made sure that her feelings of discontentment remained hidden, although she did voice them to Jenny. She found it to be cathartic, releasing her frustrations about Jenny, to Jenny, herself. She always ended such discussions by giving Jenny a tight hug, and telling her how much she loved her.

At the time of Jenny's birth, Valerie, at fourteen years old, was fairly naïve, and uninterested in matters regarding mature subjects, such as Jenny's diagnosis of Down syndrome. Because she disregarded previous conversations her parents attempted to have with her about the trials that Jenny would face in her life, there wasn't much that Valerie knew about her sister's condition. Now, at seventeen, she was disappointed in herself for not taking the time to understand the uncertainties that Jenny will, most likely, encounter.

In all probability, Jenny may eventually have difficulties with her vision, and hearing. She could also have problems with her thyroid, and she had already been diagnosed with a congenital heart defect. But the maladies didn't define Jenny. She was like any other child; she had emotions, she liked ice cream, and her best friend was Trixie. Jenny could grow up to live a semi-independent life, needing limited support or she could be dependent on someone for the rest of her life.

At almost three years old, Jenny had mastered crawling, but had not yet taken baby steps without assistance. Her communication consisted of pointing, screaming, and clapping her hands. She was a sweet baby, extremely lovable, and very cuddly. She had a cute little nose, and rosy red cheeks. Her eyes were almond-shaped, slightly slanted, and when she laughed, they disappeared in the creases of her face as her cheeks seemed to squish upward. Her hands were tiny, while her smile was enormous. Frank enjoyed making her laugh. She liked when he played peek-a-boo with her, and was especially delighted when he blew raspberries on her belly. But nothing amused her more than when her father mimicked devouring her itty-bitty hand by putting it in his mouth, which Valerie found to be disturbing.

Maybe she would go with her father when he took Jenny to the park. Her father liked when she tagged along on his outings with Jenny. And her mother liked it too, because she was able to have the whole house to herself.

After working for various construction companies, and holding a top management position with one of the biggest companies in Texas for the last twenty years, Frank was now ready to enjoy the fruits of his labor by taking an early retirement. Because he had always worked long hours, he had not had the opportunity to experience the everyday, hands-on parental duties that Anna assumed with their three older daughters. With Jenny, he would be able to be more involved in his role as a father.

As a result of his thrifty spending, and wise savings, he was able to pay off the note on their house within fourteen years. His savings and investment savvy had allowed him several resources from which he drew funds for their day-to-day living expenses.

When Valerie arrived home, she walked in on Anna, as she sat in the living room, quietly crying to herself. Being careful not to disturb her, Valerie was able to back out of the room, and sneak out the back door. She wondered why her mother was crying. After a few minutes of waiting out in the backyard, Valerie re-entered the house. This time, she made sure to let her presence be known.

"Mom, Dad, I'm home."

"Valerie, I'm in the living room," Anna hollered back. "Hi, honey, how was your lunch? Did you meet the boy?"

"What boy? What are you talking about?"

"Valerie, you know what boy I'm talking about. So, what happened?"

"Why do you think something happened?"

"Because I know you like that boy, and he likes you, and you came home early. You don't have to tell me about it if you don't want to. Your father is upstairs, getting Jenny ready for the park. Do you want to go with them or do you want to help me fix supper?"

"I think I'll go with them, if that's alright."

"Sure, you can tell me about the boy another time. Or I can wait until the two of you get back from your honeymoon, he can introduce himself then."

"Oh, Mom."

"Are you still going out to the drive-inn tonight with your friends?"

"No, I blew it off. I'll stay home with you, and Dad, and Jenny tonight."

Valerie went to the kitchen to find her father preparing the diaper bag for an outing to the park. He filled the bag with junk food; cookies, potato chips, and a couple of sandwiches. He also packed Jenny's bottle, some treats for Trixie, and a thermos filled with iced tea.

"Dad, you don't have to take a sandwich for me. Supper should be ready soon after we get back."

"Okay, I didn't. Are you coming to the park with us?"

"Yes, Daddy, if you want me to."

"Of course! I'd love it if you came with me and Jenny. Trixie is coming with us, she'd love for you to come along too."

Frank strapped Jenny in the stroller, and tethered Trixie to the handle. He said his goodbyes to Anna, then he and Valerie began the eight-block excursion to the park. Valerie had to step up her pace to keep up with Frank's long strides. She couldn't ask him to slow down for her; she knew her father, that would make him walk faster.

"Valerie, is everything alright with you?"

"Yeah, Dad. Everything's alright with me. But that's what I wanted to ask you; is everything alright with you and Mom?"

"Of course, why do you ask?"

"Well, earlier this afternoon, I walked in on Mom. She was sitting on the ugly chair in the living room, and she was crying. Why was she crying? What happened?"

"I don't know why she was crying; I wasn't there. Why didn't you ask her?"

"Because, I was afraid. What if she was sad because of you? I don't know, like maybe you were going to get a divorce or something."

"Valerie, your mother and I will never get a divorce, till death do us part. I love her very much, and I have for the past twenty-seven years. I would never leave her, and she would never leave me. Besides, if she left me, who else would want her? The woman has got four kids. No man wants a woman with four kids, especially four girls," he said, with a chuckle.

"Well, I just want to know why she was crying. I'm starting my senior year of high school, it's a happy time for me. But I can't be happy if Mom is sad."

"Valerie, you've grown up so much, Your mother and I are very proud of you. You're a good girl, you've always made good grades, and you help around the house without being told. You help us with Jenny because you want to, not because you have to. I remember when Jenny was born, and the doctor told us that she had Down syndrome, and would have developmental problems all her life. There are some things that she will never be able to do; she'll need someone to take care of her for the rest of her life. I cried when the doctor told us, I just broke down and cried. Your mother said to me, 'It's going to be alright, Frank. The baby will be alright. We're going to take good care of her.' I told her, 'I'm not crying because of the baby. I know that we're going to take good care of her, just as we have our other girls.' 'Then what's wrong?' she says to me. I told her that I was crying because I didn't want the baby to be a burden to you, Valerie. I think that may be the reason why your mother was crying this afternoon. We both think about that, we don't want you to be burdened."

"Dad, I don't know why you think that I'll be burdened."

"Cupcake, there's going to come a day, when your mother and I won't be here anymore. About a year ago, we had a meeting with Mike, it was a legal matter."

"What was it about, Dad?"

"Valerie, I'm 55 years old, your mother is pushing 44. I'm not saying that we're old, because we're not. We're still young; we can climb mountains, we can swim oceans. We can even have another baby, if we wanted to. Maybe not your mother, but I certainly could sire another child. Not that I'd want to without your mother. She's what makes it fun, you know?"

"Dad, I don't want to know that you and Mom are still doing *it*. Please, you're my parents! Why can't you be like normal people and watch TV when you go to bed? Or read a book or something? Or here's a new idea; go to sleep."

"Valerie, lighten up. I got myself fixed."

"Dad, I don't want to hear this."

"Why? I thought you'd be happy to know that I got myself fixed."

"Dad, I'm going home."

"Wait a minute. I just told you that I got myself fixed, so, you wouldn't worry about more babies coming along. The point is that your mother and I are still young enough to enjoy life, and each other, but we don't want to have any more accidents. You know, Jenny was an accident. And so were you; you were conceived on the night of your uncle Jimmy's wedding to that woman who didn't like dogs. That should have been a warning to him; if a woman doesn't like dogs, she probably can't be trusted."

"Dad, that doesn't make sense."

"Who cares? Anyway, your mother had a little too much to drink that night. She's very seductive when she drinks."

"Dad, you were telling me about your meeting with Michael," Valerie said, trying to steer the awkward conversation back to the matter at hand.

"Right, the meeting. Well, your mother and I made our wills. Do you know what a will is?"

"Yeah, so when you die, everybody knows who's going to get your things, like the house, and your car. Is that it?"

"Yes, but Valerie, it's so much more than that. It's Jenny. We had to decide on what will happen to Jenny. Who would take care of her? I don't want her to be a burden to anyone. There are places where she could live, and someone would always take care of her."

"What kind of places, Dad?"

"Maybe we should talk about this another time."

"No, Dad. Let's talk about it now. We can talk in front of Jenny. She doesn't understand what we're saying."

"We don't know that, Valerie. Not for sure."

"Daddy, don't worry. I'll take care of Jenny if anything happens to you and Mom."

"That's very sweet of you, Cupcake. Thank you, but I don't want you to do that. I want you to go to college, get a degree, and use it."

"It doesn't matter what you want, Dad. If you're talking about a time when you and Mom won't even be here, then it doesn't matter. I'm telling you that if anything happens to you and Mom, I'm going to take care of Jenny. I don't want her to go to one of those places where we'll never see her again. I have nothing against those places, I'm sure they're fine. But Jenny is my baby sister, and I'll take care of her. No matter what."

"Valerie, thank you for saying that."

"Dad, you and Mom aren't going to die for a long time, anyway. But when you do, I'll take over caring for Jenny. I will, Dad, no matter what."

"Thank you for loving your sister, and wanting to take care of her. Mike told me the same thing. He said that he and Priscilla would take her in to live with them. Priscilla's working at the law firm now. She's doing big things over there, she won't have time. But, Valerie, I want you to go to college."

"I'll go to college, Dad."

"Good, and I want you to get a degree that you can use. Don't be like Delores; she doesn't use her degree. She could be anything in the business world, but she works at the gym selling memberships. I don't get it. I'm just glad that she has Jeff. The best thing she ever did was marry him, and give me a grandson. You know that I love you girls, but now, with Kevin, he's the missing piece of the Negron puzzle. I am now complete."

"I know, Dad. You've been the only boy in this family for a long time, but now you have Kevin. Dad, what if, after I graduate from college, I want to be like Mom? You know, take care of my kids instead of work. Would you still be proud of me?"

"Of course, Valerie. I am always proud of you. But staying home with the kids is work too; don't think that it's easy. It's not easy caring for, and raising Jenny, with all of her needs. And it wasn't easy raising Delores, she was so wild. Now raising Priscilla, that was a piece of cake. She never gave us any trouble, and she did good in school. Just look at her now, she's a successful lawyer."

"What about me, Dad? Was it easy raising me?"

"Do you know what burdensome means?"

"Yes."

"How about complicating?"

"Of course."

"Challenging?"

"Yes, Dad."

"Grueling?"

"Yes, Dad. It's like this conversation."

"What about hindrance?"

"No."

"Okay, we got one. Valerie, raising you has put a hindrance on your mother's and my intimacy."

"Dad. I didn't know what hindrance meant, but I know what intimacy means."

"Oh, sorry, Cupcake. You're smarter than you look, you get that from me."

CHAPTER SIX

I Think I Love You

For some, the first day of school is filled with hysteria, and turmoil. For others, there can be excitement, and adventure. For Valerie, it was filled with wonder, and worry. Wondering if she would see the guy from Andy's Handy Pharmacy; and worry, just in case she did. There were only two high schools in town; the one that she attended, Thomas Jefferson High, and the rival high school, Audie Murphy High. That meant there was a fifty percent chance that he attended the same high school as she.

Valerie and Karen had the same class for first period. She arrived a few minutes late, handing the teacher an admittance note before taking a seat next to Karen; who saved her a spot by placing a textbook on the desk next to hers. Slightly sticking out from between the pages of the book, was a note addressed to Valerie.

"I found out his name! It's Patrick!" is what Karen wrote.

Valerie wrote back, "Whose name is Patrick?"

On her next note, Karen wrote, "The guy you like from Andy's Handy Pharmacy."

Valerie wrote back, "I don't like him anymore."

"Why? Are you still embarrassed? You shouldn't be. Everyone does stupid things to make a fool of themselves every now and then," Karen wrote.

"How do you know his name?" Valerie asked on her return note.

"I asked Sarah Beth, she's best friends with Minerva, who is going around with Hector."

"So, what!" Valerie wrote.

Karen wrote back, "So Hector works at Andy's Handy Pharmacy. That's so what!"

"You need to mind your own business!!" Valerie wrote.

"I'm helping you get a boyfriend," Karen wrote.

"Now everyone is going to know that I like him. Do me a solid, worry about getting your own boyfriend."

Before handing over the note, she noticed that the teacher, Mrs. Strash, was no longer sitting at her desk. Valerie looked around for her; since she didn't see her anywhere, she assumed that it was safe to proceed. She stretched out her arm to drop the note on Karen's desk. Before the delivery was completed, the note was intercepted by someone who had big hands with hairy knuckles. Mrs. Strash was not an exceptionally big woman, but she did have big hands with hairy knuckles. A lot of the kids called her Gorilla Hands, so did some of the male teachers.

"Ladies, thank you for the note," said Gorilla Hands. "I'll take this, and see you both after school for detention. I'm sure that I'll get a laugh when I read it, it can't be that interesting. Will I be amused, Miss Negron?"

"No, Miss Goril ... uh... Mrs. Strash."

"I won't?"

"Yes, ma'am."

"I will?"

"No, ma'am."

"Which is it, Miss Negron? Shall I read it out loud to the class, and let them decide?"

"No, ma'am. Please, don't do that."

"Alright, I'll read it later, in the teachers' lounge. You girls better not be late for detention," Gorilla Hands said, sternly.

"No, ma'am. We won't."

Besides teaching lesson plans, one of the duties of the high school teachers was to discourage the students from exchanging personal notes in the classroom. One way to do this was to confiscate the notes, and put students on notice that their personal notes would be read at a later time, by the teacher. Most of the teachers threw the notes into the trash, but there was a small group of female teachers, Gorilla Hands being one of them, who liked to read the notes. Sharing these notes with each other in the teachers' lounge was something they looked forward to; it helped to break up the monotony of the day.

Depending on who authored the notes, some teachers might find them to be amusing. However, in the case of notes written by Amy Lopez, most found her notes to be quite exhilarating. Amy's notes were infamous; they dripped with the sensual details of her many seductions. Luckily, the identity of Amy's conquests always remained anonymous. That being said, not only did Amy spill on the racy details of her illicit performances, but she also described the location of those liaisons; some of which happened to be places on campus that only the faculty would have access. There were four younger male teachers on staff, could one or all four have been participants in Amy's tantalizing games of amorousness? Only Amy knew for sure. Amy's notes provided an escape to a place of ecstasy that someone might only be able to experience vicariously through Amy, herself.

After school, Debra waited for Valerie and Karen in the hallway where the detention was held. She sat on the floor, in front of a set of lockers, doodling Brando's name on her book cover. The girls missed the pep rally, but would be able to go to the senior inauguration. It wasn't a school sponsored event, but it was a Jefferson High tradition, held at DeMarco's Pizzeria. A few of last year's seniors would be on hand to kick start the festivities. They would do a few choruses of the fight song, then a few shouts of, "Who's gonna win the game tomorrow? I can't hear you! Who's number one? I can't hear you!" It was like a pep rally, but without the cheerleaders.

Because Mr. DeMarco, the owner of DeMarco's Pizzeria, was alumni, Jefferson High class of '54, he closed the restaurant to outsiders for this one night of tradition. Next to the prom, this was the biggest social event of the year.

When they got to DeMarco's, Debra and Brando went off on their own. Valerie and Karen looked for a place to sit. Because the restaurant was packed, there were no empty tables. The best they could hope for was to find some friends who may already have a table. Karen spotted Cory.

When he noticed her, he waved them over to his table. Karen and Cory were awkward towards each other. They weren't officially going around yet, so they avoided a greeting that involved physical contact of the arms or lips. Instead, they shook hands as if they were conducting business.

"I looked for you after school, Karen. I couldn't find you anywhere," Cory said.

"Really? Were you going to ask me something important?"

"No, I just wondered where you were."

"Oh," Karen said, as her heart sank. "We had detention hall. Gorilla Hands busted me and Val passing a note."

"Oh, Gorilla Hands is tough," Cory said. "Hey, I heard that some guys saw her over the summer at South Padre Island. She's got a pretty good body, she doesn't look too bad in a bathing suit, for an older woman; I mean, if you're standing far enough away. Except for her hands, of course. If only she had a bathing suit with matching gloves, then she'd be a knockout, for an older woman. That's what one of the guys said. She was with a few other old ladies, and a couple of old guys. They looked like they were partying. I didn't know old people still partied. That's weird."

"That is weird," said Karen. "I think once you hit twenty-five, your days of partying should be over."

"Hey, y'all don't mind if someone joins us, do you?" asked Cory.

Valerie and Karen looked at each other while shrugging their shoulders.

"Do either of you know Patrick Cole?"

Before the girls had a chance to wonder if Patrick Cole was the same Patrick from Andy's Handy Pharmacy, Patrick Cole stood before them. It was, indeed, the same guy. Still a little embarrassed by what happened the last time she saw him, Valerie quickly began rummaging through her purse, pretending to look for something. When she looked up, her eyes gazed upon Patrick's dark, slightly curly hair. Once their eyes met, she abruptly broke their gaze, and went back to searching through her purse.

"Hey, Patrick. Gimme me five, man."

"Hey, Cory. What's happenin' man?"

"Nothing, dude. Do you know Karen and Valerie?"

"Nice to meet you," said Karen. "I'm gonna get a soda. Does anybody want anything while I'm up?"

"Let me go with you," Cory said.

Karen left the table with Cory, leaving Valerie to face Patrick alone.

"So, your name is Valerie?" he asked. "I'm glad to finally know your name."

"What are you talking about?" asked Valerie. "I've never even seen you before in my life."

"Come on, you know that we've met a few times."

"You must be mistaken."

"If you say so. Well, Valerie, I just ordered a pepperoni pizza. It should be ready soon. You can have some if you'd like."

"No thanks, Paul," she said, as she tried to hide the true feelings of love that she had for pizza.

"It's Patrick."

"What's Patrick?"

"My name. It's Patrick."

"Are you sure? I thought I heard Cory say that your name is Paul."

Valerie had this subtle conversation going on with Patrick; but another conversation to herself was going on in her head. 'Oh, Patrick, I'm so happy that I'm finally meeting you. It's been a long time since that first time we saw each other. I haven't been able to get you out of my mind. I think I love you! Are you going to ask me to marry you? Because I'm ready to say yes!'

"I'm absolutely sure my name is Patrick," he said, interrupting the private conversation she was having with herself. "But if you'd like to see my drivers' license, I'd be happy to show you."

"No, that's alright. I believe you, Paul. I mean Patrick."

"You disappeared on me the other day. When I went back to clean up the spill, you were gone."

"I had to leave, I had to meet friends. Uh, I mean, what are you talking about?"

"I'm talking about that day, when I was working; remember? You bumped into me, and my tray went flying?"

"No, I wasn't there," Valerie adamantly denied.

"You just said that you had to leave to meet friends."

"No, I didn't."

"Yes, you did. It was you. You knocked my tray right out of my hands, and sent everything flying to the floor. I haven't seen you since."

"Alright, I confess. I'm sorry that I took off. I was embarrassed about bumping into you, and I still am."

"No need to be embarrassed, Valerie. I'm the one who dropped the tray. I hope my pizza is ready soon, I'm hungry."

"Well, do you like donuts?"

"Yeah, I like donuts."

"Do you want a Hertz donut?"

"Sure. Do you have a donut with you? Where is it? In your purse?"

Valerie, using her thumb and index finger, pinched Patrick's arm, and twisted her wrist to ensure slight pain.

"Ouch!"

"Hurts, don't it?"

"Oh, I get it. Hurts, don't it; like Hertz donut. That's very funny, it felt like a pretty ladybug tickling my arm. Hey, I'll go get the pizza now, but I'll be right back. Don't take off again."

Handing her two dimes, he said, "Here, put some music on. By the way, you're foxy."

Patrick disappeared into the crowd. Realizing how foolish she just acted in front of him, yet again, she contemplated a disappearing act, herself.

"Why did I do the Hertz donut?" she asked herself. "He probably thinks that I'm a doofus or a dipwad."

She was unable to think clearly, as she flipped through the pages of the tabletop jukebox. After a few minutes, she was able to decide on what songs she would play; being extra careful not to choose a slow song. Debra and Brando joined her at the table.

"Was that Patrick Cole I saw a few minutes ago at this table?" asked Brando.

"I guess that's his name. Do you know him?" Valerie asked.

"Oh yeah, we're buddies."

"Is he going around with anyone?" asked Debra, while looking at Valerie.

"Not that I know of. Why do you ask? You already have a boyfriend. You're not going to dump me for him, are you?"

"Of course not," said Debra. "I was just wondering."

Patrick returned to the table with his large pepperoni pizza. Karen and Cory also returned to the table, holding hands. Valerie wondered if Patrick was going to hold her hand too. She thought that she should prove to him, and herself, that she was not the clumsy girl he saw that day at Andy's Handy Pharmacy. She wanted to show him that she was an independent, sophisticated, and graceful woman. She could even be a take-charge woman. She decided that she would show him how graceful, and sophisticated she could be, by being the one to take-charge and hold his hand.

As she slid the 16-inch pizza pan over to give herself room to take-charge, she inadvertently knocked over Patrick's soft drink, spilling the entire contents, including the ice. The area of the table in front of Patrick got wet, causing him to swiftly move his arm. He jumped out of his seat, as the soda and ice flowed off the table, and onto his lap. Her friends laughed at her. Patrick grabbed Valerie's hand, giving it a reassuring squeeze. Then he took a slice of pizza, which was a little soggy from the spilled soft drink, and gave it to Valerie, before serving himself a slice, which was also soggy.

Valerie was on cloud nine for the rest of the evening. She felt that she had found her Prince Charming. Though he didn't try to kiss her goodnight, he did hold her hand; and she sensed the attraction was mutual.

CHAPTER SEVEN

Burning Love

It had been weeks since the night of the senior inauguration. Valerie had hoped Patrick would have asked her out on a date by now. With Trixie by her side, she lied on her bed, flipping through a magazine, while listening to Donny Osmond sing to her through her record player. She had it set to continuously repeat the song.

As the song played, for the umpteenth time, her thoughts were of Patrick. Since the night at DeMarco's, she had seen him several times; at school, and at the football games. But either some or all of the gang had been there too, so they had not been able to share any other special moments as they had that night at DeMarco's. She was disappointed. Maybe he didn't like her as much as she thought he did, or as much as she liked him.

"He thinks I'm a spaz," she said to herself. "I guess I am a spaz. No wonder Didi is always calling me Dipwad; I am a dipwad. Trixie, what should I do to forget about him? Huh, girl? What should I do? I know what I'll do! Why didn't I think of this before? I'll just get another boyfriend. What's so hard about that? I'm pretty sure that Jason would jump at the chance to be with me. He's been in love with me since forever. He is sort of a dork, but, yeah; that's what I'll have to do. I'll let Jason be my boyfriend. Patrick will see me with dorky Jason, and he'll know that he had his chance, and he blew it."

Trixie barked at Valerie, as if to say, 'that's not such a good plan.' Valerie thought that before she went to the extreme of committing herself to Jason, she would first make an attempt to call Patrick. She had a phone in her bedroom, but first she would have to locate it; her room was in disarray. She found the phone cord, then followed it to locate her pink princess phone, which was buried under a pile of clothes, on a chair. While holding the receiver with her left hand, she used her right index finger to shakenly dial Patrick's phone number. She had his number memorized even though she had never actually called him before. After dialing a few numbers, her father knocked on her bedroom door.

"Valerie, are you busy?" he asked.

"No, Daddy. Come in," she said, as she hung up the phone.

"You have company waiting for you in the living room."

"Who is it? Karen or Debra?"

"Neither, it's a boy named Patrick."

Valerie ran towards the door to slam it shut, nearly slamming it on her father.

"Get out! What did you say, Dad? Who is it? What name did you say? Are you kidding around with me, Dad? It's not funny. You have to tell me the truth. Who is it? Who's here?"

"I said, Patrick. It's a boy named Patrick. Who is he, Valerie? Is he a boy you like?"

"Dad, when did he get here?"

"Oh, he's been here for at least half an hour. Is he a boy that you like?"

"Half an hour! That's almost thirty minutes or something like that! Jump back! Why didn't you tell me sooner?" Valerie asked, frantically.

"Look, Valerie, I want to know what this boy is to you. Do you like him, or what?"

"Dad, I can't talk about this right now. I have to get ready. Look at me, I look freaky-deaky. I need to fix my hair, I need to put on some makeup, I need to change my clothes. Change to what? Dad, I don't know what to wear! Should I go wholesome, or sexy? I don't have sexy clothes, so I guess I'll have to go wholesome. Dad, what do you think?"

"I think you've answered my question."

"What question?"

"Valerie, I asked you if this Patrick was a boy that you like. By the way that you're acting, I can see that you do. I'll go talk to him for a while, until you're ready. You make yourself real pretty, Cupcake. Go wholesome, leave the sexy to Delores; it'll give us something to argue about later. And don't forget to use some mouthwash."

"Dad, we're out of mouthwash, remember? It was on the list of things that we need. Mom was supposed to go to the store this morning. Why didn't she go? Dad! Do I need it? Does my breath smell?"

"No, you should be okay. Just don't get too close to him."

Frank left Valerie's room, and closed the door behind him. He was tickled about Valerie's reaction to her potential suitor. After about twenty minutes, Valerie made her grand appearance in the living room. She had brushed her teeth, and changed her clothes. She wore a sleeveless, navy blue tiered mini-dress, which was a hand-me-down from Delores. Because of the difference in their height, the hemline of the mini-dress covered most of Valerie's thighs; hanging about an inch above her knees. The same dress, when worn by Delores, revealed much more leg. It was a sexy dress on Delores; on Valerie, it looked wholesome.

Delores always complimented her mini-dresses by wearing sexy high heeled shoes or her white, faux leather go-go boots. Valerie wore brown Mary Janes with an inch and a half chunky heel, which she wore with white knee-high socks. Though she usually didn't wear make-up on the weekends, she put on a little blue eyeshadow, and black mascara. Her long hair was styled with clips to hold some of it in place on top of her head, leaving some of her hair to hang down. Her matching earrings, bracelet, and belt topped off her outfit; macramé jewelry, which she made herself.

Patrick was on the floor playing with Jenny and Trixie. He jumped to his feet when Valerie entered the room. Frank also stood up; he noticed his daughter looking a little more womanly than she usually did.

"Hi, Valerie," Patrick said. He stood in awe of her beauty.

"Hi, Paul," Valerie said to him.

"Paul? I thought you said your name was Patrick."

"It is Patrick, sir. Wow, Valerie, you look outta sight!"

"What?" asked Frank.

"Very pretty. She looks very pretty, sir."

Patrick approached Valerie, stopping short of embracing her. He handed her a bouquet of random, colorful flowers.

"These are for you. I didn't know what your favorite flowers are, so I got them all different."

"Thank you, Patrick. They're beautiful. I see that you've met my parents, and my baby sister."

"Yes, your mother has been very nice, and I've enjoyed playing with Jenny. She's cute. We're great friends now."

"Jenny likes Patrick," said Anna. "Don't you, Jenny?"

"So does Valerie," Frank said, under his breath.

Anna heard Frank's comment, and under her breath, she said, "Yeah, I know."

"Valerie, I asked your father's permission to take you out tonight. Would you like to go out with me?"

"Yeah. Where are we going?"

"Well, there's this Italian restaurant; not DeMarco's, but another place. It's downtown, supposed to be really good."

"That's fab! I've been wanting to go there," said Valerie.

"Which place is that?" asked Frank.

"Never mind, Frank," Anna said.

"I just want to know, maybe I'll take you there sometime, Annie. It's fab."

Frank opened his wallet, and took out two $20 bills. He walked over to Patrick, and handed him the money.

"Here, I want you to take this. Treat my daughter to a nice time, or a fab time."

"Oh no, Mr. Negron. You don't have to do that, but thank you. I have my own money that I've been saving up for tonight."

"How long have you been saving for?" asked Valerie.

"Since the night at DeMarco's, the senior inauguration."

Valerie bashfully looked at Patrick, while Frank took notice of Patrick's eyes, which were transfixed on his daughter.

"I'll put these flowers in water, then we can leave. Mom, do we have a vase?"

"I'll take care of that for you, dear. You go on now, go on your date."

"Okay, Mom, thank you. Bye, Jenny." She picked Jenny up, and gave her a quick kiss.

"Wait, Valerie," said Anna. "Why don't you take a sweater? It's going to be chilly out."

"I'll be fine, Mom. Don't worry."

"I'm not worried, but it's going to be a little colder than it was last night. I think you need a sweater."

"Mom, I'll be fine," Valerie said, with a little irritation in her voice.

"Annie, she'll be alright. It's not cold out," Frank said.

"Alright. I'm only a mother. What do I know?"

Patrick walked behind Valerie, towards the door.

"Bye, Mrs. Negron, Mr. Negron. I'll have her home by 9:30."

"Make it 10:00," Frank said. "Give me a hug, Valerie, then you can go."

As Valerie hugged her father, he whispered in her ear, "You look so pretty, Cupcake. Remember, don't get too close to him. Otherwise he might not ask you for a second date. You know, because of your bad breath. You really needed that mouthwash. Oh, and don't order anything with garlic. That'll just make it worse." He waved them off, "Have a good time, kids."

While walking with Patrick towards his car, Valerie's mind filled with thoughts of having bad breath. She was swept off her feet by Patrick and his charm; but what if he tried to kiss her goodnight? Should she return the kiss? She didn't want to scare him away with her bad breath. She hoped that he wouldn't try to sneak in a quick peck as he opened the car door for her. He was certainly a gentleman, holding out his hand to help her get in. After he closed the door, without trying to kiss her, he ran around to his side of the car to get in.

Patrick drove a 1969 Oldsmobile Cutlass Supreme. It was red with a white vinyl top; fully equipped with air conditioning, and an AM radio. It also had an 8-track player, which Patrick installed himself. The car belonged to his brother-in-law, Steve, who gave him full access. The only stipulation was that Patrick was responsible for paying for the gas, and car maintenance. He also had to do well in school; he had to earn A's and B's.

The restaurant was in the town square. As they made their way through the bustling square, the words of her father continued to repeat in Valerie's mind. She wondered if she had a breath mint or chewing gum in her purse. She decided to open her purse to check. In doing so, some of the contents fell out, and onto the ground. Instantly, she was overcome with anguish as she quickly tried to retrieve her things which had fallen out. Patrick bent down to help her. He picked up her powder compact, which was now broken. He also picked up her hairbrush, and a tube of lipstick. He reached for a white, narrow object about six or seven inches long. As his fingers touched the cushioned object, Valerie quickly grabbed it away. She avoided eye contact with him, as she shoved what turned out to be a sanitary napkin, back into her purse. She realized that the task of rummaging through her purse as she walked next to Patrick, was not going to refute the image that he probably had of her being clumsy.

"Oh, I know what that is," said Patrick. "No reason to feel embarrassed. I have a sister; I know about these things. Sometimes my sister calls me at work to ask me to buy some for her before I come home. The guys at work tease me about it; now that's embarrassing."

"Gum. I was looking for gum in my purse. Do you have any?"

"Gum? It's in the car, I'll be right back."

"I am a dipwad!" Valerie said to herself.

Upon returning to Valerie, Patrick handed her a stick of gum. Without looking directly at him, she accepted, unwrapped, and put it in her mouth. The walk to the restaurant was awkward and quiet. Once they arrived, they had to wait for a table. Outside the restaurant were several benches, and a large fountain which housed a statue of a cherub. Continuing to avoid eye contact, Valerie sat on the ledge of the fountain while maintaining small talk with Patrick.

"Here, make a wish," Patrick said. He reached into his pocket, and pulled out a few coins, handing one to Valerie. "I'll make a wish too. Let's toss our pennies in together. Ready? On three; one, two, three. What did you wish for, Valerie?"

"Well, it's a little embarrassing." Valerie slowly lifted her head to face Patrick. She gathered up her courage, and looked him straight in the eye. "I wished that for the rest of the time that we are on this date tonight, that I won't spill a drink on you. Or that I won't make you drop anything, or that I won't drop anything either. That's what I wished for, Patrick. I know, I'm dumb."

"You are not dumb, Valerie. And it doesn't matter about your wish. What if it doesn't come true? What if you knocked the table over, and a plate of spaghetti and meatballs ends up on my lap? Or a bowl of hot soup flies off, and lands on my head? Who cares? I wouldn't want you to feel bad about that. I wouldn't care, because it doesn't matter. Those things aren't important. Being with you on this date tonight, that is what's important. I've been thinking about this night for a long time. I had two pennies, Valerie, and I made two wishes. One wish just came true, I hope I get my other wish too."

"We just tossed the pennies, how could your wish have already come true? What did you wish for?"

"I wished that I could see your pretty eyes. I haven't seen them since we got out of the car."

Hearing Patrick's wish removed Valerie's humiliation, this made her smile.

"Cool beans! I just got my second wish!"

"What was your second wish?"

"My second wish was that I could see your pretty smile."

"Thanks, Patrick."

Valerie felt confident again; but not confident enough to make her want to order anything with garlic. When the waiter took their order, she ordered a small plate of spaghetti, with no garlic bread. Patrick ordered a generous portion of lasagna with extra garlic bread, and a side of three slices of pepperoni pizza. He excused himself from the table for a few minutes, after which, the waiter brought their food. Valerie knew that the polite thing to do would be to wait for him before starting to eat; but seeing the scrumptious pizza set before her, combined with the heavenly smell of sauce and pepperoni, she found it hard to resist. Her temptation got the best of her.

"I'm sure that he wouldn't mind if I had a small piece," she said to herself.

She cut off the tip of the triangle, and ate it. It was delicious, better than DeMarco's. She cut another small piece, and ate it, leaving half of the slice for Patrick.

"If he's not back in ten seconds, I'm going to eat the rest."

She counted ten seconds, skipping the numbers four, five, six, and seven. When she reached the number ten, she finished off what was left of the slice. Then she covered her tracks by getting rid of any evidence of there having been a third slice. Just as she swept away the last crumb from the plate, Patrick returned to the table.

"Sorry to keep you waiting. The dryer in the men's room wasn't working, and there were no paper towels. I had to shake my hands dry."

"That's alright, Patrick."

"Thanks for not eating without me."

"No problem."

"Didn't I order three slices of pizza?"

"No, only two."

"I'm sure I said three."

"No, you said two."

"I'm pretty sure that I said three. I'd better ask."

"Patrick, you don't want the waiter to get into trouble, do you? He's probably new."

"Yeah, you're right. I only wanted two slices anyway. I was going to give the third slice to you, so you could try it. I heard that this pizza is better than DeMarco's, that's why I wanted you to try it. But I'll give you one of these, and I'll just have one slice, instead."

"Thanks, but you go ahead and have both, I'm fine with my spaghetti."

"Well, if you're sure."

"Yes, I'm sure. Thank you."

After dinner, they took a stroll around the square, to and fro a few blocks, before returning to the car.

"I wish I had listened to my mother, and brought a sweater."

"Here, Valerie, take my jacket. It's getting pretty cold out. Your mother sure is nice, your father is too."

"Patrick, is it true that you were at my house for half an hour before my father told me that you were there?"

"Yeah, thirty or forty minutes."

"Why were you there so long? What was my father telling you?"

"He wasn't telling me anything. I'm the one who did most of the talking. I like you, Valerie. I just want to make sure that I do this right. If

I didn't have your parents' permission, especially your father's, we wouldn't be on this date tonight. I wanted to talk to your parents because I want them to know who I am. Otherwise, how could I expect them to trust me with their daughter?"

"Oh, I guess that's a good thing. I like you too, Patrick. Do you want to know something that I did when I was a kid?"

"Sure, what's that?"

"Well, I've known Karen and Debra since kindergarten. Debra is bossy, Karen is very sweet, but I was the one that everyone was afraid of."

"Why were they afraid of you?"

"Because I told them that my father was a serial killer. And that I could easily have anybody killed if I wanted to."

"What? Valerie, why would you say that?"

"I was just joshin', Patrick. Debra had a slumber party when we were in the fifth grade, there were lots of girls there. Amy Lopez was there, she was mean. I didn't like her, neither did Karen, but she was Debra's friend. Anyway, we told scary stories but nothing ever scared Amy. I just wanted to make up a story that was super scary so that it would scare her, and make her cry; but I also had to make it as real as possible. I thought that if I had a real person in my story, it would be more believable."

"Did Amy believe it?"

"Not at first, but a few weeks later, something happened that changed her mind."

"What happened?"

"Well, do you know those woods over off the highway when you go past the mall, and past the stadium?"

"Yeah."

"Well, they found a man's body out there. He was stuffed in a garbage bag, and his head was smashed in. They said on the news that there had been other victims that were killed the same way in other towns in Texas, and that it was probably done by a serial killer."

"I remember that, Valerie. The police called him the Smasher. For a long time, my mom was afraid to let us play outside. My sister said that she heard that the Smasher lived here, in Crystal Springs. Valerie, did you tell everyone that your father was the Smasher?"

"I didn't have to, Amy's big mouth did it for me. Everyone thought it was true, so I let people think what they wanted to think."

"Valerie, that was terrible for that man's family."

"I know, it was terrible. And I felt sorry for the man's family, it was a real bummer. I did confess to Karen and Debra. They didn't believe it anyway; they know my parents. But I was a kid, and I really didn't like Amy."

"Well, Valerie, if you really didn't like Amy, then that makes it okay. I guess."

"No, I know it doesn't make it okay. But dumb ole Amy Lopez has been super nice to me ever since. Even now, when she sees me, she goes out of her way to say hello."

"Amy Lopez? Is she the girl who always wears super short mini-skirts?"

"Yeah."

"And really tight sweaters?"

"Yeah, that's her."

"Sometimes she wears low-cut blouses. She has a pink blouse with blue trim, and blue buttons, the top button is missing. The second button looks like it's going to pop off, it's just hanging by a thread. Every time she wears it, me and the guys always wonder, 'is today the day that she'll lose that button? If she sneezes, will it pop off? If she laughs really hard, will that make it pop off?' Yeah, we always wonder about that. Sometimes the guys will make her laugh, you know, to see if it'll pop off. So far, no luck."

"Yes, Patrick! That's dumb ole Amy Lopez! So, I guess that you know her?"

"Oh yeah, she goes out of her way to say hello to me too," Patrick said, wearing a lustful grin, which quickly vanished when he caught the disapproving look on Valerie's face.

In an attempt to take Patrick's mind off of Amy Lopez, Valerie started a rumor about her.

"You know they're not real, right? She puts socks in her bra. Don't be fooled, Patrick, she's only an A-cup."

"Really? An A? Are you sure? I mean… I don't care. Who cares about Amy? She's nothing to worry about. I mean, she's not nearly as smart as you. If they're not real, then she really doesn't have much going for her. I mean, don't get me wrong, she does have a pretty face too. And her hair is so long, and pretty. Sometimes she flips her hair back, it has lots of body. I mean, her hair; her hair has lots of body. I mean... nothing. Never mind. She doesn't hold a candle to you, Valerie. She's so..."

"Yes, Patrick, never mind!"

"Um... uh ... so, Valerie, your baby sister, Jenny, she's cute. She doesn't really talk, does she?"

"No, not much. Didn't you notice that she looks a little different than other babies?"

"Yeah, I did. But I didn't want to be rude, so I didn't say anything. Why does she look like that?"

"Well, she has Down syndrome. Do you know what that is?"

"No, I've never heard of that before."

"Well, I'm not exactly sure what it is or what it all means, all I know is that she develops slow. You know, she learns slow. Something about X,Y,Z chromosomes, or whatever. We don't know what she'll be able to learn yet, because there are some people with Downs that have jobs, and get married, and do things like that. But there are some who can't. It just depends on her own personal development. My parents say that she'll never be able to live on her own, she'll have to live with someone for the rest of her life."

"Is she going to live with you?"

"I don't know."

"Well, if she does, then whoever you marry will have to be cool with it."

"What do you mean, Patrick?"

"I mean, whoever loves you is going to love you, no matter what. If that means that someday Jenny will live with you and your husband, well, yours and your husband's love will have to be strong enough to accept Jenny into your lives. Yours will have to be a passionate love, a burning love with a flame so strong, and hot that it will withstand whatever circumstance your marriage encounters. It might start out as a little spark, just a little glow that might produce a little warmth. But then it'll ignite, it'll explode; a fiery blaze that will spread like a raging wildfire, out-of-control. A burning love so intense that the red-hot flames between the two of you produces a scorching heat that'll melt everything around you. Then when you're apart from each other, you'll thirst; an unquenchable thirst that only you and your husband can suppress. Don't you think so, Valerie?"

"Huh?"

"Burning love. What I just said about burning love."

"Um, yeah, Patrick. It's hot in here."

"We're outside, Valerie."

"I know. But it's still hot in here."

"Take off my jacket. I want to ask you something."

"Yes! Yes! Yes! My answer is yes!"

"It is?"

"I mean, what? What do want to ask me?"

"I really like you, Valerie."

"I like you too, Patrick. What do you want to ask me?"

"Well, Valerie …"

"What do you want to ask me, Patrick? Ask me! Ask me!"

"Are you …"

"Yes, Patrick! My answer is yes!"

"… going around with anybody?"

"Oh! Um … no. I'm not going around with anybody. I'm not, Patrick. I'm on the market. I mean, I'm ready. No, I mean I'm available. I'm trying to say that I'm not going around with anybody. No one. There's no one. Not at all. I'm free."

"Good. Because I want to ask you if you would go around me."

Patrick reached into his pocket, and removed a dark blue, velvet, drawstring bag. Valerie looked on with wonder as he removed a sparkling, quarter carat diamond ring, hanging from a shimmering gold chain.

"My sister gave me this ring. It was our mother's; our father gave to her when he asked her to go around, back then they called it going steady. It's a promise ring, I'd like you to have it. Do you want to go around with me? Do you want to think about it?"

"Yes!"

"Yes, you want to think about it?"

"Yes. And no, I don't."

"Yes, you want to think about it? And no, you don't want to go around with me? Ouch. Okay."

"No! Patrick. Yes! Yes, I want to go around with you! And no, I don't want to think about it. I don't have to think about it. I'm sure that I want to go around with you. But are you sure about this ring?"

"My parents died when I was twelve; it was a car accident. My sister and brother-in-law raised me. Valerie, this ring is special to me, and so are you. Yes, I'm sure that I want you to have it. I think I'd better get you home now. I know your dad said we can stay out until 10:00, but I want to earn his respect, so, I'll have you home by 9:30 instead. Is that alright?"

"Yeah, that's alright," Valerie said.

"Alright, let's get you home."

CHAPTER EIGHT

A Beautiful Morning

Valerie looked at the calendar, which was hanging on the inside of her closet door. It was the fourth Thursday of November, better known as Thanksgiving Day. The house would soon be swarming with relatives. Valerie got dressed, opened her jewelry box, and carefully removed the diamond that Patrick gave her. She spent a few minutes admiring it before putting in on, after which, she spent a few more minutes admiring the way it looked on her neck. Eventually, she made her way downstairs to the kitchen.

"Good morning, Mom and Dad. Good morning, Jenny." She picked up Jenny from her high chair to give her a kiss before sitting her back down. Frank was sitting at the table, reading the newspaper.

"Good morning, Valerie," Anna said. "You seem to be in a good mood."

Valerie gave her mother a kiss, being careful not to get too close to her, as her hands were inside the carcass of a turkey.

"It's a beautiful morning!"

"Cupcake, every morning the good Lord lets me open my eyes is a beautiful morning. What makes this morning so beautiful to you?"

"She's in love, Frank. Are you hungry, Valerie? Would you like me to fix you some breakfast?"

"No thanks, Mom. Do you need any help with anything?" she asked, in hopes of getting a rejection.

"No, honey. But thank you for offering, you're very sweet."

"Valerie, what are your plans for this beautiful morning? Anything special?" asked Frank.

"Well, Daddy, it is Thanksgiving. As you can see, Mom is preparing a great meal with, hopefully, pumpkin and apple pies."

"Aunt Gina will bake pies, Valerie," said Anna.

"That's right, Cupcake. Aunt Gina will be here, along with everyone else. What are you going to wear today, when everybody comes over for Thanksgiving dinner?"

"Who is everybody?"

"Well, there's us, your sisters, and their husbands."

"Also, your uncle Danny, and aunt Gina," Anna added. "And your uncle Jim, and his new wife."

"What? Uncle Jim is married again? Since when?"

"Your uncle got married last weekend in Las Vegas," Frank said. "And your new aunt's name is something like Thelma or Velma. No, wait. It's Bonnie, because I teased him about him being Clyde. She'll be here this afternoon, ask her yourself. I can't believe my baby brother is married."

"Why can't you believe that Uncle Jim is married, Dad? Uncle Jim gets married all the time. I can't wait to meet my new aunt."

"Frank, her name is Nancy. Jim's wife is Nancy," said Anna.

"Well, I was close when I said Naomi. Oh, and one other person will be here," Frank said.

"Who is that, Daddy?"

"I forgot his name. I think it's Paul."

"Paul? Who's Paul?" asked Valerie. "Mom, who's Paul?"

"Valerie," Frank said, "I thought you knew Paul?"

"I don't know anyone named Paul."

Valerie took out a bottle of orange juice from the refrigerator, and started to pour herself a glass. After a few seconds, it dawned on her that her father was referring to Patrick. "Paul!" she exclaimed. Her excitement caused the orange juice to overflow from the glass, to the counter, and finally, to the floor. "Dad! Do you mean Patrick? Is Patrick coming over for Thanksgiving? Hotdog! Why didn't you tell me sooner? He probably thinks I'm a doofus because I didn't invite him myself."

"He doesn't think that, Valerie. I told him that it was your idea to invite him, so don't worry about it."

"I don't have anything to wear!" She ran to her bedroom, leaving a mess of orange juice for her mother to clean.

As everyone began to arrive at the Negron household, Valerie was still trying on outfits; she couldn't decide on what to wear. She narrowed down her choices to two dresses, when someone knocked on her bedroom door.

"Can we come in?" asked Delores.

"Didi! Priscilla! I'm so glad to see you."

"Hi, Doll. What's new?"

"I hear that someone has a boyfriend, and he's really cute," said Delores.

"Did Dad tell you? I think Dad likes him. He invited him over for Thanksgiving."

"Yes, Dad told us a few minutes ago," Priscilla said. "Well, tell us about him."

"His name is Patrick Cole, and he's real cute! He's a fox! He's tall, and his hair is dark, a little curly. He's a senior, like me. He used to go to Murphy, but transferred to Jefferson this year because his family moved. He has a job, he works at Andy's Handy Pharmacy. He's really nice, and fun to be with, and he makes me smile. He's really good with Jenny too, and she likes him. Look, he gave me this ring. But I didn't know that Daddy had invited him to come over today. I wish I had known because I have nothing to wear."

"That's a beautiful ring, Valerie. But what do you mean by saying that you have nothing to wear? You have a closet full of clothes," said Priscilla.

"Pretty clothes, my hand-me-downs," Delores said.

"I know, Didi. They're pretty, and I'm grateful. But some are too sexy, and I can't fill out the top part out quite the way that you do; unless I use socks. But I would be nervous about using socks. What if they fell out? That would be a nightmare!"

"Well, I wouldn't know about that; I've never had to use socks," Delores said.

"Don't worry about that, Val. Mom called me a few days ago, and told me all about your new boyfriend. I got you something, and you won't need socks."

Priscilla handed Valerie a shopping bag, which contained a new dress. Valerie removed the dress from the bag, and held it up to her body.

"Priscilla, it's beautiful. Thank you!"

"Well, I didn't get you a dress or anything, but I'll do your hair, and make-up," Delores said.

"Didi, thank you. I would love that."

"Okay, Dipwad, let's make you beautiful."

As the house began to fill up with relatives, Valerie anxiously paced the floor. She started in the living room, moved into the dining room, before returning back to the living room.

"Hey, why don't you sit down? He'll be here soon," Jeff said to Valerie.

She sat on the couch next to him, squirming in her seat.

"Valerie, don't be nervous. You're a very pretty girl, and you're smart. There's no reason for you to be nervous about anyone."

"Thank you, Jeff. This is my first boyfriend. When Didi was my age, she already had a ton of boyfriends. I'm not pretty like Didi."

"Yes, you are. And don't ever forget that. You're beautiful on the inside too."

"Thanks, Jeff."

"So, what's this guy's name, Patrick? He'd better be good to you or he'll have to answer to me." Jeff kissed Valerie on her forehead before walking away.

Patrick arrived with a bouquet of red roses for Valerie, and a single yellow rose for her mother.

"Thank you, Patrick. I love my roses!"

"And I thank you too, Patrick. I love my yellow rose! I'm the Yellow Rose of Texas!"

"How about if you dance for me later, Annie? You can put that rose between your teeth, and show me what you got."

"Daddy, we have company," Valerie said.

"Sorry, Cupcake."

"That's okay, because this is the best Thanksgiving ever."

Before long, the air was filled with the sensational aroma of a combination of spices, masking the subtleness of burnt dinner rolls. The blending of scents served as an informal notice that dinner was ready. The lavish meal was set up on the kitchen counter, elegantly arranged with the turkey in the center, and a cornucopia of the trimmings on one side. On the other side, was an assortment of decadent, scrumptious desserts. Relatives overflowed on two elongated tables; one table for the older generation, and one table for the younger generation. As Frank prepared to give the Thanksgiving blessing, he was interrupted by Michael.

"Priscilla has an announcement to make. Go ahead, honey."

"No, you do it, Mike."

"No, I want you to do it, honey."

"No, darling. You should be the one to do it."

"Oh, for crying out loud. Priscilla is pregnant," Delores annoyingly blurted out.

"Thanks for spoiling it, Didi," said Priscilla.

"Sorry," Delores said.

As congratulations were offered to Priscilla and Michael, Delores secretly slipped away from the table. After a short period, she nonchalantly returned. Her momentary absence had gone unnoticed by everyone, except her husband.

Some belched, others hiccupped, while Frank broke wind; just about everyone gave some indication that they may have overindulged. The blame for this irresponsible behavior was placed on Anna and Gina, because they prepared the delicious meal. Nevertheless, after an adequate intermission from eating, it was time for dessert.

"Mom, do you have any whipped cream? I don't see any," asked Delores, as she stood in front of the refrigerator, with the door wide open, rifling through the contents on the shelves.

"Delores, that was the one thing I asked you to bring. If you didn't bring it, then we don't have any."

"No worries, Mom. I'll run and get some, be right back."

"Didi," said Jeff, "don't leave. We don't need whipped cream."

"Nonsense. My mother wants whipped cream, so I'm going to get her whipped cream."

"Delores, I don't need any whipped cream. There is no need for you to go anywhere. We are all having a good time, enjoying ourselves," Anna said.

"Well, just think how much more we will enjoy ourselves if we have whipped cream. I'll go get some."

"Delores," Frank said, "no one needs whipped cream. Besides, the grocery store is closed. Sit down with your husband."

"Dad, I'll go to the drug store, it's open. I'll be right back."

"Andy's Handy Pharmacy is closed today. Andy believes in family time, so he closed the store," said Patrick.

Glaring at Patrick, Delores said, "Big Tex Pharmacy is open 24 hours."

At once, Delores was gone; leaving her family in bewilderment.

"Priscilla, do you know what's going on with your sister?" Anna asked.

"No, Mom, I don't. Let's not let Didi ruin our Thanksgiving. Let's enjoy the day."

"Patrick, let's see if we can catch a game on the boob tube. We'll have our dessert in the living room," Frank said.

"Football? I'm in," said Jim.

He grabbed his wife's hand to lead her to the living room. She pulled her hand out of his, and said, "I think I'll help the girls serve the dessert, then wash the dishes, sweetheart."

"Thanks, Aunt Nancy," Priscilla said.

"Yes, thank you, Nancy," Anna said. Turning to Gina, she added, "I really like her."

The football game on TV had already started. The team that Michael and Jeff were rooting for was doing quite well. Frank, Danny, and Jim were going for the other team, which was not playing up to par, according to the Negron brothers. The excitement of the game caused Jim to let out a few curse words, prompting Frank to smack him on the back of his head.

"Sorry, Frankie."

"It's alright, Jimmy. It gives me an excuse to smack you."

Valerie and Patrick sat on the floor, careful not to block the view of the TV, which was a floor console. Valerie's disinterest in the game caused her eyes to roam.

"If you're bored, Dollface, why don't you help out in the kitchen?"

"Excellent idea, Mikey," Danny said. "And would you mind bringing your dear uncle another piece of pumpkin pie?"

"Sure, Uncle Danny. Come with me, Patrick."

Until now, Valerie had been able to sidestep the kitchen. Anyone in or nearby was certain to be recruited to carry out a role in tidying up the aftermath of what once was a sparkling clean kitchen.

"Mom, do you need help with anything?" Valerie asked. "I'll be happy to help after I take Uncle Danny a piece of pie."

"No, thank you, Valerie. We're almost finished. Why don't you and Patrick take Trixie out?"

"Mrs. Negron, would you like to come with us for a walk?"

"No, but thank you for asking. You're a very sweet young man, Patrick. Thank you again, for my yellow rose, and for coming, and spending Thanksgiving with us. I've enjoyed getting to know you, and Frank thinks highly of you; I want you to know that. Your sister has done a fine job in raising you. Frank told me about your parents; I'm very sorry, dear."

"Thank you, Mrs. Negron. You and Mr. Negron have been very kind to me. The whole family has been great."

The unsettledness that Anna was feeling, brought upon by Delores, was gone, and replaced by the fondness that she felt for Patrick. She was happy that her daughter had found a companion who possessed many of the qualities essential for a prospective mate, just as she had found in Frank, many years before. The serene moment was disrupted by the sound of the phone ringing.

"I'll get it," Valerie said. She ran to answer the phone, which was hanging on the wall in the kitchen. She was quick, catching it on the second ring. Wearing a look of irritation on her face, Valerie stretched out the ten-foot cord to reach her mother, and handed her the receiver.

"It's Didi, for you, Mom."

"Delores, where are you?" asked Anna.

Priscilla casually walked into the living room; she held her right hand in a fist next to her cheek, as though she was holding a telephone receiver. Without using her voice, she mouthed, 'It's Didi'. Jeff and Frank promptly got up from the ugly chair, and couch, respectively, and speedily made their way to the kitchen.

"Is that Delores?" Frank asked, before snatching the phone out of Anna's hand. "Delores, you tell me where you are. Tell me right now."

"Dad, I'm at the hospital."

"Are you alright?"

"I'm fine. I'm visiting a friend."

"Delores, your family is here. Your husband and son are here. I'm sure that your friend will understand why you need to come home."

"I'm tired, Dad. I'm going to stay here a while longer, then I'm going home. I'm not going back to your house."

"Delores Joan, you need to get back here. You need to get back to your family, to your husband," Frank said, sternly.

"I already told you, I'm visiting a friend. When I am ready to leave, I'm going home."

"Delores, come home now. Hello? Hello? Are you there? Delores? Annie, our daughter hung up on me."

"I'm sorry, dear, but you should not have scolded her. I'm not saying that you were wrong, but you know Delores, she doesn't listen to you, anyway."

"Jeff," Frank said, "Delores says she's at the hospital visiting a friend. Do you know who her friend is?"

After a brief pause, Jeff reluctantly answered, "Yes, Frank, I do. But I don't want you to get involved."

"Jeff, talk to me, son. Delores is my daughter, and I love her. But I know her, and I know you; you're a good man. Tell me who's she with."

Jeff hesitated before answering, "Her friend, they work together at the gym. They've been spending a lot of nights together, their gym rendezvouses. She said she was working out; she didn't mention the kind of work out she was getting. Anyway, he is also married, and his wife found out. She called me, and I confronted Didi. We had a big fight, she told me to leave."

"What do you mean, she told you to leave?" Frank asked.

"She told me to leave. I've been staying with a friend. Before today, I hadn't seen her in over two weeks. I wasn't going to come over today, but she said that I should, so I can take Kevin for a few days."

"Jeff, you are always welcome here. Even if you and Delores get a divorce," said Anna.

"Annie, nobody is getting a divorce! Jeff, why is he in the hospital?" asked Frank.

"His wife, she has a lot of brothers."

"What did they do? Beat him up?"

"If they had just beat him up, he'd be alright. They nearly killed him."

"I wish they had killed him."

"Frank, you don't mean that."

"No, Annie, I don't. I'm sorry for saying it. It's just that ... that girl is impossible! Why can't she be happy with one man? Priscilla is happy with one man. Gina is happy with one man. You're happy with one man, aren't you, Annie?"

"Of course, darling. I'm very happy to be with only one man."

"What about Elvis Presley, Mom? Wouldn't you rather be with Elvis Presley than with Daddy?" asked Valerie.

"Well, of course, dear. I love your father, but c'mon; apples and oranges. I have apple pie all the time, that's your father. Just once, I would love to taste the orange. Do you know what I mean? For his lips to gently touch mine, for our bodies to press up against each other, for my heart to flutter, as never before…"

"Annie, do you mind? I'm standing right here!"

"I'm sorry, Frank."

"We're married, you know."

"I know. I'm sorry. Please forgive me."

"Well, I guess, but you'll have to make it up to me. Tonight, in the bedroom, wear that black nighty I bought you. I know it's a little ripped from the other night, but it'll still get the job done, huh, Annie?"

"Oh, I wish that Delores hadn't forgotten the whipped cream. Wouldn't that have been great, Frank?"

"Oh yeah, if only we had whipped cream. Annie, do you remember that one day, Valerie was at school, and Jenny was with Danny and Gina, you made vanilla pudding, and we went back to bed, and we ate the pudding in bed, and you got a little on you, and I …"

"Mom, Dad, please! Can you give it a rest? We were talking about Didi," said Priscilla.

"I'm sorry, Princess. Delores, yeah. What is wrong with my middle daughter? I just don't get it. Annie, I can't stand by and let our daughter ruin her marriage. I'm going to tell that girl a thing or two. And I'm going to do it right now."

"Frankie, you're angry. You shouldn't talk to her when you're angry," said Danny.

"Frankie, she's a grown woman. This is between her and her husband," Jim said.

"She may be a grown woman, but she's still my daughter. I'm going to find her. I have to talk to her. I'll choose my words carefully. I can't let her throw her life away. Jeff, do you know which hospital she's at?"

"I don't know," said Jeff.

"Well, there are only three in town, I'll find her. I'm not going to let her throw her life away. If she wants to throw her life away, it'll be over my dead body."

Frank grabbed the keys to his pickup truck that were hanging from a hook on the wall in the kitchen.

"Annie, I'm going to get our daughter."

"I'm coming with you," said Anna.

"Frank, you need to calm down," Gina said. She stood in his way to block him from leaving.

"Gina, I love you. You're like my sister," Frank said. He hugged her, and gently lifted her feet off the floor, moving her out of his way so that he could leave.

"Annie?"

"I'm right behind you," Anna said.

"Daddy, please don't go anywhere. Leave Didi alone, let her do what she wants. No matter what you say to her, she's going to do what she wants."

"Princess, I love you."

"Gina, will you watch Jenny for me?" Anna asked.

"Of course, Anna. You go with your stubborn husband, he's a mule. I'll take care of Jenny."

Anna ran outside to get into the pickup truck. Frank was already seated inside, about to start the motor. Gina hollered at Frank from the doorway.

"Frank, Delores is going to do what Delores wants to do. You can't stop her. If she wants to ruin her life, she will."

"Over my dead body!" he yelled back.

"You're a mule, Frank! You're a stubborn mule!" Gina hollered.

Frank peeled out of the driveway. Anna didn't have time to close the door on her side of the pickup, but the swift speed of which Frank drove off created a velocity high enough that it slammed the door shut for her.

Gina turned to her husband, and said, "Your brother is a stubborn, old mule!"

"I know, my love," said Danny. "He always has been."

Following a day of food, fun, enchantment, and drama, it was time for Patrick to leave. Valerie walked her boyfriend outside, and they spent a few moments on the porch, where Patrick, awkwardly, and endlessly, thanked Valerie for the invitation to spend the holiday with her. During what they believed to be a private moment, Patrick gently, and tenderly kissed Valerie goodnight. An intrusive clan, made up of Valerie's family members, witnessed their romance by peeking out the front window.

As Valerie turned the doorknob to let herself into the house, her nosey family quickly scattered about to various locations of the living room. Michael was sitting on the couch, along with her two uncles. Her new aunt, Nancy, sat on Jim's lap. They were intensely watching something on TV. Valerie noticed that it was a commercial for feminine hygiene products, so their enthusiastic interest didn't add up. Jeff and Priscilla sat on the loveseat, having a serious conversation about diaper rash.

"Do I put the cream directly on his winky or just around it?" asked Jeff.

"Well," Priscilla replied, "I think you're okay with putting it on the winky. I don't know for sure because I've only changed Valerie's and Jenny's diapers; and neither of them have a winky."

Gina was sitting on the ugly chair, thumbing through a magazine. Even as her eyes focused on the pages, she didn't realize that she was holding the magazine upside down.

"Excuse me," Valerie said.

"Oh, honey, we didn't see you there. I was just reading this magazine, it has some very good recipes." Gina tossed the magazine; while aiming for the coffee table, it landed on the floor.

"Did Patrick leave?" Priscilla asked.

"Yes, he just left," Valerie said. "But you should know that, shouldn't you?"

"How should I know?" asked Priscilla.

Valerie skimmed the room, and took notice of the guilty pleasure expressions that everyone wore on their face. She squinted her eyes, as though using them as weapons, to shoot daggers at her nosey family.

"I know you all were spying on me, and I don't appreciate it!"

"We weren't spying on you!" said Priscilla.

"We did no such thing!" said Gina.

"That's absurd!" said Michael.

"We've been sitting here, watching TV," said Jim.

"Why would we do that?" asked Jeff.

"We're sorry, Valerie," said Danny.

"Why were you spying on me?"

"Okay, we were spying, but just for a minute. Please forgive us, but you looked so cute," Gina said.

"Valerie, we didn't mean to do it," said Jeff.

"Valerie, don't be mad," said Priscilla.

"Why did you do that to me? I would never do that to any of you."

"Yes, you would," Michael said. "You have spied on us before. Remember, Priscilla? Once when we were making out here in this living room. We were on the green velvet couch, the one your parents had before your dad bought this couch."

"Yeah, I remember. Valerie was hiding right there by the doorway."

"I was five, and Daddy scolded me for it."

"Valerie, sweetheart, I'm sorry. I'm new to the family, the last thing that I'd want to do is make you angry," said Nancy.

"I'm not angry with you, Aunt Nancy." said Valerie.

"Valerie, you were thirteen, not five," Michael said. "But we're sorry, Dollface. Don't be angry with us."

The sound of the doorbell seemed out of place, as no one was expected to visit at that hour.

"I'll get it," Valerie said, "maybe it's Patrick, maybe he forgot something." Valerie opened the front door to find two men standing on the porch. "Hi, come in," she said, leading them into the living room. "Policemen are here," she said to her family.

CHAPTER NINE

Seasons In The Sun

I t was the dreaded visitor that no family ever wants to have knocking on their door; law enforcement. They did not pay visits for joyous occasions, they had bad news to deliver, and that was obvious to everyone, except Valerie. With only three family members who were not present, Priscilla's imagination fled to a region unknown to her. Grisly, dreadful thoughts dominated her consciousness before she was able to reflect on the splendor of those whom she cherished, but were absent; her parents and her sister.

"Is this the residence of Frank and Anna Negron?" asked one of the officers.

"Yes," Priscilla said, "they're my parents, but they're not here right now."

"No, ma'am. We regret to inform you that there's been an accident."

"No," Priscilla said, softly.

Though still oblivious to the purpose of the officers' visit, Valerie was spooked by the demeanor of her sister. Hesitantly, she approached her, and gradually put her arms around her.

"The driver of the pickup truck, Mr. Francis Robert Negron, was heading west on County Road 86. He lost control of the vehicle; he and his passenger, Anna Maria Negron, were ejected. I'm sorry, they've both been pronounced dead at the scene. We are truly sorry for your losses," the police officer said.

"No, no, no, no! This can't be!" Priscilla sobbed, uncontrollably.

Michael gathered her and Valerie in his arms, and held them tightly. The second police officer offered his condolences, then they both left the house.

"No! This isn't happening! No! It's not happening! God, why?" Priscilla asked, between sobs.

Valerie's naivete ceased when she ultimately grasped reality, and the tragedy became evident. Echoing the cries of her sister, she could scarcely fathom the demise of her parents. Priscilla decisively placed blame for the catastrophe on Delores. Though no one declared that they were in agreement, it was not the time for such a conversation.

With the passing of hours, eventually, everyone drifted off to sleep. Danny and Gina slept in Valerie's room, while Jim and Nancy slept in the guest room. Priscilla slept in Michael's arms, while he slept on the couch. Jeff, while holding his son, fell asleep on the ugly chair; his feet resting on the mismatched ottoman. Valerie curled herself into a ball on the loveseat. As dawn approached, the family awoke in succession. Feelings of disbelief remained in the hushed ambience of the house. Nancy put on a pot of coffee while Gina searched through the refrigerator, looking for something to fix for breakfast. She found half a dozen eggs, so, she sent Danny to the grocery store to buy more. Jeff was the first to shatter the silence by starting a dialogue.

"I have to find Didi. I have to tell her what happened."

"I don't want to see her right now," Priscilla said.

"Priscilla, she has to be told," said Gina.

"I have to find her, I have to tell her about her parents," said Jeff.

"You go on, honey," said Gina. "Nancy and I will keep an eye on Kevin for you."

"Yes," Nancy agreed. "You take whatever time you need."

"Thank you," said Jeff.

"Jeff," Priscilla said, as she grabbed his arm, "tell her what happened, but tell her not to come back to this house. We don't want her here. But you will always be welcome. My parents loved you."

"Your parents also loved Delores, she's still their daughter. And they wouldn't want you to be angry with her. I have to find her, and when I do, she will be welcome to come back to this house. This is her parents' house, and they would not want her to be turned away by her own sister."

Jeff walked out the door, leaving Priscilla to make peace with her feelings towards Delores.

"No one has ever made my brother do anything that he didn't want to do," Jim said. "He had his own free will, and that's why he left last night. Your mother went with him, because she didn't like to spend too much time away from him; neither one of them liked to be away from the other for too long. You can't blame your sister for that. At least they went together. Frankie and Anna are together, forever."

Valerie, still sleeping, awoke to the sound of voices. She sat up, and listened carefully. She couldn't make out what was being said, but she did recognize the voices to be that of her parents. She got up, and followed the sound, which led her to the front porch. She saw her parents sitting on the porch swing.

"Mom, Dad? Is that really you?" she asked.

She slowly moved towards them.

"Wait, honey. Wait right there," Anna said to her.

"Why?"

"Valerie, we just came to say goodbye."

"Cupcake, there are a few things that I need to say to you. First of all, your mother and I want to make sure that you go to college. Promise us that you will go, and that you will finish. We want you to get a degree."

"I do want to go to college, Daddy. I don't know what I want to be yet, maybe a teacher."

"Valerie, you'll make a wonderful teacher. You've always made your father and me proud, I want you to know that."

"I know, Mom. You've told me before, many times."

"There's something else; do you remember that day at the park when we talked about what might happen to Jenny after your mother and I are gone?"

"Yes, Daddy, I remember."

"We don't want you to feel guilty. Michael will ultimately have the final decision on where Jenny goes. You're young, and we don't want to burden you. We want what's best for you, and for Jenny."

"Dad, I told you that I would take care of Jenny, and I will. I promise."

"You're a good girl, Valerie. But trust whatever decision Mike makes. He'll do whatever is best for both of you, alright?"

"No, Dad. I know what is best for me, and what is best for Jenny. I will do what is best for both of us. She's my sister, and I'm going to take care of her."

"Whatever Mike says," Anna interjected.

"And one more thing," Frank added, "I know that you and Delores are always giving each other a hard time. I guess that's what sisters do. Sometimes you tend to jump the gun without knowing all the facts. I'm sure that you're upset with Delores right now, but don't be. You don't know all the facts."

"I hate Delores right now, Dad. So does Priscilla. We both hate her."

Valerie's eyes welled up with tears.

"Priscilla is my princess, she's a sensitive girl. She doesn't hate Delores, she's just upset right now. But she's logical, and smart. It might take her a few days or so, but she'll come to realize that what happened was not Delores' fault; it's just something that happened. But you, on the other hand, you've always been emotional. That's not always a good thing, Valerie. That leads you to be a little over dramatic, at times. When people are too emotional, they can't think logically. You're blaming Delores for something that she had no control over. You can't do that. You said that you hate your sister? You're letting your emotions control you, Valerie. If you love us, then you can't hate Delores. She's our daughter too, and we love her."

"I will try not to hate her. But right now, I do. If you really are not coming back, then it will be hard for me not to hate her."

"You can be angry, but don't let that anger fester inside you, then it becomes hate. You don't have to promise me right now, but at some point, you have to let it go, Cupcake. What happened was not Delores' fault."

"Valerie, do you know why I always liked to go everywhere with your father?"

"No, Mom. Why did you like to go everywhere with Dad?"

"Because, I always thought, if something ever happens to Frank, and the Lord takes him away from me, then I want to be with him so that we can go together. I don't want to live without him. I know that I have you girls, but you'll do what kids do. You'll grow up, and move away, start your own lives. I love you girls, but I love your father in a different way. I never wanted to imagine my life without him. Now I'll never have to."

"But what about Jenny, Mom? She needs you."

"I love Jenny, but she's a baby. She won't even remember me."

"But I need you too, Mom. I'll remember you."

"I know you will, Valerie. But I have no say-so about this. My life is over, I have to go."

"If you and Dad are really not coming back, then I do blame Didi. If she hadn't left yesterday, then you and Dad wouldn't have gone after her. You would still be here. This is her fault."

"Cupcake, I made the decision to leave. Delores didn't ask me to go out looking for her. I did that because I love her. She's my daughter. You have no idea what Delores has been through, or what lies ahead for her."

"Valerie, Delores is going through a lot right now. Just love her."

"Okay, Mom, Dad. I'll try to love her. But I won't like it."

"Valerie, before we go, I want to tell you about the shoebox. If you look under mine and your father's bed, you'll find a shoebox. There are a few things that I'd like you to have for your wedding to Patrick, and a few other mementos."

"What's in there, Annie? Where are the love letters that I wrote to you? I mean, I don't mind if Valerie reads them. They're my beautiful expressions of love to you. But you know how Valerie is. She doesn't want to know that we have feelings, and do things, how we love each other."

"Oh yeah, Valerie. The letters may be a little risqué for you. I know Priscilla would not appreciate them either. But Delores would sure love to read them, give them to her."

"I want them," said Valerie. "I may not read them, but I want them."

"Well, share them with your sister," Anna said. "Valerie, will you do something for me? When you have kids, if you have a boy, will you name him Robert? I've always liked that name. Remember, it's your father's middle name."

"Okay, Mom. I'll name my first son, Robert."

"Thank you, sweetheart."

"Well, if your mother gets to pick out your son's name, then I want to pick out your daughter's name. After all, you got to pick my daughter's name."

"Alright, Dad. If I ever have a daughter, what do you want me to name her?"

"Anything but Myrtle."

"Oh boy, Frank! My grandmother is not going to be pleased with you."

"Uh oh, Dad. You're on great-grandma's naughty list."

"Don't worry about your father. I'll look after him, as I've always done for these many years. Now you have to go in the house, Valerie. It's time, sweetheart. We love you, always remember that."

"No, Mom. I won't go in the house unless you come with me."

"We can't go inside the house, Valerie," Anna said. "We have to be going."

"No, Mom. Don't go. I don't want you to go," Valerie said, her sobs becoming increasingly profound.

"We have to go, but we love you," said Anna.

"Mom, I need you to stay. Please stay. Daddy, don't go. At least, let me hug you. Please let me touch you, just one more time."

"Valerie," Frank said, "we can't do that. We must go. But we'll always be in your heart. You won't see us, but we'll be right there. And we'll be there when you start your life with Patrick. Don't let anyone tell you that you're too young. Eighteen is not too young. Your mother was younger than that when I fell in love with her. I know that boy loves you."

"Do you think so, Daddy?"

"I know so."

It was becoming increasingly difficult for Valerie to maintain her composure. She steadfastly refused to go into the house, for fear of never seeing her parents again.

"Valerie, we're all on this earth for just a short time, a season. Your mother and I have had a good life; a great marriage, and we made great kids. We've had a good season. The days that lie ahead will be sorrowful, but the sun will shine again for you, Valerie. Trust me, it will. Your season is just beginning, and you'll share your seasons in the sun with Patrick. There will be many seasons in the sun for you, Valerie. Now please be a good girl. I love you, Cupcake, and I always will, but it's time for you to go into the house."

"Yes, Valerie. It's time for us to leave. I love you, always, my sweet daughter. This is very difficult, I can't say goodbye. Please, listen to your father. Go into the house."

"Valerie, where are you, Doll?" Priscilla called out.

"Your sister is calling for you, Valerie. Go in the house," Frank said.

"I'm out here, Priscilla," Valerie called out.

"Why don't you ask Priscilla to come out here?"

"Alright, Dad. I'll be right back. Don't leave."

Valerie ran into the house, and called out for Priscilla. She found her in the living room, sitting on the loveseat.

"Priscilla? Mom and Dad, they're outside. Come outside with me."

"Valerie, come here, Doll."

"Didn't you hear me? Mom and Dad are outside. Come outside with me."

"Sit down here with me, for a few minutes. Mom and Dad want you to sit with me. Come on, come now, and sit."

Valerie walked towards Priscilla, and sat next to her. Priscilla wrapped her arms around Valerie.

"I love you, Doll."

"Priscilla, come outside with me. Mom and Dad are on the front porch."

"Okay, I'll go outside with you. But first, I want you to do me a favor. Open your eyes."

Valerie opened her eyes to find herself on the loveseat, curled up in a ball. Priscilla was next to her, kneeling on the floor, caressing her forehead.

"Wake up, Valerie. Patrick is here," said Priscilla.

Without saying a word to either Priscilla or Patrick, Valerie leapt to her feet; without delay, she ran out to the front porch, calling out to her parents. Priscilla and Patrick followed after her.

"Mom, Dad! Come back! Please come back!" Turning to Priscilla, she said, "They were here just a few minutes ago. Mom and Dad were here, Priscilla. I talked to them; they were right here. Mom was sitting on the swing, and Dad was sitting next to her. Then he got up, and stood right there. I'm telling you the truth, they were here; just a few minutes ago."

Taking Valerie into her arms, Priscilla comforted her little sister. Michael watched, in grief, from the doorway. Patrick assumed the role of comforter by taking Valerie from Priscilla's arms, into his own. In an attempt to persuade Priscilla, Valerie reiterated, "Mom and Dad were here, just a few minutes ago. They were right here."

In the days that followed, the family was faced with the unpleasantries of making the final arrangements for the unexpected deaths of Frank and Anna. Patrick was given the honor of serving as a pallbearer. The day of the funeral would be the first time Delores would see her family since Thanksgiving. Despite the fact that she was a married woman, she was accompanied by her lover when she arrived at the service. Having been released from the hospital only a few days before; his chest was tightly bandaged, and his face was still slightly bruised. One of his knees had been broken, so he relied on Delores, and the use of cane to help him get around.

She entered the funeral home, and sat in the back, on the last row. Her plan was to slip out immediately after the service concluded, without being seen by anyone. She carefully scanned the room, taking notice of those who attended. She saw Jeff sitting next to Priscilla on the front row. On the second row, behind Valerie, was her mother's sister, Teresa. Although Teresa and Anna only saw each other occasionally, they shared a close bond. Teresa's husband, George, and Frank, were also great friends.

A few rows over, she saw Frank and Anna's friends, Mr. and Mrs. Ladson. Valerie's friends, Karen and Debra, were also there, with their boyfriends; their parents sat in the row behind them. A few rows away from them, on the arm of a new man, was her old friend, Jennifer. Delores, still regretful about what happened between her and Jennifer, was happy to see her friend with somebody new. Sitting next to her uncle Danny, was her cousin, Mario. They seldom saw each other, and she missed his friendship. Although she had never met Frank's dear friend, Max, he was there with his daughter and her husband. There was no way anyone would be able to predict the significant role one member of Max's family would have in Delores' future.

Lastly, she noticed a woman whom she recognized from Jeff's office. She was sitting alone. She and Delores had never been formally introduced, but she had seen her on a few occasions. The encounters between the two were not very friendly. Delores found her presence to be puzzling, and a bit uncomfortable. Unfortunately, Delores' well thought out plan to slip out quietly became unraveled when she was spotted by Kevin, who was sitting a few rows from the back, in the arms of one of Anna's relatives. Upon seeing his mother, he cried out to her. His faint cry rang loudly in the stillness of the room, catching the attention of everyone, including her estranged husband.

Jeff turned around and spotted Delores. The eye contact between the two lasted a mere second. As a result, it led Jeff to make a decision to confront his wife. Hoping to evade him, she hastily exited the building, leaving her lover trailing behind.

"Your son is calling you," Jeff said, as he caught up with Delores in the parking lot.

She dug through her purse to look for her keys, while giving Jeff the cold shoulder. He grabbed her by her arm, and repeated his previous statement.

"Your son is calling you."

"Jeff, I just can't see him now. I'll pick him up tomorrow afternoon."

By now, her adulterer caught up with them, and took it upon himself to get involved in a private matter between a husband and his wife.

"I'm Johnny," he said to Jeff. He stuck his hand out as a gesture.

Refusing to shake hands with the man whom his wife had taken up with, Jeff sized him up. Despite the bruising on his face, it was evident that he was a good-looking man. As a result of Jeff's rejection of his pseudo token of goodwill, under the guise of a hand shake; Johnny decided to step up his game by showing Jeff the prominent role he thought he had in Delores' life. Having heard the banter between Delores and Jeff, he steadfastly justified her conduct towards her son.

"Listen, Jeff, Delores has been through a lot. She's still trying to process everything that happened with her parents. Naturally, she's upset. You shouldn't take it personally, and neither should your son. I can give you a call when she comes around."

Jeff, being completely repulsed by the obnoxious suggestion presented to him by his rival, found his presence to be distasteful. He was highly offended that Delores gave him so much leeway concerning their son, and the manner of which he spoke to him. Entirely out of his character, he set off an altercation by slamming his fist into Johnny's mouth, which was immediately followed by a second punch to his nose. Hearing Delores' screams, pleading for him to stop, he stepped back to examine the devastation of his rage, and the destruction of his marriage. Delores' pleas were not necessarily for Johnny's benefit, but for Jeff's; she didn't want him to end up in jail if Johnny decided to press charges for assault. Jeff shared an acrimonious glance with the woman he loved. Before getting into the car with Johnny, she had a couple of questions for Jeff, which caught him off guard.

"What is that woman to you? And why is she here, at my parents' funeral?"

Arduous days follow the death of a loved one. Somehow, amid the trials and tribulations, life must resume to normal; not as it once was, but as it will be. Valerie, as anyone in her situation would be, was left with an enormous cross to bear. A dismal existence while learning to live without those who are most treasured, those who will forever remain close at heart.

A great uncertainty loomed through her mind; what was to become of her and Jenny? At the age of seventeen, she was not quite ready for the world of obligations and responsibilities of living independently. Nor was she ready for the commitments and accountabilities that she would be charged with if appointed conservator over Jenny. Still, the promises made to her father occupied her thoughts; promises that were given freely of her own will, not as rhetorical responses to requests made by him.

A temporary resolution concerning Valerie's and Jenny's living arrangements involved their relatives that resided in Crystal Springs. The plan was that everyone would alternate spending one week living in the Negron house to look after Valerie and Jenny. Valerie gave this plan two vehement thumbs down.

"I promised Dad that I would take care of Jenny," Valerie said. "I'm sure there's money in his bank that we could use to live. And I could learn how to drive Mom's car. Michael, Mom and Dad said that you would have the final say. Please trust me. I'm not a baby. I can do this."

"When did Mom and Dad say that to you, Valerie?" Priscilla asked.

"The day they came to see me, to say goodbye; the day after Thanksgiving. I know that you don't believe me, but I am not lying. They were here."

"I believe you, sweetheart," Gina said. "I know your father would do whatever he had to do to see you one more time, your mother too."

"Thank you, Aunt Gina. Priscilla, you don't have to believe me. I won't be mad at you, because I know it sounds crazy."

"Well, I believe that you believe it; if that counts for anything."

"Yes, it does, thank you. Does this mean that I can stay here with Jenny, and take care of her by myself?"

"Not by yourself," Jim said. "If Mike is in agreement, you can live with Jenny, but we're all just a phone call away. What do you say, Mike? Will you trust the Small Fry to be on her own? We will all be here for her. Besides, I can't stay here for a whole week, and have her in my hair. She'll cramp my style with the ladies. Do you know what I mean? I can't bring a woman here, and entertain her, the way that I like to entertain women."

"Excuse me?" Nancy asked. She was a bit annoyed, and surprised by his comment.

"Baby, I'm sorry. I don't know why I said that. I'm not thinking straight."

"I guess that's understandable, with everything that's happened," Nancy said. "But watch yourself, Jim."

"Uncle Jim," Priscilla said, "Aunt Nancy is a very sweet woman, and I like her, we all do. So don't blow it! I'm going to tell you something that I frequently told my dad; we don't want to know about your sex life! What is it with you, Negron men? You always have to brag, and boast about your conquests. Dad did that all the time, and you do it too. Uncle Danny, you never do that. Thank you."

"I never brag about my sex life because I don't have a sex life," Danny said.

"What? You watch your mouth! Or you're never getting it again," Gina said.

"Sorry, my love," said Danny. "I just meant that it would be nice if we could share our special moments together more frequently. If you're worried about me bragging it about it afterwards; I promise I won't, my love."

"We'll talk later," Gina said, sternly.

"Well, I don't consider it bragging, just stating a fact," Jim said. "We, Negron men, have never had any problems in the bedroom. No siree Bob. We've always been virile. And my brother, he was something else. Him and your mother were always going at it. They were like rabbits. God bless them."

"Uncle Jim, don't tell us anymore!" Valerie said. In order to tune him out, she stuck her fingers in her ears, and began to sing, "la la la, la la la, la la la."

"Mike, if it makes you feel better, I'll drive around randomly at all hours of the night," said Jim. "If I see a red Cutlass in the driveway, there's gonna be trouble."

"No sir, I wouldn't do that," Patrick said.

"Jim, Patrick is a good boy. Leave him alone," Gina said.

"Yeah, I guess you're right," said Jim.

"Valerie, are you going to be ready to learn to drive tomorrow afternoon? I'll teach you," said Jeff. "If you want, I can teach you to drive the mustang."

"The mustang? That old car? It's over ten years old. No, thank you. Who would want to drive an old mustang? Not me."

"I think it's pretty classy," said Patrick.

"Well, Mike, what do you say?" Jim asked. "I feel comfortable with this decision."

"Me too, Mikey," Danny said. "I trust Valerie. She's smart, and responsible. But I still want you to have a life, and enjoy yourself, Valerie. Gina and I are close by, we'll babysit every Saturday."

"And I'll come by every morning to get Jenny off to her daycare," Gina said.

"Jimmy and I will babysit every Friday night, so you and Patrick can go out on dates," said Nancy.

"Mikey, the four of us are close by. We'll be here during the week too. At a moment's notice, if need be," said Danny.

"Let's give it a try," Michael said. "But I can't stress this enough, Valerie, this arrangement is temporary. I'll reevaluate things as we go along."

"Thanks, Michael. I won't let you down," said Valerie.

"You're welcome, Dollface. And you'd better not," said Michael.

CHAPTER TEN

All I Have To Do Is Dream

A few months had passed since Valerie last saw her sisters. She mused over Delores; hoped that she was safe, yet, she still had much resentment over what she considered to be Delores' role in the death of their parents. She remembered that her father wanted her to let go of her anger, and not blame Delores for the accident. She was not ready to do that. Though she hadn't seen Priscilla, they maintained close contact, speaking on the phone at least twice a week.

With the baby due at the end of May or early June, Valerie was curious about Priscilla's pregnancy weight gain. Her phone conversations with Michael included a little game, which he called, *Guess how much weight your sister has gained.* Priscilla was gaining an excessive amount of weight, which she attributed to the pregnancy, as well as stress associated with mourning. Michael attributed it, mainly, to pizza, cheesecake, and Mexican food, with the pregnancy having a minor contribution.

The senior prom was just around the corner. Valerie and her friends, with Jenny in tow, went shopping for their prom dresses. Valerie knew it would not be easy for her to find the one special dress that would not only be the right color, and have the right fit, but would also be sexy, in a modest way. A few days before the prom, Priscilla and Michael planned a visit to spend some time with Valerie and Jenny. Their stay would be long enough to attend Valerie's graduation.

Priscilla arranged a day of pampering for Valerie and her friends by taking them to get facials, manicures, and pedicures. Jenny also got a manicure and pedicure; along with a new dress and shoes. Priscilla had an extra surprise for the girls; a gift bag containing high quality, glamorous cosmetics, body lotion, and a small bottle of expensive perfume. The girls excitedly experimented with new shades from their eyeshadow palettes so that on the night of the prom, they would be ready to use their new colors.

Priscilla intended to help the girls get ready for their big night. However, since her unborn child vied for her attention, all she could do was sit in a chair in Valerie's bedroom while the girls got ready. Her thoughts reflected on the upcoming milestones in Valerie's life, and how the void created by their mother's absence might affect her little sister. She also wondered about Delores; whether her continued reckless behavior was the effect of losing their parents.

"Thank you for taking me and my friends for our girls' day out, and for our make-up. I love my make-up," Valerie said.

"You're welcome. I hope that tonight is special for you," Priscilla replied.

"It will be. I wish Mom and Dad were here. I miss them. I know you're thinking about them too, I can tell."

"Yes, I was thinking about them. I wish they were here to see how pretty you look tonight for your prom."

"I always wonder why they had to die. Why did God let them die? I'm sure that Jenny misses them too."

"Valerie, no one knows why things have to happen, but the Bible says, *To every thing there is a season, and a time to every purpose under the heaven. A time to be born and a time to die.* It was Mom and Dad's time to die."

"Like that song on the radio?"

"Yes, just like that song on the radio."

"Mom and Dad are in heaven, right, Priscilla?"

"Yes, they are. They're in the Promised Land, walking on streets of gold. One of Dad's favorite Bible verses is in the book of John. It says, *In my Father's house are many mansions: if it were not so, I would have told you. I go to prepare a place for you.* Mom and Dad are living in a mansion, Valerie."

"I wonder what they're doing in a big mansion."

"Well, if God allows a married couple to have intimate relations, then I think you know what they're doing."

"Yes," a giggling Valerie replied.

"But do you know what else I was thinking about?"

"No, what?"

"Well, I was just thinking about how I have never been to a prom."

"What? You didn't go to your prom?"

"No, I didn't. I was fifteen years old the night of my prom. I didn't really have any friends in high school. The other girls in my class didn't like me, because I was younger, and smarter than they were. And the boys, well, to them I was a kid."

"Oh, Priscilla, I'm sorry. I didn't know that you didn't go to your prom. I remember Didi's prom, because Dad was really mad that night. He didn't like the dress she wore. It was red, and it showed off a lot of everything, if you know what I mean. It went really low in the front, and in the back too; she couldn't even wear a bra. And it had a slit that went really high, it showed off her legs. She might as well have been naked; that's what Dad said. Then Mom said, 'Don't give her any ideas, Frank.' Then Dad said, 'this is all your fault, Annie.' I don't see how it could be Mom's fault."

"Was the dress pretty?"

"It was pretty and real sexy."

"That sounds like a dress Didi would wear."

"She didn't get home until 5:00 in the morning, and she wasn't even wearing the dress! It's a good thing Dad was in bed, snoring away."

"What was she wearing?"

"Some guy's letterman jacket, and a great big smile."

"I'm so jealous. No, I'm not. Because soon after my prom, the prom I didn't go to, I met Michael. We dated, and fell in love, then he asked me to marry him. I was head-over-heels in love, so I said yes. And besides that, just look at him. He's so handsome. A lot of other women wanted to be with him, but he loved me, and chose to spend his life with me. Now we're going to have a baby."

"Your dates are here," Michael called out, from the other side of the door.

"They'll be right down," Priscilla shouted. "I'll tell the guys that you will be out in a few minutes. Come on, girls. Let's hurry."

A special occasion commands an extraordinary mode of transportation to the exclusive destination. Patrick, Brando, and Cory each contributed towards the cost of renting a limousine. They picked out a white, stretch limo with black leather seats. They got a good deal on it because it was an older model, and the seats were torn in a few places. The ripped seats were held together with duct tape, which was starting to lift up at the corners. It also had a retractable sunroof, which was stuck in the open position. Fortunately, there was no rain in the forecast, so the guys weren't too concerned. But to be on the safe side, the limousine company provided umbrellas, for an additional forty dollars. As the girls joined their dates, Patrick took Valerie's hand, and held back from going outside with the others.

"So, when is this baby coming?" he asked.

Priscilla awkwardly answered, "Anytime now."

"I remember Thanksgiving when I first met all of you."

"Yeah," Priscilla said, "I'll never forget that Thanksgiving. You two should get going. They're waiting for you outside."

"Okay, but first, I want to say something."

"What's that?" asked Michael.

"I want you to know that I will be respectful to Valerie, tonight. I'll bring her home on time."

"I know you will," Michael said. "You two have fun." He pushed Patrick and Valerie out the door, said goodbye, and shut the door behind them. Jeff joined him and Priscilla in the foyer.

"What was that all about?" asked Jeff.

"Oh, nothing," Michael said. "Patrick is going to ask Valerie to marry him."

"What?" Priscilla asked.

"Did he tell you that?" asked Jeff.

"He doesn't have to tell me anything. That's just what I know," Michael said to them.

"You're crazy," Priscilla said.

"We'll see," Michael said.

"Yeah, we'll see," said Priscilla.

"Yes, we will," said Michael.

The prom experience was everything that Valerie dreamed it would be. The venue was beautifully, but oddly, decorated. Ordinarily, school events would be decorated using the school colors of purple and white, however, the student council, in an effort to save money, exploited the bicentennial commemoration by using decorations entirely of red, white, and blue. The decorations were free, leftover from the art club. The band, Project Terror, was a popular band, known for playing a variety of Motown, and rock and roll, as well as their own original songs. They were in high demand in Austin, Houston, and San Antonio. Because its members were former Jefferson and Murphy High graduates, (classes of 1969, 1970, and 1971), they were true to their Crystal Springs fan base.

With the exception of her uncle Jim's occasional wedding receptions, Valerie had not had many chances to strut her stuff on the dance floor, but she had the steps, and the rhythm. She could do the bump, the hustle, and the funky chicken. Fortunately, Project Terror played several slow songs too, allowing dance partners to experience a closeness that they would otherwise miss out on. Knowing a good thing when it comes along, Patrick seized this golden opportunity to create some unforgettable memories for him and Valerie.

After the prom, many of the seniors took the party to various restaurants, and nightspots. Patrick, Valerie, and their friends, went to Steak and Ale. For the three couples, the gathering would prove to have a momentous purpose. College and vocations were decided, aspirations were professed, and friendships were reaffirmed. Once the limousine driver left the Steak and Ale parking lot, there was only one destination remaining, which was Valerie's house. From there, Brando and Cory would drive their girlfriends home. Patrick's intention was to stay with Valerie for a little while after; maybe watch a little TV, which, hopefully, would lead to a make-out session on the couch.

"I had the best time that I've ever had in my whole life," Patrick said, as they walked up to the front porch. "Thank you, Valerie. Thank you for going with me to the prom, and for these past few months that we've been together. I love you."

"I love you too, Patrick. I realized it the day of my parents' funeral. There is no way that I could have gotten through that time without you. I still can't believe that they're gone. I miss them so much."

"I know you do, Val. I miss my parents too."

"I still think about that day after Thanksgiving. It's okay that you don't believe me; but I saw them, Patrick. I know it wasn't a dream, it was real. I saw my parents. But now if I want to see or talk to my them, it has to be in a dream. I close my eyes, then all I have to do is dream. Your parents are gone too; do you ever dream about them?"

"Sometimes."

"Oh, Patrick, I wish I had met your parents."

"Me too, Val. My parents would have loved you. I didn't know your parents for very long, but I miss them too. Your dad told me that he fell in love with your mom when she was sixteen years old. He loved her from the minute he saw her. That's much like my parents' story too. They met when they were both seventeen, and got married right after high school. My dad joined the army; the only way he could take my mom along with him, was if they were married. They would have got married anyway, that just helped move things along faster. The same with my sister and her husband; they would have married anyway, but after my parents died, they got married sooner so that he could help my sister raise me."

"I hope to meet your sister and her husband soon."

"You will, Val, very soon. I know that you dream about your parents, but what else do you dream about?"

"Lots of things."

"Like what?"

"Sometimes I dream about Jenny, and what it would be like if she didn't have Down syndrome. Sometimes I dream that she is just regular like us; at least for one day, maybe a few days. I love Jenny, but sometimes I wish that we could talk to each other; have real conversations. I wish that God would give us just a few days to have that sister experience; that we could hang out, and be real sisters and real friends. I could give her advice on boys and makeup, and things like that. And she would annoy me, just like I annoy Didi. Don't get me wrong, I love Jenny just the way she is, but I would love to have those few days with her. Just a few days. That would be a wonderful gift."

"Well, Valerie, I'm sorry that you'll never get that gift."

"That's alright, Patrick. I know that I'll never get that gift. That doesn't change how I feel about Jenny. I love Jenny. And I hope that she forgave me for what I did."

"What did you do?"

"Do you remember a couple of weeks ago, when her hand got burned by the iron?"

"Yes, I remember. It was an accident, Valerie."

"Yes, but it was still my fault. I should have been more careful."

"You have to forget about that. I'm sure that Jenny has."

"Patrick, she'll have a scar forever. Every time she sees her hand, she'll be reminded of what I did."

"Valerie, we all have accidents. Sometimes they will leave scars; sometimes scars can serve as a reminder that we went through something terrible, and have overcome the tragedy. That's life. Jenny's scar is from a little burn on her hand. Think of the brave men and women who served in Vietnam. Why are you making a big deal about a little scar on Jenny's hand?"

"You're right, Patrick. I guess I feel guilty about it."

"You shouldn't feel guilty about that. If anyone is guilty, it's me. If I hadn't called you on the phone, you wouldn't have knocked the iron over, and Jenny wouldn't have got burned."

"That's true! So it's really your fault, Patrick!"

"I guess so. Can we sit out here on the swing before going inside? I have something for you."

"For me? What is it? I love getting gifts!"

"Valerie, I love you."

"I know, Patrick. We already said that we love each other. Where's my gift?"

Patrick got up from the porch swing, and reached into his pocket, taking out a little black, velvet box. He stood for a few seconds before getting down on one knee.

"Oh, I like the box. It's so soft," Valerie said.

She snatched the box out of Patrick's hand, which led him to stand up. His attempt to grab the box back from her was unsuccessful.

"Valerie, give it back."

"Why? You said it was for me," she said, clenching the box in her fist. She moved around the porch, struggling to keep Patrick from prying her fingers from the box.

"Valerie, let go. I want to give it to you the right way. Let go."

"You said it was for me, so buzz off. It's mine."

"What's going on out there?" asked Michael, through the closed screen door.

His boisterous utterance was unexpected, startling Valerie and Patrick in such a way, causing them to lose their balance, while at the edge of the porch. With her arms stretched out, swinging in a circular motion, Valerie hoped to regain her footing. Ultimately, it was her own demand for dominance which led her to tumble off the porch, down to the ground below. In an attempt to catch her before she plunged down, Patrick descended instantaneously. The hard landing, two feet below, caused the little black, velvet box to fly out of Valerie's hand.

"Valerie! Patrick! Are you alright?" Priscilla called out.

Michael and Jeff ran down to help them.

"What were the two of you doing? You weren't fighting, were you?" asked Jeff.

"No, sir. I mean, no, Jeff. We weren't fighting."

"Well then, what's going on?" asked Michael.

"Mike," Priscilla interrupted.

"Will one of you please tell us what is going on?" asked Michael, while ignoring Priscilla.

"Mike!" Priscilla said, for the second time, with a bit more enthusiasm in her voice.

"I had a gift for Valerie, and she got a little excited. She grabbed it out of my hand before I had a chance to give it to her," said Patrick.

Priscilla let out a deafening scream. "Michael! I've been calling you! My contractions started."

"Your contractions started?"

"Yes, they're coming every five to seven minutes. I tried to tell you in the house, but you ignored me. You were so busy watching TV with Jeff; it was as if I didn't exist."

"I heard you, I wasn't ignoring you."

"Well, you wouldn't take your eyes off the TV to see how I was doing."

"We were watching the beauty pageant, Priscilla. It's not like we get to see it every day. Right, Jeff?"

"Don't get me involved," said Jeff.

"Mike, you didn't have to watch it. I should be more important to you than Miss America!"

"It wasn't Miss America, it was Miss USA. And besides, you ignore me all the time when you're watching Starsky and Hutch, so that makes us even."

"Michael!" Priscilla howled, as her rage erupted with such force that she grabbed him by his shirt to pull him towards her. "Michael, this baby is coming! You need to take me to the hospital, right now!"

"Alright, honey, let's go. Valerie, do you want to come with us?"

"Valerie, I can stay with Jenny. She's fast asleep anyway," Jeff said.

"I can stay with you, Jeff," Patrick volunteered.

"No, that's okay, Patrick. You go with Valerie. I'm taking care of Kevin, I can take care of Jenny too. What's one extra kid? It'll be no problem. I'll call Aunt Nancy or Aunt Gina if I need any help," said Jeff.

"Jenny is my responsibility, so I will stay," Valerie said.

"No," said Jeff, "I'll stay, you go with your sister."

"How about if I stay?" Priscilla asked, sarcastically. "Because in a few more minutes, I may not need to go to the hospital. I can have the baby right here on the lawn!"

Fed up with Michael's lack of urgency at getting her to the hospital, Priscilla grabbed his hand, and bit him hard, on the flesh at the base of his thumb. Doing so, the bite broke the skin, releasing traces of blood, which trickled through Priscilla's lips, and down Michael's hand.

"I don't care if Valerie comes with us or not, you need to take me to the hospital! Now! Right now! Right now! Right now!"

"Alright, let's go. I need to see a doctor too. Look what you did to my hand; I'm bleeding."

"Mike!"

"C'mon, Valerie! You're wasting time! Priscilla is about to have a baby, and I think I may need a tetanus shot. Patrick, are you coming? Let's go!"

The drive to the hospital was filled with shrieks and shrills, owing to an infant's demand to make his or her debut into the world. Priscilla hoped that she wouldn't deliver the baby in the car, but since the contractions had already launched the sequence of events, it was out of her control. When they arrived at the hospital, Priscilla was whisked away to the delivery room. Valerie sat in the waiting room with Patrick. Reminiscing about the night Jenny was born, she shared her recollections with him. His contribution to the conversation included bold assumptions of the pair assuming parental duties, in the course of time. Certainly, after they were married, if that was to be.

Finally, after a period of time that lasted well into the following morning, Frank Andrew Branham made the scene. Valerie was finally able to see her sister, and meet her new nephew. Upon entering Priscilla's room, she went to her bedside, leaving Patrick standing in the doorway. She watched as her nephew snuggly bonded with his mother.

"Should I be here?" asked Patrick, who was standing in the doorway.

"Sure, you should. You're practically family," Michael said, waving him in with his left hand, which was wrapped in gauze.

A familiar voice coming from the hallway, behind Patrick, asked, "Can I be here?"

"Didi," Priscilla cried out, extending her arm as a gesture. Delores hurried to her sister's side, and held her as they quietly wept. After a few moments, she moved to the other side of the bed, where Valerie stood. She gathered her little sister in her arms, and held her close.

"Didi," Valerie asked. "Where have you been?"

"We can talk later," Delores said. She shifted her attention to Priscilla's new son, and asked if she could hold her new nephew. Upon cradling him, she said, "Look at this little one, so sweet and innocent."

"I remember when you were sweet and innocent, Didi," Priscilla said.

"I don't know that person," she replied.

"You are that person, Delores. I know that you're hurting. Let me be there for you, I'm your big sister. We can get through this together."

Without a further exchange of words, the alliance between Priscilla and Delores resumed to its natural state. For Valerie, the sisterhood remained shattered.

CHAPTER ELEVEN

I Heard It Through The Grapevine

For the past few days, Gina and Nancy had their heads together, preparing for a double celebration. Not only to celebrate the arrival of the new baby, but also to mark the occasion of Valerie's upcoming graduation from high school. Relatives and friends from out of town would also attend. Patrick, in the meantime, had been troubled about the whereabouts of his gift to Valerie. Where was the little, black, velvet box? Since the night it was lost, he and Valerie had spent hours looking for it. Before the guests arrived, Valerie and Patrick made one last attempt to find the box. Valerie's repeated requests about the contents of the box went unheeded.

"I can't imagine what happened to the box. I've looked, and looked for it. I don't know how far it could have flown when it left your hands, but every inch of this yard has been combed. I wonder if Trixie found it, and buried it somewhere, but I didn't see any recent dirt mounds," Patrick said.

"I'm sorry, Patrick. You had a surprise for me, and I ruined it. Please don't be mad."

"I'm not mad. I didn't expect you to grab the box, otherwise, I would have held it tighter; but I'm certainly not mad about it. You were just having fun."

"Thanks for not being mad about it, Patrick. You're very sweet. But tell me, what was in the box?"

"Let's find the box first, Valerie. Then you'll find out what's inside."

"I wish you would tell me. I know it has to be jewelry. Was it a ring or earrings? The box was too small for it to be a necklace or bracelet. Tell me what was in the box, Patrick, I'm dying to know."

"You're not dying, Valerie. I didn't want you to find out like this, by me telling you. I wanted to see your face when you opened the box. Your aunt Gina is making a huge meal for a couple of celebrations, I want to add one more thing to the list, one more reason to celebrate."

"What is the one more reason that you want to add to the celebration list?"

"Do you want to know what was in the box?"

"Yes, Patrick, that's what I've been asking. Will you please tell me what was in the box?"

"Well, like I said, I wanted to see the look on your face when you opened it. But I guess it would be alright if I just told you. It's a mood ring, Val. I got you a beautiful mood ring."

"A mood ring? Really? I was hoping it was diamond earrings. I've always wanted diamond earrings. But a mood ring? How nice."

"Sorry, Val. I didn't mean to disappoint you."

"Oh, Patrick, you didn't disappoint me. Really! I think a mood ring is lovely! It really, truly is. I hope we find it."

"Sure, Valerie."

"No, really! I'll love it! My stone will always be a bright color when I'm with you."

"How much time do you think we have before your aunts are finished cooking, and everyone gets here?"

"Umm... maybe an hour? Why?"

"Come on. That's just enough time."

"Enough time for what?"

"Come on," he said. He took Valerie's hand, and led her to his car.

"Where are we going, Patrick?"

"I want to show you something. We're going to the mall, no more questions until we get there. Come on, let's go."

"Patrick, it's Sunday. The mall is not open on Sundays."

"They repealed the law, remember? Let's go."

A clueless Valerie followed Patrick's lead as they wandered through the mall, bypassing several shops until they approached a jewelry store.

"After you, Mademoiselle," Patrick said, as he extended his arm to direct Valerie inside the store. "Hi, do you remember me?" he asked the saleswoman behind the counter.

"Yes, Paul," she said.

"Patrick."

"Yes, Patrick. How are you? Is this your girl?"

"Yes, this is Valerie. Can I see a ring, like the one I bought?"

"Certainly."

She opened a case, and took out a diamond ring.

"This is very similar."

"Thank you," he said to the saleswoman.

Holding the ring between his thumb and index finger, Patrick got down on one knee, looked at Valerie, and said, "Valerie, I love you with all my heart. I always have, ever since the first moment that I saw you, and I always will, until I take my last breath on earth. Will you marry me?"

He slipped the ring on Valerie's finger. She was awestruck; her knees buckled, she got chills, and her heart raced so fast that she thought it might explode in her chest. It took a few moments before she was able to restore her presence of mind, hitting a few snags while finding her voice; she was not a smooth talker under pressure. What flowed through her lips seemed to be wordless mumbles, eventually evolving into the phrase, "Yes, Patrick, I will marry you!"

The proposal, and subsequent acceptance, brought down the house with applause and cheers from the small crowd of spectators, who watched as the events unfolded. Valerie, not accustomed to having the spotlight shone on her, audaciously held her hand high to flaunt the precious stone. Her radiant smile quickly disappeared as Patrick removed the ring from her finger, and returned it to the saleswoman.

"I hope you find your ring, and congratulations," she said to Patrick.

"Thank you," Patrick said, as he took Valerie's bare hand, and walked her out of the store.

Wishing she had a diamond ring on her finger, she wore a frown on her face as they walked through the mall, back to the car. Eventually, the frown was replaced by a huge grin when she was struck by the realization that she was engaged to Patrick.

"Are you happy, Valerie?"

"I am so happy, Patrick! I can't believe it. I'm going to marry you. I'm the luckiest girl in the world. Woo-Hoo!"

"I'm the one who is lucky. I'm going to marry the most beautiful girl in the world. I love you very much, Valerie. I only wish our parents were here to see us get married, but I know in my heart that they are happy for us. My sister is happy for me, she can't wait to meet you."

"I can't wait to meet her, Patrick. What's her name? Susan? She'll be my sister-in-law."

"Yeah, her name is Susan."

"Let's plan the wedding. I don't want anything big. I just want family, and our closest friends to be there. I want to marry you right now, Patrick! But I have to ask you something, something very important."

"What is it? Anytime you ask anything of me, my answer will always be yes."

"Well, there's Jenny. We're a package."

"I know that, Valerie. Remember our first date? When I said that whoever you marry will have to be cool with Jenny?"

"Yes, I remember when you said that."

"And do you remember that I talked to your father before we went out that night?"

"Yeah, I've always wondered what the two of you talked about."

"I told your father that I was in love with his daughter, even though we hadn't started dating yet. I told him that I fell in love with you when I first laid eyes on you, and that I was going to marry you. And that someday, after he and your mother have passed on, that I was going to have Jenny move in with us. I would take care of you for the rest of your life, and together with you, we would take care of Jenny. That's what I told your father, Valerie, and that's what I'm going to do."

Valerie was anxious to get home. Surely, everyone had arrived by now, and she could not wait to announce her engagement to her friends. When they arrived at the house, there were a number of cars parked in the driveway. Brando, Cory, Debra and Karen were sitting on the front porch. As Patrick and Valerie walked up the walkway, Brando hollered at them.

"Come on you guys! Everybody's waiting."

"Where have you been?" Debra asked.

"Guess what?" asked Valerie.

"Whoa, whoa. Hold on, Valerie," said Patrick. "Now is not the time. Be patient."

"There you are," Jeff said, while standing at the front door. "Everyone's been waiting on you two. We're hungry, come on."

"I'm sorry to keep everyone waiting," Patrick said.

Entering the house, they were greeted with questions, and phrases such as; "Where were you guys?" "Everybody's been waiting for you." "Do you know how to tell time?" "We're hungry."

"Come on, we have lots to celebrate," Michael said. "Does everyone have a glass?"

Danny and Jim handed out glasses. They were disposable champagne glasses that Gina bought for this special occasion. Jeff popped the cork on one of the champagne bottles, and began to fill the glasses. Michael got the second bottle ready.

"We have a few toasts to make, so be sure to take small sips," Michael said.

"Let's hurry with these toasts," Gina said. "Everybody's hungry, and I don't want my meatballs to get cold."

"Alright," Michael said. "First of all, I have to mention Frank and Anna. I miss them terribly; I know that we all do. Frank was good to me when I asked for his daughter's hand in marriage. Priscilla was very young and beautiful, and a bit naive. I was the older man. The sophisticated, incredibly handsome, extremely wise, charming, older man."

"Mike, get to the toasts," Priscilla said.

"Alright, but first, let me ask a question. I thought about this last night, I've always wondered; does anyone know how in the world the rumor got started that Frank was the Smasher? Remember the serial killer a few years ago?"

Debra, Karen, and Patrick shrugged their shoulders, and looked at Valerie. Valerie looked at her blouse, and straighten her clothes to avoid eye contact with anyone.

"What?" Gina exclaimed.

"Who's been saying that, Mikey?" Danny asked.

"It's been a rumor for some years now," said Michael.

"My brother, the Smasher? Yup, I can believe it," Jim said. The family was flabbergasted by his comment. "What is everybody looking at me for? He was my brother. I loved him, but every time we had a pet, it wound up dead. Tell them, Danny."

"He's right. We always wondered how Sparky died," Danny said.

"And Butcher," Jim added.

"Shame on you, Jim. And you too, Danny. My own husband, talking malarkey," Gina said.

"Wait a minute, darling," Danny said. "We loved our brother, but animals did tend to die a lot. Jimmy, remember when Frankie killed those chickens?"

"That's right, the chickens," Jim said.

"Uncle Danny, Uncle Jim," said Priscilla, who was annoyed with her uncles, and the conversation, "the two of you, and Dad, grew up on a farm; killing chickens were part of your chores. And Dad told us about your dog, Sparky, who died at the age of fifteen. And Butcher got run over by a car."

"Yeah, I guess so," said Jim.

"Your brother was the Smasher, Jimmy?" asked Nancy.

"What do you know about it?" asked Jim.

"I heard the rumor when I lived in Fort Worth."

"How did you hear about it in Fort Worth?" asked Valerie.

"I don't know, I heard it through the grapevine. That's the reason my family never wanted me to move to Crystal Springs after my divorce; they were afraid for me. Did they ever catch the real Smasher? I told my family that they did; I didn't want them to worry when I accepted a teaching job at Murphy High."

"I never heard that they caught him," Michael said.

"Michael, why did you have to bring up Dad being the Smasher?" asked Priscilla.

"I think it's funny," Michael said.

"You think it's funny that my father was a serial killer?"

"He wasn't the Smasher, honey. People just think that he was, not all people, I'm sure. It was a silly rumor."

"I've never heard that Frank was the Smasher," said Jeff. "I heard it was some guy from Amarillo, but they caught him. He's in prison now, everyone can relax."

"I'd love to know how the rumor got started, that's all I meant," said Michael. "Who started it, anyway? Frank was a great guy, he could never hurt anyone. That's what makes it so funny. He thought it was funny too, so did Anna."

"My parents knew?" Valerie asked.

"Priscilla, it's funny, but let's move on," Michael said. "Where was I? I wish Frank and Anna were here. Let's raise our glasses to Frank and Anna. We miss you, and we'll always love you."

Everyone raised their glass simultaneously, and said, "To Frank and Anna." Then everyone took a sip of champagne. Michael raised his glass for a second time.

"To Priscilla's and my newborn son, Frank, named in honor of his grandfather."

Once again, everyone raised their glass simultaneously, and said, "To baby Frank." They took another sip of champagne. Michael raised his glass for a third time.

"To the graduates; Valerie, Patrick, Debra, Karen, Brando and Cory; congratulations. We wish you all the best that life has to offer."

For a third time, everyone raised their glass simultaneously, and said, "To the graduates; congratulations."

"One more," Patrick said, as he raised his glass. "To me and Valerie. I proposed, she said yes. We're getting married."

CHAPTER TWELVE

Because

The announcement caught everyone off guard, except for Michael, whose earlier prediction was right on the money. Because everyone was fond of Patrick, he was already considered to be a part of the family.

"Let me see your ring, dear. Did this handsome young man get you a ring?" Gina asked.

"I'm sure that Patrick got her a ring. He's not a cheapskate like Brando," Debra said.

"A cheapskate?" asked Brando.

"I love you," said Debra.

"Where's your ring?" asked Karen.

"Well..." Valerie said, as she looked around the room, sheepishly.

"So, the little box you lost in the front yard, was that the ring?" Michael asked, before he burst out laughing.

Sorrowfully, Valerie said, "Yes, my engagement ring is lost."

After a moment of empathy towards Valerie's lost ring quandary, dinner was served. As they began their meal, Patrick divulged every detail of his first effort to propose to Valerie. Then he told of his second, more successful try at the jewelry store.

Much later; after the last meatball was devoured, and the last slice of garlic bread was swallowed, and the last glass of wine was gulped down;

Gina and Nancy cleaned up the kitchen while Michael, Jeff, and their two uncles caught the NBA playoff game on TV. The San Antonio Spurs were playing against the Charlotte Hornets. It was a bittersweet game since the Hornets stole the star player from the Spurs. Priscilla was in her old bedroom, nursing her baby, and keeping watch over Jenny. Patrick, Brando, and Cory hung out on the front porch. In hopes of finding the ring, Patrick retraced the steps leading to the moment when he and Valerie fell. His re-enactment failed to produce results.

Valerie, Karen, and Debra sat on Valerie's bed, listening to records, and talking about what the future may hold for each of them. Valerie had a burning question for her friends.

"Okay, now that the prom is over; am I the only one who has never done it?"

"Yeah, Valerie, I guess you are," said Debra.

"Valerie, you should have gone all the way with Patrick on prom night. We're women now," said Karen.

"No, Karen, she did the right thing. Valerie, there's nothing wrong with waiting. That's how it's supposed to be; you fall in love, and if you decide to spend your life with him, then you get married."

"Well, Deb, you're not married, and you gave it up," Karen said.

"No, Karen, I'm not married, yet. But Brando loves me, and I love him, and we're each other's first. We're getting married in a couple of months. Does Cory even love you? He seems like a player."

"He's not a player!"

"Well, he's been with Amy Lopez. Anyone who's been with Amy Lopez is a player."

"Oh, Debra, I know all about when he was with Amy Lopez. That was last summer. Besides, maybe I'm the player. Did you ever think of that?"

"Karen, you're not a player," said Valerie.

"Well, she's not a virgin, either," said Debra.

"Karen, Debra, we're best friends. We shouldn't be fighting. We'll all be married soon, except for you, Karen. Patrick has never even tried, you know. We've made out a bunch of times, and we've talked about it; but we both want it to be special. We both want to be married first."

"You wait for marriage, Valerie. It will be special. It will be very special," said Debra.

As the day came to a close, and everyone left for their prospective homes, Michael and Priscilla sat down in the living room with Valerie and Patrick to discuss wedding plans.

"I am so happy for you, Valerie. Mom and Dad would be happy for you too." Priscilla said, as she hugged her little sister.

"Yes, they would," Michael said. "Valerie, Patrick, I wish you all the joy, and happiness, the world has to offer. Eighteen years old, your both young. When your …"

Valerie interrupted, "Michael, we may be eighteen, but we're …"

"Just a minute, Valerie," Michael interrupted Valerie's interruption. "I'm not saying that you're too young. Let me finish."

"Okay, I'm sorry," Valerie said.

"Eighteen years old, you're both pretty young. When your sister married me, she wasn't much older than you are now."

"Oh," said Valerie.

"Marriage is a big step, it's the biggest you will ever take. But I've seen you grow up, you're a very mature young woman. Patrick, I think that you are also mature, and quite capable of providing for my little sis-in-law."

"Thank you, Mike," said Patrick.

"Do you know what Mike said on the night of your prom?" Priscilla asked.

"No, what did he say?" asked Valerie.

"Right after the two of you walked out the door, Mike said to me and Jeff, 'He's going to ask her to marry him.' Didn't you say that, Mike?"

"How did you know what I was going to do?" Patrick asked.

"I just knew. I'm a pretty swift guy. I am very happy for both of you. Let's talk in the morning. It's been an exciting day. There's still matters to discuss about Jenny."

"What about Jenny?" Valerie asked.

"In the morning," Michael said. "Patrick, it's late. Are you going to drive home? You can stay on the couch, if you'd like."

"Yeah!" he answered, overly enthusiastic.

"Don't forget, I'm in the room next to Valerie's," Michael said, sternly.

"Oh, I know. I wouldn't…. umm…. you don't have to worry," Patrick said.

"I'll get you a blanket and pillow," Valerie said.

As Valerie, Priscilla, and Michael started to walk out of the living room, Priscilla asked Valerie, "So, maybe a fall wedding? Or next winter?"

"We were thinking about next week, after graduation."

"What?" Priscilla asked, stopping dead in her tracks. "There's no way. That's not going to happen."

"Why not, Priscilla? That's what Patrick and I want to do."

"Yeah, why not Priscilla? That's what they want to do. What's wrong with that?" asked Michael.

"It takes time to plan a wedding. Where are you going to have it? What about the food? Patrick, what did your parents say? I'll bet your mother would agree with me."

"My parents died years ago. My older sister, and her husband, raised me. She's all for us getting married. She told me that unless Valerie wanted a big wedding, we should keep it simple."

Priscilla replied, "Well, I think that if the two of you love each other, your love will be strong enough for you to wait. At least a few months."

"With all due respect, Priscilla, we don't want to wait. I love Valerie, and she loves me. We want to start our lives together right away," Patrick said.

"It's too soon."

"Priscilla," Michael said, "either he loves Valerie, or he doesn't. Patrick, do you love her?"

"Yes, I love her. I love Valerie."

"He loves her, Priscilla."

"I just don't want them to rush into marriage. They need to be sure. It takes time to be sure."

"No, Priscilla, we're not going to wait," said Valerie.

"You're not thinking straight, Valerie. Why won't you wait? Why does it have to be now? Give me one good reason why you can't wait."

"Because," Valerie said.

She took her sister's arm, and led her to the couch, they both sat down.

"We had a wonderful day, last Thanksgiving, until the accident. We never thought that when Mom and Dad left the house that night, we'd never see them again. We expected them to come home, but they never did. And they never will. Patrick never thought that he wouldn't ever see his parents again, either. They died in a car accident, just like Mom and

Dad did. We're not promised tomorrow. I'm going to marry Patrick next week, and even next week is not promised. To answer your question about why we won't wait; because, we won't."

"Look, Priscilla," Michael said, "it's their decision, not yours."

"I'm sorry. I just want you to be sure."

"I am sure," said Valerie.

Over the next few days, Valerie and Patrick planned their wedding, and the events that would take place after the wedding. Patrick would move into the house after he and Valerie were married. The two of them insisted that they could be full-time college students, and raise Jenny. They would have long days, driving back and forth to San Antonio, but they felt that they could handle it. After all, Valerie had been going to high school, and caring for Jenny since the death of her parents. She did have lots of help from her aunts and uncles, who assured them that they would continue to be of help for as long as she and Patrick needed.

Patrick would receive his portion of the inheritance left by his parents, while Valerie would continue to receive funds from an annuity set up by her father. Their combined resources would get them through their college years, with an ample amount available for use at their discretion. Michael's financial advice, and sophisticated business savvy, would allow their capital to grow by leaps and bounds over the next several years.

There was still the matter of Frank's remaining estate. Before he died, he set up a trust to be bequeathed to whomever would care for Jenny. Michael would determine who would be Jenny's legal guardian. For the time being, he was comfortable letting Valerie and Patrick assume that responsibility. However, he reserved the right to re-evaluate the situation as he deemed necessary.

The wedding would be held on the Sunday, following graduation. It would be at the house, in the backyard. A reception and dance would follow. As a wedding gift, Jeff would hire a DJ to provide music. Now all they needed was a dance floor. Jeff and Michael worked together to build a makeshift platform to be used for that purpose. Karen and Debra would both stand as bridesmaids, while Priscilla and Susan, Patrick's sister, would be matrons of honor. Jenny, of course, would be the flower girl. Brando and Cory were Patrick's groomsmen, while his best friend and brother-in-law,

Steve, would serve as his best man. The remaining unassigned wedding duty was giving the bride away; Valerie had to choose someone to assume that responsibility.

Although she loved her uncles dearly, they hadn't been as involved in her life growing up as Michael had. Before his marriage to Nancy, Jim's womanizing and numerous marriages, didn't allow him to spend very much time with his niece. Danny and Gina spent a few years living in San Antonio, while Mario, attended private school. Loving her as much as they did, her uncles relieved much of her anxiety by suggesting to her, that Michael would be a logical and laudable choice to fill in for Father of the Bride duties.

"My brother would be so proud of you, Small Fry. You've become quite a woman. I wish Frankie could walk you down the aisle, but since he can't, I think Mike would be a good fill-in. But I will always be here for you," said Jim.

"I'm here for you too, honey. Gina and I love you more than words can say. I wish my brother could be here for his Cupcake, as she gets married, but I know that Mikey will do a fine job walking you down that aisle. And I know that my brother is looking up at you with pride."

"Looking up? Where do you think our brother is, Danny?"

"Uncle Danny, heaven is up, so Daddy will be looking down."

"Sorry, Frankie. That's what I meant."

Valerie found Michael with Jeff, working in the backyard, on the makeshift dance floor.

"Michael, can I speak to you about something. It's not private, Jeff; you don't have to leave."

"Sure, Dollface. What's on your mind?"

"I wish my dad was here to give me away; but since he is not, I have to ask someone else if they would do me the honor. You've known me since I was a little girl; if you don't mind, I would like you to give me away at my wedding."

"Of course, I don't mind, Dollface. It would be my honor."

"Thanks, Michael. Jeff, you are very special to me too. I want you to do another job that my father is supposed to do. Would you dance with me? When they play the first song that's supposed to be for the father and daughter to dance together, I want you to dance with me."

"I have two left feet, but I'd love to. Thank you for asking me."

"Thank you, Jeff. Dad was right. He always said that you two were the best sons-in-law that any father could ask for. You're also the best brothers-in-law that any sister could ask for. I love you guys."

CHAPTER THIRTEEN

Two Out Of Three Ain't Bad

The graduation ceremony was long and boring, as most graduation ceremonies are. Delores went to the ceremony, incognito. She broke up with Johnny, and started drinking more; a habit she picked up after her parents died. She met a new man. He was nice, and somewhat good looking, though she didn't have any romantic feelings towards him; he was just something to do to pass the time. Her looks were beginning to suffer; though nothing that a little root touchup, and mascara, couldn't fix. Her wardrobe wasn't very flattering either, she started to dress sloppy. She used to wear clothes that hugged her curvaceous figure, now she wore baggy clothes to hide it. She wanted her old life back, but felt that she was stuck with her new life, and the choices that she made; choices which led to decisions made in haste, with regrettable outcome. She wondered how her life became such chaos. What started out to be a few problems in her marriage, became self-destructive fury after the deaths of her parents.

After she gave birth to Kevin, she was hit with the baby blues, not to be confused with postpartum depression. She was adamant when explaining it to Jeff.

"Babe, I'll be fine. It's just a mild case of the blues, that's why it's called the baby blues. I'm not depressed; I just need something, but I don't know what. I want to be a good mother to our son, but before I can do that, I have to shake off these blues. Otherwise, I won't be good for anyone, including you. Maybe it's because I still have a couple of extra pounds on me. I've never had extra pounds, I've always had a great body."

"You're not that heavy, Didi," Jeff said. "All women gain weight when they're pregnant. And all women maintain a little of the extra weight after they give birth, it's natural. But you're still beautiful. Extra weight on you does not diminish your beauty."

"I'm not that heavy? What are you saying? Are you saying that I have extra weight? That's the same as being fat. That's just great! My husband thinks that I'm fat."

"Didi, I'm sorry. I didn't mean to imply that you're fat. You still have an incredibly gorgeous body."

"Still? Even though I'm fat, right? You're saying to me, that even though I am fat, I still have a gorgeous body? That's not possible. But thank you, Jeff. Thank you for confirming that I'm fat."

"Didi, that's not what I'm saying, honey."

"That's okay, I'm fat. You should be glad that I'm not in denial, because I'm going to do something about it. I'm going to start working out at the gym."

"The gym where you work?"

"Yeah, I'll have to stay afterwards. It's the only way that I'll be able to get a really good work out. I'll be back to my old self in no time."

"Didi, you're already there all day? Can't you get a work out during the day, while you're there?"

"No! I can't! I need to lose weight. I want my sexy body back."

"Why is losing weight so important to you?"

"Well, maybe because I worry about my husband's roving eye."

"What are you talking about?"

"Not what, Jeff. Who? Who is she? What's her name?"

"What do you think you know?"

"Is there something to know, Jeff?"

"Let's talk about this."

"I guess you've answered my question. I guess there is something to know."

By the end of the graduation ceremony, Delores meant to be in her car, ready to drive away. Instead, she was lost in thought, and did not realize that the crowd was moving towards the exit. She had to scramble to get to her car before anyone saw her. As she made her way through the parking lot, she heard someone call out after her. Rather than turn around to see who was calling her, she walked at a faster pace. As she reached for the door of her car, with her keys in her hand, someone touched her shoulder. She still did not want to acknowledge this person, who was persistent in trying to get her attention.

"Didi, why won't you answer me? I've been calling you!"

Delores wasn't sure that she recognized the female's voice, but she reluctantly turned her head to see who it was. Standing before her, was Jennifer, her friend from high school. When her eyes met Jennifer, the accrued misery, beginning with the death of her parents, all at once erupted, and she found herself seeking comfort from her former friend. Jennifer's husband, who had been walking a few feet behind them, had now caught up.

"Bob, this is Delores; Didi, my good friend who I haven't seen in a long time. Come on, Didi, let's go. Let Bob drive your car, and you ride with me. I want you to come to my house, we can talk. Come on, where are your keys? Give them to Bob."

Jennifer put a crying Delores in her car, then they drove away. Bob, driving Delores' car, followed as they headed for their home. When they got to Jennifer and Bob's house, Bob gave Jennifer and Delores privacy.

"Didi, what happened? You look awful. I have never seen you look awful."

"I'm sorry, Jennifer. I'm sorry about Jeff," Delores said, through tears.

"Didi, that was a long time ago. I've moved on. I'm married to Bob, and we are very happy! We have two children, life is great! You were my friend, Delores; what you did hurt me. But only for a while, then I got over it. I met Bob. I called you, I wanted to tell that I wasn't mad or hurt anymore; I wanted to tell you about Bob. I left so many messages, but you never returned any of my calls. Not one."

"I'm sorry, Jennifer."

"Don't be. If Jeff hadn't broken up with me, I probably would have missed out on meeting Bob. Everything happens for a reason, Didi. Sometimes we can't see the wonderful things that God has in store for us, in the midst of the trials in our lives. But we have to step back from the situation, and let

Him do His stuff. It's obvious that you're going through something right now. I'm sorry, but things will get better for you. I don't know when, but they will. I'm sorry about your parents, Didi. They were very nice, I liked them. Remember when we used to eavesdrop on them during their lovemaking sessions? Frequent lovemaking sessions, I might add."

"Oh yeah. I sure do. But if you lived in that house, you couldn't help but eavesdrop. My parents had an awesome marriage, and sex life. My sister and I were accustomed to their sexual encounters. There was no way that we could ignore them. They were often, and they were loud."

"Yeah, I know. I was there too, remember? I couldn't imagine such high pitches coming out of your mother. Do you know that I could never look your father in the eye? What a way to learn about sex! I will forever appreciate your parents."

"Yes, they were something else. I miss them so much. I miss the talks I used to have with my mother. We had some wonderful talks. I miss the relationship I had with my dad. We always argued, mostly about the way I dressed or how many boyfriends I had. But we always made up afterwards. I kept him on his toes, he always said that to me. I loved them more than anything, and now they're gone. It's my fault, you know?"

"Didi, don't you dare blame yourself. It was an accident. I heard what happened, it was not your fault. Your parents would not want you to blame yourself. Priscilla doesn't blame you. I ran into her the other day, she told me that she hadn't seen you for a while. She hopes that you're doing alright. She told me everything about Thanksgiving; she thinks that's why you're staying away. She doesn't blame you, Didi. She misses you. She had Jenny with her; she's a cute baby. I'm flattered that your mother named her Jennifer."

"Her name is not Jennifer, it's just Jenny. Valerie chose the name. Do you remember Valerie?"

"Of course, I do. Valerie, she's quite a girl. You saw her graduate, huh? Can you believe that she's getting married Sunday? Where did the time go? I remember when she was a little girl, and I'd go to your house; she would be there, wanting to hang out with us. Do you remember the one time when she was eight or nine years old, and she …"

"What did you say? What's happening on Sunday?"

"Your sister, Valerie, she's getting married. You didn't know?"

"No. I had no idea."

Jennifer went to the kitchen, and got a bottle of wine from the refrigerator. She poured two glasses.

"Let's have some wine. Remember when we used to drink the cheap stuff? This is much better. Didi, you didn't answer me before. I asked you what happened? You look a mess. You look like you're on drugs. Are you on drugs?"

"No."

"Did you and Jeff break up?"

"It's complicated. Are you sure that Valerie's getting married Sunday?"

"Yes, Priscilla told me about it. Didi, now that you know about it, are you going to go to the wedding?"

"No, I wasn't invited."

"Delores! You probably were not invited because your family doesn't know how to get a hold of you. I think you should go, Didi."

"No, it's not a good idea."

"Why not?"

"No one wants me there. Especially Valerie."

"Didi, she's your sister. It's the most important day of her life. She loves you."

"Well, Jennifer, two out of three ain't bad."

The day of Valerie and Patrick's wedding, like most wedding days, was filled with anxiety. The ceremony would take place at 6:00 in the evening. The late start would allow plenty of time to take care of those last-minute details. Considering that it was a short engagement, and the wedding was planned within the same week that it took place; it stood to reason that every detail of this wedding, was a last-minute detail.

Patrick had not yet replaced the diamond ring; Valerie didn't want him to. She was adamant about finding the ring that she lost. They would continue to look for it, after they got back from their honeymoon, which would be a camping trip to Big Bend National Park. It was a logical honeymoon destination, considering that both Valerie and Patrick enjoyed camping.

"How does the saying go?" Debra asked. "Something old, something new, something something something. I don't know. Does anybody know?"

"Something old, something new, something borrowed, something blue," said Karen.

"I have something borrowed," said Valerie. "Priscilla let me borrow this gold bracelet, Michael gave it to her on one of their anniversaries. I still need something old, something new, and something blue; let me think about that. Wait a minute! I can't believe that I almost forgot about the box! I'll be right back."

Valerie ran out of her bedroom, and returned a few minutes later. She had a large shoebox, which she placed on the bed.

"What's that?" asked Debra. "It looks like a giant shoebox, probably from a pair of your dad's work boots."

"It is," said Valerie. "My mom told me about this box that she kept under the bed. She said that there would be something for me, for my wedding day, in this box. Alright, here I go; I'm going to open the box now."

Valerie opened the shoebox. Inside was an envelope, *For your wedding*, was written across the front. It was stuffed with $572 in denominations of ones, fives, and ten dollar bills. There was also a black velvet box that contained a pearl necklace, and matching pearl earrings. A note inside the velvet box, read:

Valerie,

My darling daughter, this pearl set will fulfill the "something old" that you need for your wedding day. My mother wore them on her wedding day, I wore them when I married your father, and Priscilla wore them when she married Mike. I hope you will wear them on your wedding day. They belong to you now. I love you.

Mom

"Look at this. It's a bag from Frederick's of Hollywood," Karen said. "What do think is in there?"

"Knowing my parents, I'm afraid to look."

"I'll open it," said Debra. "Look! It's your something new, and something blue! It's your garter, and it's blue! The price tag is still on it, so it's brand new!"

"Can you use the same thing for new and blue?" asked Karen.

"I'm pretty sure that you can." said Debra.

"Look at this," Valerie said, holding a few bundles of letters tied together with purple ribbons. "There must be hundreds of letters. These are love letters that my dad wrote to my mom, before they got married, and throughout their marriage."

"How sweet," Karen said.

"It's not sweet, they're probably X-rated. I'm not reading them," said Valerie.

"Can I read them?" asked Debra.

"No, you can't," said Valerie. "You know, I'm glad that I remembered about this box. It has everything I need, everything my mom wanted me to have for my wedding day."

"I'm glad that you remembered too," Debra said. "When did your mom tell you about the box?"

"The last time we talked. It was our last conversation before they left this earth."

Valerie put on her garter, and wedding dress, then looked at herself in the full-length mirror. She hadn't removed the curlers from her hair, and wasn't finished applying her makeup, but she could admire her wedding dress. Her dress was white, which captured the essence of her virtue. It was floor length, and didn't have a train. The upper front had a square neckline, and was made of satin with lace. She bought it two days earlier at a thrift store. It was not only a perfect fit, but it was also very pretty, and clean. It looked fairly new, except for a slight tear on the seam of the waistline. Gina was able to fix it up easily. Incredibly, the dress cost only $15.

Debra and Karen both wore their prom dresses as bridesmaid dresses. Valerie, using her new cosmetics that Priscilla bought her, applied her makeup, while Debra and Karen began to remove the large curlers from her hair. All at once, the girls noticed a familiar face staring back at them in the mirror. Valerie immediately turned around to see her sister, Delores, standing inside the doorway.

"Didi, what are you doing here?" Valerie asked.

"You don't seem happy to see me," Delores said.

"I don't seem happy? I'm getting married today. This is the happiest day of my life, with the exception that Mom and Dad are not here. They should be here. Dad should be here to give me away, and to dance with me, before handing me off to my husband. He's not here to do that, Delores. Michael is giving me away, and Jeff will dance the first dance with me."

"That's nice that Jeff will do that for you."

"That's nice? Jeff is heartbroken."

"I know. I meant that it's nice that he'll do that for you. It's nice that you can depend on him."

"Yes, I can depend on him. He's happy to do it, even though you broke his heart. Do you know how much you've hurt your husband? Do you know how hard it was for him to see you with another man at Mom and Dad's funeral? Do you even care? I don't want you here today, Didi. I don't want you to upset Jeff."

"I'm sorry that I came. I just wanted to see you on your wedding day."

"When you went to see Priscilla in the hospital, I was so happy to see you. Then you left again, like I didn't matter."

"Of course, you matter. You're my little sister, that's why I'm here," Delores said.

"Well, why weren't you here on Thanksgiving? If you had been here, then Mom and Dad would still be here. Dad wouldn't have left to go look for you. We all told him not to go, but he didn't listen to anyone, because he wanted you to be here. We all wanted you to be here, with your family, where you belonged. But you left, so Dad went after you. And Mom went with him."

"I'm so sorry, Valerie."

"You are so selfish, Didi, and you always have been. Your coming here today is selfish. Of course, I want to talk to you, and straighten things out. But do you think that I want to do that today? On my wedding day? I don't want you here."

"Okay, Valerie. I just wanted to see you on your wedding day. I'll leave. But before I do, let me ask you a question. Do you know how hard it was for me to see that woman at my parents' funeral?"

"What woman? What are you talking about?"

"Why don't you ask Jeff about the woman? Never mind."

"Delores, why did you come here?"

"You're my little sister. It's your big day. I love you."

"Really? Well, Didi, I guess two out of three ain't bad."

"Didi, you're here! I'm so glad you came!" Michael said, excitedly, as he entered the room.

"Talk to you later, Mike," Delores said, before walking out the door.

"Wait, Didi. Aren't you going to stay for the wedding?"

"I can't believe that she showed up," said Valerie.

"It's okay, don't cry, Dollface. You're getting married today. It would be nice if Delores could stay, and be here for your wedding, but it is your wedding."

"Michael, you want her here? After everything that she's done, you would want her here?"

"She's done nothing to you, Valerie. And yes, I would want her here. She is still your sister. She should be here, but it's your wedding. I know that your parents would want her to be here."

"Well, my parents aren't here, because of her."

"Your parents aren't here because of an unfortunate accident. It had nothing to do with Didi," said Michael.

"Do you want me to try to catch her before she leaves, Val?" Debra asked.

"What?" asked Valerie.

"Valerie, Didi is like my big sister too. She should be here."

"Valerie," Karen said, "can't you put everything aside, just for today? I don't have any sisters; I have you, Debra, Priscilla, and Delores. Let Debra catch her, and bring her back."

"Why are you girls upsetting me?"

"Never mind," said Debra. "Let us help you finish getting ready."

"Do you want Patrick to see you with all this junk in your hair?" Michael asked. "What is this? A sponge?"

"Michael, these are called curlers," Valerie said. "Do you think she left? Do you think anyone saw her? I hope Jeff doesn't see her."

"Valerie, Didi meant no harm."

"Michael!" Valerie snapped.

"Don't worry about Jeff. He's a big boy, he can take care of himself. He doesn't need you to protect him. Is this how I'm walking you down the aisle? With you looking like this?"

"No, of course not."

"Well, Patrick's going to think that you're standing him up. Look at the time."

"Oh no! We need to hurry!"

"Come on, we'll help you," Karen said.

"Michael, we'll call you in a few minutes," Debra said. She shooed him out the door.

It was an emotional time when Pastor Craig introduced the newlywed couple. The absence of the bride's and groom's parents created a void felt by everyone.

"Ladies and Gentlemen," Pastor Craig announced, "may I present, Mr. and Mrs. Patrick Anthony Cole."

Valerie wondered what Delores meant when she said to ask Jeff about a woman being at their parents' funeral. She wondered if she made the right decision by banning Delores from her wedding. Time would tell.

CHAPTER FOURTEEN

Everything I Own

After seventeen years of marriage, Valerie and Patrick were expecting their third child. Because she was in her first trimester, her pregnancy had not been announced. She fulfilled the promise made to her mother by naming her firstborn son, Robert. Her second child, also a boy, was named Matthew, after Patrick's father. Robert was seven years old and Matthew was five. This time around, Valerie was hoping for a girl. Whether the baby would be a girl or boy, it was already decided that this would be the last child for them. When he or she is old enough to start kindergarten, Valerie would go back to work, teaching at the elementary school.

It was 6:00 in the morning, Valerie woke up with a cramp in her leg. She closed her eyes, waiting for the pain to subside, hoping against all likelihood, to fall back to sleep.

"I might as well get up," she said to herself.

Patrick was already showering, he had a busy morning ahead of him. Since becoming a trial lawyer, he worked with Michael and Priscilla at their law firm in San Antonio. He didn't have to be at the office until 10:00 that morning, but he was going to head out a little early. He needed to return the rental car that he had been using while his Mustang, the same Mustang that Frank bought many years before, was being repaired.

Occasionally, he had cases in Crystal Springs; sometimes he worked them pro bono. He loved the residents of his home town, and gave back to the community as often as he could.

Valerie made her way downstairs to find Jenny sitting at the kitchen table. She was singing a song that she made up as she went along; her lyrics were unintelligible. She was also drawing pictures using her crayons; something that she enjoyed doing often. To those who didn't know Jenny, looking at one of her drawings probably looked like something drawn by a five-year-old child, not a twenty-one-year-old adult. But to those who knew this twenty-one-year-old adult, every one of her drawings was a masterpiece. Valerie picked up one of the finished drawings; it looked to be a self-portrait of Jenny wearing a graduation cap and gown, complete with a tassel. Jenny was about to complete her time in the public-school system. Though not officially graduating from high school, her Certificate of Completion would be part of the graduating class of 1993.

There are many people who have Down syndrome, and are high functioning; leading independent, or semi-independent lives. Jenny is not one of them. She's low functioning; not able to learn to read or write. She also doesn't know her numbers beyond the number ten, nor does she know the sequence or value. Her communication skills are limited, although she does know a few words, and a few signs in American Sign Language. Besides using the few words that she knows, her primary method of communication is using common gestures; including pointing, nodding her head, and shrugging her shoulders. Her understanding is also very limited. She says yes to just about everything. Actually, she says "yeah". Yeah is one of the few words that she can pronounce clearly, although she does not always understand its definition.

"Why are you up so early, Jenny?" asked Valerie. "Did you draw something?"

"Ree," Jenny said, as she nodded her head.

Ree is the name given to Valerie by Jenny. Since Jenny is not able to pronounce the consonant sound of the letter V, she shorted Valerie's name to Ree.

"That's a pretty picture, Jenny, I like it. Are you hungry? Do you want me to make breakfast?"

"Yeah," she said, nodding her head.

Valerie opened the refrigerator; she took out a carton of eggs, and a package of bacon. She held them up to show Jenny.

"Jenny, do you want bacon and eggs?"

A smiling Jenny nodded her head, and said, "Yeah, pizza hut."

Valerie put the bacon and eggs on the counter. She opened the pantry, and took out a box of oatmeal. She held it up, then asked, "Jenny, do you want oatmeal?"

"Yeah, pizza hut."

Valerie put the box of oatmeal on the counter, next to the bacon and eggs. She took out a loaf of bread from the breadbox, and took out a bottle of maple syrup from the pantry. She held them up for Jenny to see.

"Jenny, do you want me to make you some French toast?"

"Yeah, fren tow pizza hut," Jenny said.

She nodded her head, clapped her hands, and displayed an enormous smile, because French toast happened to be her favorite meal for breakfast. Pizza hut was a generic term that Jenny often used to describe a meal.

"Jenny, which would you like for breakfast? Bacon and eggs, oatmeal, or French toast? Which would you like?"

Jenny nodded her head, clapped her hands, and said, "Yeah, pizza hut."

"Alright, we'll have French toast. But first you need to take your medicine. Will you come here so I can give you your medicine?"

Valerie, touched her right middle finger to the palm of her left hand, and moved it in a tiny circle, which is the sign for medicine in American Sign Language.

"Yeah," Jenny said.

"Okay, well come on," Valerie said, motioning for Jenny to go to the kitchen counter. Jenny takes a few prescriptions on a daily basis. Since she is unable to swallow pills, Valerie crushes them for her, and gives them to her with a spoonful of applesauce.

"I don't smell coffee," Patrick said, walking up to Valerie to give her a kiss.

"Pak!"

"Good morning, Jenny," Patrick said, giving her a kiss on her forehead.

"Patrick, you don't smell coffee? Jenny, do you smell coffee?"

"Yeah," Jenny said, enthusiastically.

"Patrick, Jenny smells coffee."

"Very funny. Your sister is very funny, Jenny. Why do you have all this food out, Val?"

"I asked Jenny what she wanted for breakfast. I'll put it back. Would you like something before I put it back?"

"No, thanks. I want to make sure that I have plenty of time to turn in the rental car, and pick up my Mustang. If I have time, I'll pick some breakfast up before I get to the office. Did you call Didi? Valerie, you need to call her."

"I don't see why I have to call her. She knows Jenny's graduation is coming up. She should already know the date. Jessica knows about graduation, and I didn't say a word about it to her. She just made it a point to know."

"Valerie, I know you're upset about Didi's new husband, but you have to back off. The two of you have come a long way these past couple of years. Look at how long it's taken you to get back to having a relationship with her. Don't let her new husband get between the two of you. Jeff has moved on, he's now with Jessica. And Didi is now with Bill."

"He's a creep, Patrick. And I don't trust him."

"It's her choice, and her life."

"Yeah, you're right. Besides, Didi will become bored, very soon; then he'll be gone," Valerie said, satirically.

"I need to get going. Let me have a kiss. Give the boys a hug for me. See you tonight, Val. Bye, Jenny."

"Bye bye, Pak" Jenny said, waving to Patrick as he walked away.

Making a phone call to Delores would be troublesome for Valerie. She repressed bitterness towards her sister; because of the death of their parents, and because she believed that Delores had destroyed her marriage to Jeff. For many years, she held onto the hope that Delores and Jeff would restore their marriage. There were several reconciliations throughout the years. On two such occasions, their reunions also resulted in two more children; Emily was twelve years old, and Nicole was ten.

Kevin, being the oldest of Frank and Anna's grandchildren, was the only grandchild that Frank and Anna got to meet before they died. The years since have slowly erased whatever memories Kevin had of his grandparents. He treasured the keepsakes given to him by his aunt Valerie; photographs, and small mementos, which once belonged to Frank.

Delores and Jeff didn't have an official custody arrangement. It seemed to work out with Delores having them about 40 percent of the time, and Jeff having them about 60 percent of the time. Since there were no hard and fast rules about the arrangement, they divided the time according to Delores' schedule. Kevin was old enough to come and go between his parents as he pleased. The girls preferred to stay with Delores, but since she had a continuous battle with her demons, sometimes they went weeks without seeing her. Because there are some ways in which a father can not take the place of a mother, Delores' absence was hard on the girls, especially Emily. She was becoming a teenager, and had already begun to experience the monthly burdens of becoming a young woman.

Priscilla and Michael's children were Frankie, who was 17, Lauren was 15, and Monica was 13. In total, Frank and Anna had eight grandchildren.

For the past several weeks, Valerie had an additional responsibility to deal with; she had to find a day-program for Jenny to attend. Once Jenny completed her time in the public school system, she needed somewhere to go, and something to do. She couldn't spend her days doing nothing at home. Just as any other human being, Jenny needed a purpose. She needed a reason to get up every morning, to be productive, and to have a social life. After much thought and consideration, Valerie and Patrick decided on a facility where Jenny would attend, beginning the Monday after graduation. With that heavy burden off her shoulders, Valerie would now be able to shift her focus on planning a graduation party for Jenny.

Before she could think about calling Delores, Valerie needed to get Jenny and the boys ready, and off to school. She noticed that her keys were not hanging on the hook where she thought that she left them. She searched through her purse; she didn't find her keys, but she did find a store receipt for a magazine, and a bottle of nail polish. She also found the melted remains of a candy bar. On a hunch, she looked on the dresser in her bedroom. Next to her jewelry box, was the magazine. Under the magazine, were her keys. Driving Jenny and the boys to school and back, would allow Valerie time to prepare herself to make the dreaded phone call to her sister. Much to her surprise, the ten-minute phone conversation between her and Delores was pleasurable. It included an invitation to lunch, which Valerie reluctantly accepted.

They met at a restaurant downtown in the square. It was the same storefront that housed the Italian restaurant where she and Patrick dined on their first date many years before. It was now a different restaurant, serving Tex-Mex food; Valerie and Patrick dined there frequently. The food was delicious; they served homemade flour tortillas, which Valerie found to be quite easy to overindulge.

"Valerie, I'm glad you came. I went ahead and ordered you the enchilada plate. I know how you love enchiladas. Is that alright?" Delores asked.

"Yeah, that's what I usually get, enchiladas. It's been such a long time since you and I have had lunch together, Didi. Let's see, I think I was in elementary school, and you were trying to impress an older man who had kids, so you brought me along on your date. Do you remember?"

"I'm sure that wasn't the last time that I took you to lunch, Valerie. But I do remember when you tagged along with me when I had lunch with Gary."

"Gary? Was that his name?"

"Yeah, Gary Martinez."

"Martinez? Didn't you have a friend whose last name was Martinez?"

"Yeah, Cindy."

"Was he Cindy's father?"

"Yeah, Valerie. He was Cindy's father."

"Cindy, the cheerleader? You dated her father?"

"Yeah, but she didn't make the varsity squad. She lost out to me."

"You've got to be kidding. She lost out to you?"

"What's so surprising about that, Valerie?"

"Didi, she kicked higher than you could. She could do the splits, you couldn't. And she had already been a cheerleader. She even went to cheerleader school. There's more to being a cheerleader than yelling, '2-4-6-8, which of you guys wants to be my date?' That was so unfair to Cindy."

"Well, aside from that; I was prettier."

"Prettier, Didi? Or were you just easy?"

"Both. Valerie, why are you being so hostile?"

"Alright, I'm sorry. But you dated Cindy's father? That's gross. You were a teenager. Wasn't he old? Wasn't he married to Cindy's mother? And what did Cindy have to say about that? Did she call you Mommy?"

"He wasn't that old, Valerie; and Cindy didn't know. Her parents were separated at the time; they ended up getting a divorce. And besides, I may have been a teenager, but I was still a woman. A woman with needs."

"Oh, I should have known that you would go behind your friend's back to get a man. Well, that makes everything right, in your world. Look, I didn't come here to talk about your sex life when you were a teenager. Do you want to help me plan Jenny's graduation party?"

"No, I'll leave that up to you, but I will bring potato salad, and deviled eggs. Jenny likes my deviled eggs. Valerie, there's something that I'd like to discuss with you."

"What's that?"

"Well, I'd like to help you with something else concerning Jenny. You and Patrick have done an excellent job raising Jenny, all these years. I know Priscilla helps, every now and then, but you do most of the work."

"It's not really work. Patrick and I love taking care of Jenny. I've taken care of her all of her life. What is this about, Didi?"

"Well, I was just thinking, maybe I can do more. I haven't been fair to you. I'd like to take Jenny off your hands, you know, to give you a break. She can stay with me for a while, just for the summer. It can be longer or shorter. A few weeks, a month, even a weekend, whatever you say."

"Maybe you can do more? You've never offered to help with Jenny before, even when Mom and Dad were alive. You have three children who live with their father because you've abandoned them. Now you think that you should do more for Jenny? Just when I try to give us a chance to be sisters and friends, you do something selfish. But you try to disguise it as being so sweet, and kind, and helpful. But I know you, Didi, and I'm not falling for it. Goodbye, I'm leaving."

"Wait, Valerie. I want to be more involved in Jenny's life, so does Bill. You can't deny me that."

"I can, and I will. The answer is no. You cannot be more involved in Jenny's life. I don't trust your motivation, and I certainly, don't trust Bill."

"Valerie, this is not solely your decision. It's a family decision; Priscilla, Mike, and Patrick, also have a say in this. I'm only asking to be a part of her life, she is my baby sister too."

"Didi, why don't you go home? I think Bill needs to make a beer-run, you should help him."

"Why are you being so mean? I'm trying to do the right thing, I'm trying to correct my mistakes. Bill would like to get to know Jenny too."

"What? No way! There's no way that I would let a loser like Bill get close to Jenny."

Valerie stood up, pushed her chair in, and gathered her purse. Before walking away, Delores pleaded with her.

"Valerie, Bill is not a loser. What do I have to do? Do I have to get a lawyer to serve you papers in order to spend time with my own baby sister?"

"You want to get a lawyer, Didi? You want to take me to court? This isn't about Jenny. It's about Mom and Dad's estate. You want it, don't you? You want the house, the money, everything. You want everything, except Jenny."

"I don't want the house, Valerie. That's your house, and I don't care about whatever money that Dad left. I just want to spend time with Jenny. Bill and I want to spend time with Jenny."

"I have lawyers too, Didi. I've got the best there is; my husband, Priscilla, Michael, and his entire law firm."

"Valerie, I just told you; I don't want to go to court. I just want to spend some time with Jenny, that's all. I didn't mean to upset you. We can talk about this another time."

"No, we can't." Valerie started to walk out the door.

"Valerie, wait. I'm sorry for everything. You're right, I'm not a good mother. But I didn't abandon my children. I love my kids, and I do spend time with them. Not as much as I'd like, but Jeff is a good father. I'm not so selfish that I can't admit that. And I'm sorry that I haven't been a very good sister to you or to Jenny. I know that you blame me for what happened to Mom and Dad. And maybe you're right, maybe it is my fault. Believe me, I would give anything to have Mom and Dad back. I would give everything I own."

"It doesn't matter what you would give, Delores, because there is nothing that you have or could ever give, that would bring them back."

Valerie walked out of the restaurant, leaving Delores to wallow in her own misery. As far as Valerie was concerned, Delores brought it upon herself. Whatever guilt or grief Delores was experiencing, Valerie felt, was self-deserved.

CHAPTER FIFTEEN

The Long And Winding Road

Delores asked the waiter for a doggie bag so she could take home the two untouched lunch plates. She and Bill would have it later, for dinner. She opened her wallet to retrieve her credit card. After handing it over to the waiter, she smiled, amid tears, upon seeing a photograph in the clear, plastic sleeve of her wallet. It was a snapshot, folded at the ends so it would fit snug into the sleeve. The picture was taken on Christmas of 1974, the last Christmas the family shared before Frank and Anna's death. She wasn't sure if it was Michael or Jeff who acted as photographer, because neither one of them were in the picture. Those who were in the picture were Frank, Anna, Delores, and her sisters. Though many snapshots were taken that day, this was Delores' favorite. They posed in front of the Christmas tree; Frank held Jenny in one arm, while the other was wrapped around Anna's waist. Priscilla stood to the right of Anna, her head resting on her mother's shoulder. Delores sat in a chair, in front of them, while Valerie sat on her lap.

She remembered the photo session, quite well. Numerous pictures were taken, most of which, Valerie was laughing hysterically. Delores remembered that each time they were instructed to say 'cheese', she tickled Valerie, causing her to laugh. How could they possibly know that eleven months later, Frank and Anna would be gone?

Delores drove the long way home. She wanted time to herself, before going home to Bill. She let her mind drift back to that day, as it often did; to that fateful, Thanksgiving Day.

There were only two people whom Delores trusted enough to confide. One was her sister, Priscilla, and the other was her mother. Because Priscilla had just discovered that she was pregnant with her first child, Delores didn't want to burden her sister with her problems, that day. She decided to confide in her mother. Perhaps another reason that Delores chose to confide in her mother, that fateful day, was because she knew that no matter what she did, her mother would not judge her, and would always love her.

Delores made her last phone call to her mother from the hospital lobby. Her conversation was supposed to go something like:

> "Hi, Mom. I'm sorry that I left. I had to get away. I'm at a hospital, visiting a guy. He's not really a friend, but I made a huge mistake. Mom, it's bad. A couple of weeks ago, I ended up in bed with him. It was just that one time, but that led me to feel sorry for him, and ashamed of myself. It was hard for me to break it off with him, after the one time. I know, I was stupid! There's no excuse. But what led me to do that, was one day, I stopped by Jeff's office. There was a woman there, she was real pretty, Mom. She was flirting with Jeff. He didn't know that I was there, and he flirted right back with her. Mom, do you remember when I met Jeff? He was in a relationship with Jennifer. He cheated on her, with me. And do you remember how I had a hard time losing weight after I had Kevin? Maybe Jeff cheated on me, Mom, maybe he didn't. I'm not sure. But… I don't know. What should I do? Mom, I need you. I've made such a mess."

Delores wasn't able to have that conversation with her mother, because her father grabbed the telephone away from her mother, and as usual, Delores and her father's contentious temperaments got the better of them, causing Delores to hang up on her father by slamming down the phone.

Frank was prepared to look for his daughter, all night long, if he had to. By coincidence, the first hospital he stopped to search, was the hospital where she was. Frank parked his pickup truck a few spaces down from where Delores' car was parked. By the time they arrived at the hospital, Frank's temper had cooled down, and he was back to being his usual self. Frank and Anna walked into the hospital, hand in hand. Since they didn't know the name of Delores' friend, the only thing they could do was wait for Delores in the hospital lobby.

It had been a long day for both Frank and Anna. The chairs in the lobby were quite comfortable, enabling Frank to doze off, while Anna sat in silence; thoughts of her daughter's infidelity occupied her mind. Frank awoke to find his eyes being covered by the soft hand of his daughter. She used her other hand to pinch his nose, forcing him to breathe through his mouth. When Delores was a little girl, she often woke her sleeping father by pinching his nose. Though she hadn't done that in years, Frank welcomed the playful affection from his daughter.

"I'm sorry, Dad. I shouldn't have hung the phone up on you."

"I just found out from your husband, that you've done something far worse than hanging up the phone on your old man."

"I'm sorry, Daddy."

"Do you love Jeff?"

"Yes, Daddy. I do. I just … I don't know. I just …"

"You just have the passion of your mother. If I didn't keep a close watch over her, she'd be stepping out on me all the time."

"Frank! How could you say that?"

"Hey, you're the one who called me an apple pie, and talked about pressing your body up against another man. Remember?"

"Mom!"

"This is about you, Delores. Not me."

"Yes, let's talk about you, Delores," said Frank. "You're my daughter, and no matter what you do, I'm always going to love you. Always remember that. You keep me on my toes, do you know that? Ever since you were a little girl, you've been a handful. I blame your mother for that."

"Why blame Mom?"

"It's easier, and she doesn't mind, because I always make it up to her."

"Yes, Daddy. We all know how you and Mom make up. We've all heard you."

"Delores, my lovely girl. I've always called you my lovely girl, and you are quite lovely. I guess that's why all the boys have always liked you. But your lovely in another way too. You remind me so much of your mother, although you look like my side of the family. But like your mother, you have a lovely heart. Not everybody sees it, but I do. Your heart is like gold; it's kind, and compassionate, and caring, and loving. I see how you are with your sisters. That can't be easy, especially with a sister like Valerie. But you're just like your mother. You have her sex appeal, and charisma. I've always called you my lovely girl, because I see beyond your physical beauty. I wish you could see yourself the way that I see you, you're just so lovely. Let me tell you something, there's nothing wrong with you wanting to dress sexy, and be seductive, and alluring, and having a good, healthy sex life. Look at your mother; she's all those things, and so much more. She's everything to me. I couldn't live without her. But you have to limit yourself to one man. Okay? And that man is your husband."

"Okay, Daddy. I'm sorry. I screwed up so bad."

"Your husband loves you. Your mother loves you. And I love you, Delores. Now you go home, and be sexy, and wear your slinky dresses, but only for your husband. Make him realize that he can't live without you; the same way that I can't live without your mother. How about you come home with us tonight? Let's go home, and have a big slice of pumpkin pie, without the whipped cream."

"Thank you, Dad. Thanks for coming after me, and for the talk. Can I ride home with you and Mom? I'll pick up my car tomorrow."

"Sure, honey. Ride with your father and me."

"No."

"Frank, let her ride home with us."

"No."

"Why not, Dad? Why can't I ride with you?"

"I don't know. There's no reason why you can't ride with us, I just don't want you to. Follow us home, Delores. You have your own car."

Disappointed, and a little offended, Delores drove home alone, closely following her parents. When they stopped at a traffic light, Frank waved his hand out the window to get her attention. Quickly, she rolled down her window, then smiled at her father, waving back at him. He shouted at her, "I love you, my lovely girl!" The light turned green. Continuing to closely follow her parents, she turned left on County Road 86. The speed limit varied between 45 to 55 miles per hour, depending on the section of the road. It was a long and winding road.

"Frank, I'm going to get a few minutes of shut-eye. Wake me up when we get home."

"Okay, Annie. Do you want some apple pie when we get home?"

"Literally? A slice of apple pie?"

"No."

"Metaphorically? You?"

"Of course, me."

"Then yes! I do!"

"Annie, I can't wait to get you home!"

"Drive carefully, Frank. You know this is a long and winding road."

Frank put his arm around his wife. She snuggled close to him, laying her head upon his chest. As Delores followed behind them, she saw the silhouette of her parents as they closely sat next to each other. She admired their relationship, and was thankful for the relationship that she had with them. Feeling a little guilty about making them come out to look for her, she thought about ways in which she could make it up to them.

Music would help her to think more clearly. Her right hand reached across the front seat, as she tried to locate an 8-track tape. She felt two tapes on the seat next to her, she'd have to look at them to decide which one she would listen to. Taking her eyes off the road for a second, she decided that the clear winner would be rock and roll. When she looked up again, she saw her father's truck swerve in the road ahead of her. She realized what caused her father to lose control of his vehicle; a small herd of deer ran across the road. While most of the deer were lucky enough to make it to the other side, a few of them didn't make it across, and remained in the middle of the road. Delores gripped the steering wheel firmly, and hit her brakes hard, which minimized the damage to her vehicle, once it made contact with the deer.

The collision was minor, Delores' immediate concern was for her parents. She saw her father's truck swerve off the road. Frank's encounter with the deer would prove to be hazardous. Scanning the direction which she saw his truck plummet off the roadside ditch, she discovered it several yards away; it had flipped over several times before hitting a tree, and landing upside-down.

Calling out to her parents, she ran towards the direction of where the truck landed. She stumbled and fell upon, what appeared to be a mannequin. Picking herself up off the ground, her hands touched the figure, which to her surprise, felt smooth and baby-soft. Closer observation gave rise to the realization that this figure sprawled across the ground, was not a mannequin at all. It was the lifeless body of her mother. Her face was covered in blood. Her head had been split open, which created a hole that was deep and wide. Blood and tissue, possibly her brain, oozed out. Delores presumed that her mother had flown through the windshield, and had her head smashed in, possibly by a large rock nearby. Taking her mother into her arms, she cradled her, while talking to her.

"Mom, please wake up. Don't leave me. I need you, Mom. Nobody knows me like you do. Mom, you can't leave me. Dad needs you too. So does Priscilla, and Valerie. And Jenny, Mom, she's just a baby. Don't leave us. Mom, I love you. I need you in my life, so much. Dad can't live without you, and I don't think that I can, either. Mom. Mom! I can't live without you! I just can't. Please don't go!"

She held her mother tighter, as tears rolled down her face. In the distance, she heard the faint cry of her father. Not wanting to let go of her mother, she knew that she had to check on her father. Maybe there was a chance that he would survive. She kissed her mother's bloody face, then turned her face slightly, so that her cheek pressed against her mother's cheek. She heard her father cry out again. Before leaving her mother's side, she briefly paused, holding her mother for a few more minutes, while saying a prayer. Then she said goodbye.

It was a starry night. The constellations supplied the night sky adequately, with enough light for Delores to see her way to maneuver through the field. Even so, she couldn't see her father. The tall grass covering most of the ground made it difficult to determine his location. She continued to walk towards the upside-down pickup truck, while carefully watching her steps. She knew she was getting closer as she heard her father's call grow louder, despite the sound of his voice lacking strength and vigor.

"Annie? Annie? Where are you, Annie?"

"Dad, where are you?"

"I'm here, honey. How's your mother? Where is she?"

Delores didn't answer her father. Following the sound of his voice, she found him lying under the truck. His legs were mangled; one was sticking up through the shattered glass of the windshield. The other was bent at the knee, however, it was not bent in the natural position. He was covered in blood, and his body was weak. He knew that he didn't have much time.

"Daddy, I'm here."

"Delores, is that you?"

"Yes, Daddy. I'm here. You're not alone, I'm with you."

"I'll bet you're glad that you didn't ride home with us, huh?"

"No, Dad, but I have to go for help. I'll be back as soon as I can."

"No, don't leave me. Where's your mother?"

"Mom? I don't know. She's probably fine, Dad. Let me go get help."

"Delores, I always know when you're lying to me. Tell me about your mother. I don't have much time, sweetheart."

"But if I can get help, then you might make it. Dad, you could make it through this, I know you can. I love you, Daddy. I don't want you to leave me."

"Tell me about your mother. I don't think she survived. I have an ugly feeling, an ugly pain in my heart. It's worse than the physical pain of this accident. I can't feel my legs, I'm in so much pain, sweetheart, but it doesn't compare to the pain that's in my heart. I think your mother is gone. And if she is, I can't live without her. Delores, I love your mother so much that I can't live without her. You don't have to say it, I know it's hard for you to say it. But I know that she's gone. And you know it too."

"Daddy, don't leave me. I love you."

"Delores, you've always been my lovely girl. Priscilla is my princess. Valerie is my cupcake. Jenny is my baby. And you're my lovely girl. I want you and your sisters to be happy."

"Daddy. Daddy, please…"

"I will always love you, my lovely girl."

CHAPTER SIXTEEN

Sooner Or Later

When Valerie arrived home, she decided that since she hadn't had lunch, she was entitled to a bowl of Rocky Road ice cream. After serving herself several scoops piled high, she turned on the TV, hoping to catch up on her favorite soap opera. Just as she plopped down on the couch, not even having a chance to start on her ice cream, the telephone rang.

"Hello, Mrs. Cole, Kimberly Bell, Jenny's teacher."

"Hi, Mrs. Bell. How are you? Is everything alright?"

"Not exactly. A woman from the Caring Hearts facility is here. She's with a social worker from T.D.M.W. That's the Texas Department of Mental Wellness. They said that they're here to observe Jenny. Were you aware of this?"

"No, I had no idea."

"They're very pushy, asking personal questions. I've alerted my principal, he'll be here in a few minutes. He won't be happy about this, he's very protective of his students. Are you able to come by?"

"Give me a few minutes. I'll be right there."

Valerie quickly ate as much ice cream as she could within ninety seconds, then she went outside, got back into her car, and drove to the high school.

When she walked into the classroom, Jenny was seated at her desk, while the woman from Caring Hearts, and the social worker, sat at a table with Mrs. Bell. Valerie walked over to the table, and stood behind the chair that was intended for her to sit.

"Hello, Mrs. Cole," said the woman from Caring Hearts. "I hope you don't mind that I brought along Ms. Torres."

"I'm sorry," said Valerie, "I know that you're from Caring Hearts, but I've never met you. Who are you, and what do you want?"

"Oh, pardon me. I'm Lucinda Daniels, and I brought along Ms. Torres to discuss a matter concerning Jenny."

"So? What are you doing here?"

"I just told you, we're here to discuss a matter concerning Jenny," Mrs. Daniels said. She had a snarky attitude, which Valerie did not appreciate.

"I know that you're from Caring Hearts, and you've told me your names, but that doesn't explain anything to me. Do you want to get to the point? I'm a pretty busy woman, and I've got a million things to do."

During this exchange between Valerie and Mrs. Daniels, the principal arrived. Without saying a word, he stood behind Valerie.

"Mrs. Cole, there's no need to be rude," Mrs. Daniels said.

"Forgive me, but I'm still waiting for an answer, and I haven't had lunch. A bowl of ice cream isn't lunch."

"Ree, I ceem," said Jenny.

The thought of ice cream excited Jenny, so she moved to the table to sit next to Valerie.

"We'll have some ice cream later, Jenny, when we get home," said Valerie.

"I'm Mr. Garcia's assistant. You know, Mr. Garcia, the director of Caring Hearts?" Mrs. Daniels said.

"Mrs. Cole, allow me to introduce myself. I'm Brandy Torres. I'm a social worker with the Texas Department of Mental Wellness. Jenny has been assigned to my caseload. Mrs. Daniels asked me to meet with Jenny to do an assessment. I hope that's alright with you."

"Why are you asking my permission after the fact?"

"I thought you knew," Mrs. Daniels said.

"No, Mrs. Daniels, I didn't know."

"Well, why don't you sit down?" asked Ms. Torres. "We can discuss the findings, and my recommendations."

Ms. Torres gestured her hand to indicate to Valerie to sit down. Valerie sat down slowly, while leering at Ms. Torres.

"I understand that you have a busy schedule, and that your husband also has a busy schedule, which leads me to conclude that between the two of you, there really is no time for Jenny. She's just not able to get that one-on-one time that she so desperately needs."

"Excuse me?"

"If you look at her hands, you'll see that she has all sorts of skin problems; due to neglect. I'm sure it's not intentional. I can certainly understand how you, and your husband, may not have the time to properly care for Jenny. But don't feel bad. I see this a lot. It is my recommendation that Jenny be placed in a group home. You may not be aware of this, Mrs. Cole, but Caring Hearts has a few openings at a couple of their group homes. Isn't that right, Mrs. Daniels?"

"Oh, yes. We do have a few openings, but they're going fast. Rest assured, we'll take great care of Jenny. And you'll be happy to know that you can come visit anytime you'd like. Just be sure to call first," Mrs. Daniels said.

"Oh, really, Mrs. Daniels? I can come visit my own sister anytime I'd like, as long as I called first? Oh, goodie!" Valerie said, as she clapped her hands.

"Excuse me, ladies," the principal said, "you know nothing about Jenny, nothing at all. I've known Jenny for seven years, and I can assure you that she receives excellent care at home. She's happy."

"With all due respect," said Ms. Torres, "this really is no concern of yours."

"Listen, ladies, I am the principal here. Everything that is said and done in this school, is my concern. Everything that affects my students, is my concern."

"I'm prepared to take this to court, Mrs. Cole," Ms. Torres said.

An enraged Valerie responded, "You've got to be kidding me! You have no case! I have never neglected Jenny, I love her. Is this what Caring Hearts is about? Trying to convert their day clients to become live-ins at their group homes? That doesn't seem like a caring heart to me. That sounds like a greedy heart. It's all about money, isn't it?"

"Mrs. Cole, look at her hands," Ms. Torres said. "How do you explain that?"

"Ms. Torres, have you never seen anyone with eczema?"

"It's bad, Mrs. Cole."

"Yes, Ms. Torres, eczema is bad. That's why I'm taking her to see a specialist. The appointment is not until two weeks from now, Jenny's primary doctor set it up months ago. Do you know how long it takes to get an appointment with a dermatologist in this town? There are two dermatologists, and a lot of people with bad skin. Do the math! Come on, Jenny, let's go home."

"Mrs. Cole, wait. Why don't you just give the group home some thought? Sooner or later, you and your husband will realize that you need a break from taking care of Jenny, and she really wants to go."

"Oh, she does? Well, she didn't mention it to me when we chatted this morning over breakfast. When did she tell you about it? What words did Jenny use to convey that message to you? Did she say, 'Ms. Torres, take me to a group home, my sister neglects me.' Is that what she said to you, Ms. Torres? Tell me what words she used, because she only knows a few. Let's see, she knows the words: yeah, bye, pizza hut, ice cream, Wednesday, 'that's good', 'no way', 'that's mine', 'I want that'. She also knows the numbers, one through ten, though not in order, and not the value of each number. There are a few more words that she knows, Ms. Torres, but I'm pretty sure that 'group home' are not part of her vocabulary."

"Well, Mrs. Cole, you may not know your sister quite as well as you think you do."

"I know my baby sister very well. You don't know her at all. Do you know that Jenny loves to dance, and sing? She loves to color, and draw pictures. She can't swim, but she loves to wade in the water. She loves to look through my husband's dictionary, she follows the words with her finger as if she's reading it. She loves to push the shopping card when we go to the grocery store, but I don't let her because she rams into me. At first, I thought she did it accidentally, but then she kept doing it, and she seemed to enjoy it, so she knows what she's doing. She loves to watch scary movies, she finds them amusing. Yet, she's afraid of the dark, so she has a nightlight on when she sleeps. Don't you dare tell me that I don't know her as well as I think I do. No one knows Jenny better than I do."

Sensing that Valerie was upset, Jenny got up from her chair, and embraced her.

"It's alright, Jenny. I'm fine."

Jenny scowled at Ms. Torres, and shook her finger at her in a scolding manner.

"I certainly didn't mean to upset you, Mrs. Cole," said Ms. Torres.

"You've also upset Jenny," the principal said.

"Well, I didn't mean to upset anyone. Earlier, I was able to conduct an interview with Jenny. I asked her a few questions about school, and various things. When I asked her about the group home, she seemed enthusiastic."

"Mrs. Cole, may I say something?" asked the principal.

"Please do," said Valerie.

"Ms. Torres, Mrs. Daniels; you two seem to think that you know what Jenny wants, but I know my students quite well. If either of you can convince me that Jenny wants to go to a group home, I'll get Mrs. Cole and her husband to sign the necessary paperwork. But if you can't convince me, I will find great pleasure in throwing you both out on your ear."

"Mr… I'm sorry, I don't know your name," said Ms. Torres.

"I'm the principal. Who do you think that you're talking to?"

"Well, Mr… uh…" uttered Ms. Torres.

"You may call me, Mr. Principal."

"Mr. Principal, I don't appreciate your threats," said Ms. Torres.

"Mr. uh… sir," Mrs. Daniels babbled.

"You may also call me, Mr. Principal."

"Mr. uh… Principal, this is highly unprofessional," Mrs. Daniels said.

"This is my school, and we'll do things my way. I should throw you both out right now, but I won't. Because sooner or later, you're going to humiliate yourselves, and when you do, Mrs. Cole, and Mrs. Bell will join me for a good laugh. Come on, Ms. Torres, let's get this going."

After a grimacing glare aimed at Mr. Principal, Ms. Torres apprehensively turned to Jenny.

"HI, JENNY, HOW ARE YOU?"

"She's not deaf, Ms. Torres," said Mr. Principal.

"I'm aware of that," Ms. Torres snapped back.

"You watch your tone with me, lady!"

"I mean, excuse me. I ... I had her confused with another student."

"Is the other student hard of hearing?"

"Um ... no, she's not."

"I guess you showed us sooner, rather than later."

Ms. Torres tried to maintain her dignity, but it was obvious to everyone that she became flustered.

"Hi, Jenny, sweetie, do you remember what we talked about earlier?"

"Yeah," Jenny said, nodding her head.

"You seemed real interested in going to a group home. Would you like to do that?"

"Yeah."

"Group home, right?"

"Yeah."

"Okay, sweetie. I'll see what I can do about the group home."

Valerie, Mr. Principal, and Mrs. Bell shared an indulgent glance; Valerie also rolled her eyes, she was not very discreet.

"There you have it. You were right there when she said it. I didn't coax her, Mr. Principal. She has her own free will," said Ms. Torres.

"Do you think that convinced me?"

"Mr. Principal, she really wants to go," Mrs. Daniels chimed in.

"Ladies, that's Jenny's response to everything. She says yes to everything." Turning to Jenny, he asked, "Jenny, is your name Betsy Ross?"

"Yeah," Jenny said, as she giggled, and nodded her head.

"Jenny, are you married to Tom Selleck?"

"Yeah," she responded.

"I haven't seen him lately, did he move back to Hawaii?"

"Yeah, pizza hut," a hungry Jenny giggled.

"Jenny, do you think Ms. Torres will be getting a kickback from Mrs. Daniels, if she gets you to go to a group home?"

"Yeah," Jenny said, continuing to nod her head, and giggle.

Mrs. Daniels and Ms. Torres looked perturbed.

"Jenny, should I tell these ladies to go jump in the lake?"

"Yeah."

"Ladies, I agree with Jenny. Why don't you both go jump in the lake? And don't bother Mrs. Cole again. Her husband is an attorney, and he'll wipe the floor with you. Good day."

"Oh, thank you," Valerie said. She stood up to give Mr. Principal a big hug, and stuck her tongue out at Mrs. Daniels and Ms. Torres as they left the room.

"You're welcome, Mrs. Cole. I'll see you at graduation."

"Thanks, I'll see you then."

"Patrick! I'm so glad that you're home," Valerie said. She ran into his arms as soon as he walked through the front door.

"What's the matter, Val? Are you alright? Is it the boys or Jenny?"

"It was a terrible day, Patrick. I was threatened, twice, that Jenny would be taken away from us."

"What? Let's sit down. Now tell me what happened. Who threatened you?"

"Well, first it was Didi. She wants the house, and she knows the only way she can have it is by gaining guardianship over Jenny."

"Valerie, did she say that to you? That she wants the house, and guardianship over Jenny?"

"She didn't exactly say that. But why else would she want Jenny? Patrick, you know she doesn't care anything about Jenny."

"I wouldn't say that, Valerie."

"What? Do you think that Didi cares about Jenny? She doesn't even care about her own kids."

"Come on, Valerie. That's not fair."

"The kids spend more time with Jeff than they do with her."

"So what! That doesn't mean she doesn't love them. Maybe she loves them so much, that she's willing to, unselfishly, let her kids spend time with their father. Do you know that there are some mothers who receive child support, and don't even allow their children to see their fathers? And sometimes they don't even take proper care of their kids; they use the child support money on luxuries for themselves, while the kids do without. Not all mothers do that. Most mothers put the welfare of their children above all else. Didi falls in that category. She knows that the kids are better off by spending time with both parents. Maybe that's her way of loving her kids, doing what's best for them, not what's best for her. Think about it, Valerie."

"Well, alright, I'll think about it."

"Think about this too, sooner or later, you're going to have to let Didi spend some time with Jenny."

"No, she wants to take Jenny from us. She mentioned hiring a lawyer."

"Let's not accuse her of anything. Besides, do you think that I would be intimidated by any lawyer she might hire?"

"No, not at all. And I told her so."

"Who else threatened you today, Val?"

"Well, we're going to have to find a new place for Jenny. It's a long story, but let's just say that Caring Hearts isn't so caring, and they don't have a heart. They also threatened to take Jenny away from us. We were at the school when this happened."

"You shouldn't worry about that. You're married to a successful lawyer. You never have to worry about any legal matters. Did you say that you were at school when this happened? I'm surprised that Mr. Principal didn't step in. If he knew about it, believe me, he wouldn't put up with that, not for one minute."

"Mr. Principal? Don't you know his name?"

"It's hard to pronounce. Do you know it?"

"No."

"Besides, he likes being called Mr. Principal. That's what everyone calls him. I hear that his wife calls him that too, even when they're in bed."

"Patrick, how would you know that?"

"Everybody knows. Hey, that gives me a great idea."

"What's that?"

"Why don't you call me, Mr. Lawyer?"

"Patrick, I'm not going to call you Mr. Lawyer. What would people say?"

"I'm not asking you to call me that all the time. How about just when we're in bed. It could be fun. How about it?"

Patrick pulled her close to kiss her.

"No," Valerie said.

She gently bit his nose before walking away.

"Okay," Patrick yelled after her. "I'll ask you again later, when you're in a better mood."

"Not going to happen," Valerie yelled back.

CHAPTER SEVENTEEN

Don't Give Up On Us

Jenny got a standing ovation when her name was called to receive her Certificate of Completion, as did the three other special education students. Upon the recommendation of Mr. Principal, Valerie found a new place for Jenny. *Just Like You, serving those with special needs.* The staff was much friendlier, and both Valerie and Patrick were pleased.

As with every milestone in hers and Jenny's life, Valerie missed her parents a little more than usual. She wondered if Jenny remembered them at all. When looking through photo albums with Jenny, Valerie liked to point out pictures of their parents. Sometimes, when asked if she remembers her parents, Jenny's response is "yeah". But even if Jenny did not have Down syndrome, she probably wouldn't remember them; she was not even three years old when they died.

It was a hectic day at the Cole house on the afternoon of the graduation party. Besides decorating the house for the party, there was much food to prepare. The main dish would be burgers, hotdogs, and bratwurst. Patrick would be in charge of that; he enjoyed his role as the grill master. Valerie always made sure to include certain foods on the menu; she wanted to represent her German, Mexican, and Italian heritages. Those foods were bratwurst, pinto beans, Spanish rice, and Panzanella. Of course, she didn't prepare these foods herself; she delegated to those family members who, over the years, had demonstrated the tastiest recipes for these scrumptious dishes. Priscilla made the beans and rice; while Gina, who immigrated from Italy as a child, made the Panzanella.

Some of the guests included, Mrs. Bell and her husband, Mr. and Mrs. Principal, Jenny's classmates, and their families. Valerie's lifelong friends, Karen and Debra, would also be there. Karen lived in town, and was married to John, her second husband. Her first marriage to Cory ended when the rumors of his infidelity proved to be true. They had two children who lived with her and John. Debra and Brando lived in Colorado with their four children. They planned their annual Texas vacation to coincide with Jenny's graduation.

Valerie took her time deciding on an outfit to wear. Since she hadn't announced her pregnancy, she wanted to make sure that her clothes did not make the announcement for her. Looking at herself in the mirror, she realized that it was time to break the happy news. Her belly was not huge, but it was becoming obvious that she was pregnant. After finding something cute to wear, she got dressed, and made her way downstairs. Jenny was dancing in the living room, without any music.

"Awe, Priscilla must have bought her a new dress," she said to herself. "Jenny, that's a pretty dress you're wearing. I like it. Look at the pretty flowers on it. Do you like the pretty flowers?"

"Yeah, it mine," Jenny said, smiling, and nodding her head.

"Did you say thank you to Priscilla for giving you this dress?"

"Yeah, tank cu, Cilla."

"You're a good girl, Jenny. Let's go outside to the backyard, and see who came to your party."

Jenny was excited to see that her friends were already in the backyard. She went back into the house to retrieve her boom box. Once the music was blaring, Jenny could hardly keep still; she kicked off an impromptu dance marathon. Valerie was intrigued by how Jenny, and her friends, were able to communicate with each other. Since Jenny's vocabulary was limited to only a few words, she didn't understand very much of the English language, but she did seem to understand what her friends were saying to her.

Valerie wondered if Jenny's friends were on the same intellectual level as Jenny. They were more vocal than Jenny was, and had a broader vocabulary. As Jenny and her friends twirled around to the music, Valerie couldn't help feeling a bit envious. Jenny and her friends didn't have a care in the world. How wonderful would that be, to not have to worry about anything? She imagined that it would be like staying five years old forever.

Watching her children play with their cousins, and with Karen's and Debra's kids, brought Valerie much joy. She reminisced about playing with Karen and Debra when the three of them were growing up; now they all had children of their own. Seeing Delores across the yard diminished some of her joy; at least her husband was not with her. She wondered what the topic of conversation was between Delores and Priscilla; they seemed to be having a serious heart-to-heart. She hoped that Priscilla would be able to talk some sense into Delores about her wanting to take Jenny.

Valerie tried to remember the last time that she and Delores were on good terms with each other, it was probably before their parents died. There were moments throughout the years, when Valerie and Delores shared happy times; a few Christmases here and there, an occasional birthday party, or random times when their aunt Gina made a special family meal. But something always happened that caused those joyous unions to crumble. Priscilla remained close to both of her sisters, and hoped that a lasting reconciliation was on the horizon.

The party was a success, continuing well into the evening, with family and close friends being the last to leave.

"It's been wonderful seeing everybody, but this baby is wearing me out. I have to get to bed. I'm sorry, everyone," Valerie said, while yawning.

"You get to Dollface bed. I mean Doll, bed. You know what I mean. Goodnight, Faceydoll. We'll all be here in the morning, still partying. Huh, everybody?" said Michael. He was slightly intoxicated while raising a bottle of beer in the air.

"I'll walk you up, honey," Patrick said.

"Goodnight, everybody," said Valerie.

Patrick held Valerie's hand as they walked upstairs to their bedroom. "It was a great party, Val. The effort you put forth in planning was well worth it. Jenny was elated seeing everyone."

"Yeah, I'm glad that she had a good time. Patrick, has Didi talked to you about wanting Jenny to live with her?"

"Yes, she has. So, here's a question for you, Valerie; would it be so terrible for her and Bill to spend just a little time with Jenny?"

"What? Are you serious? Do you not want Jenny to live with us anymore? So much for the promise that you made to my father. Goodnight, Patrick."

"Wait a minute, Valerie. That is not what I am saying. I will always keep the promises I made to your father, and to you. All I am saying is, what I'm asking is, would it be so bad for Didi to take Jenny for a weekend? Maybe just the evening? Didi is Jenny's sister too, but Jenny doesn't even know her. Not like she knows us, and Mike, and Priscilla. She should have the chance to get to know her a little."

"Didi's had a lot of chances, Patrick. Goodnight."

"Alright, I'm sorry. I didn't mean to upset you. We'll talk about it later. I love you. Goodnight, Valerie."

Valerie awoke to find a box of dark chocolate candy on the spot of the bed where Patrick sleeps. There was a note next to it. In her haste to open the box, the note flew to the floor. After eating a piece of candy, she got out of bed, then walked over to retrieve the note, which read:

Val, I'm sorry. Please don't be angry. I love you.

"When people tell me not to be angry, it usually means that they've done something that will make me angry," she said to herself.

She quickly put on clothes before going downstairs, just in case the party-goers were still at it, as Michael said they would be. She peeked into her boys' bedroom; she saw there were a little more toys scattered on the floor than usual. It brought a smile to her face, because she knew that the messier the bedroom, the more fun the boys had. As she passed by Jenny's room, she decided not to peek in. The door was closed, so, she didn't want to cause creaking noises by opening it. She thought she'd let Jenny sleep in since yesterday was a long day for her.

When Valerie arrived downstairs, she found Michael sleeping on the couch. His head was slightly hanging off the edge, and his mouth was wide open. His neck and chest were covered in popcorn. Emily, Nicole, and Monica, who were supervised by Lauren, were taking turns throwing popcorn into his mouth. Of course, few kernels actually made the target, which was why there was a mess.

"Good morning, Aunt Valerie," the girls said to her.

"Good morning, girls. Lauren, why is your father covered in popcorn?"

"Well, Aunt Valerie, he passed out. He knows the rules."

"Aunt Valerie, you should see our dad," a laughing Nicole said. "We stuck popcorn up his nose."

"Really? Where's my camera? I'd like to get a picture of them."

"No pictures!" Jeff bellowed, from his resting spot on the floor.

The girls, not knowing that Jeff was awake, let out a little scream. Michael echoed the sentiment louder, which caused the younger girls to shriek, and run out of the room. Lauren stayed behind, laughing at her father and uncle.

"I knew you were awake Dad, and you too, Uncle Jeff," Lauren said.

"Yeah, we were awake. We're just letting you girls have a little fun," Michael said.

"Valerie, are you alright with Didi?" asked Jeff.

"Well, I don't know if I'll ever be alright with Didi. But there's no way that I will ever let Jenny go with her."

"Uh… I think you'd better talk with your husband."

"Valerie, good morning, honey," Patrick said. He brought her a cup of coffee, and gave her a kiss, then led her to the couch, where they both sat down. "I want to talk to you about something; Priscilla and I want to talk to you about something."

"What's going on?"

"I'll start," said Priscilla. "I want to talk to you about Didi."

"I saw the two of you talking yesterday. What were y'all talking about? Did she tell you that she wants to take Jenny?"

"Yes, she did. But she doesn't want to take Jenny from you, Valerie. She just wants to spend a little time with her, that's all."

"But you agree with me, right? Patrick thinks we should let Didi take Jenny for a few weekends, but I say no. What do you say, Priscilla?"

The room seemed to silence as Priscilla prepared herself to give Valerie her point of view. On the verge of speaking, the telephone rang, providing her a much welcomed interruption. As almost everyone volunteered to answer it, Valerie assigned the task to Michael.

"I'm going to get Jenny up. I let her sleep in because I'm sure that she went to bed late last night. Priscilla, I do want your opinion on this matter. I'll be back in a few minutes."

"Wait, Valerie. Jenny's not in her room," Patrick said.

"Where is she?"

"She's not here, honey."

"Patrick, where is she?"

"That was Bill," Michael said. "Didi's been in an accident. We need to get to the hospital."

"Michael, what happened?" asked Priscilla. "Was Jenny with her?"

"What do you mean, was Jenny with her?" Valerie asked.

"Let's go. We'll talk in the car," Priscilla said.

"No! I'm not going anywhere until somebody tells me what's going on. What did you mean asking if Jenny was with Didi? Patrick, where is Jenny?"

"Jenny went with Didi last night," Michael said. "They were just involved in a car accident. We need to go. Lauren will stay with the kids. We can talk later."

"Go, Aunt Valerie. I got this," said Lauren.

Valerie grabbed her purse and keys, then headed out the door, to her car. Patrick, walking next to her, attempted to hold her hand. She pushed his hand away, and walked towards the car at a faster pace.

"Valerie, wait a minute," Patrick called out.

Valerie ignored him, and rushed to get to her car. Patrick, walking at a fast pace to catch up, arrived at the passenger side of the car; moments after Valerie got in, and started the motor. He knocked on the window, but she kept her eyes focused straight ahead.

"Come on, honey, unlock the door. Valerie! Unlock the door!"

Continuing to ignore him, she put the car in reverse, and backed out of the driveway, then she sped away. She wasn't at all concerned that Patrick could have been injured in her haste to drive off.

"Why is there always a damn car accident, and why is it always because of Didi?" she asked herself.

She tearfully recalled the day when she was fourteen years old, and her parents told her that there was another baby on the way. She remembered the temper tantrum she threw, and how much she did not want her mother to have another baby. She remembered the frustration she felt with Jenny as a baby; how she wasn't learning to do things as fast as Valerie wanted her to learn. She hoped that, for these past seventeen years, she had been a good mother to Jenny. Even though they were biologically sisters, Valerie felt that Jenny was more like a daughter to her, rather than a sister.

Many times, during these past several years, Valerie wondered what it would be like if Jenny did not have Down syndrome; if she could be just a regular sister. She wondered what it would be like for Jenny and her, to have the big sister-little sister experiences. After a few minutes of driving, Valerie was able to calm down enough to realize that she didn't even know what exactly had happened. All she knew was that there had been a car accident, and Delores was driving. But who had been injured? Was it Delores or Jenny? She would soon find out who was injured, and how severe they were, as she drove into the hospital parking lot.

The rest of the family arrived at the hospital, about the same time as Valerie. Not wanting to see Patrick, Valerie went out of her way to avoid being near him; actions which were noticed by everyone. Michael was told by a nurse, that a doctor would be out shortly to inform them on what was happening. At this point, it was still unclear how severe either Delores or Jenny were injured. They waited with uncertainty, while trying to maintain a peace of mind.

Patrick thought he would comfort his wife by putting his arm around her, which resulted in Valerie exerting her arm with such force to cause her husband discomfort, and embarrassment. A second attempt to embrace Valerie, compelled her to lose control of her emotions.

"If anything happens to Jenny, I hold you responsible, Patrick! This is your fault! You knew that I didn't want Didi to take her, and you went against my wishes! I will never forgive you for this, Patrick! Never!"

"Valerie, please don't blame Patrick," Priscilla cried.

"It's alright, Priscilla. She has a right to be angry with me. Valerie, I'm sorry. I'm so very sorry. You know how much I love Jenny. I would never do anything to hurt her."

"But you did, Patrick. I can't even look at you right now. I want you to leave," Valerie cried.

"Wait, don't leave Patrick. Valerie, this isn't his fault."

"Priscilla, let it go. Call me when you know anything, I'll be at home. Valerie, I'm sorry. I love you." Patrick tried, unsuccessfully, to hold back his tears.

"Valerie, it's not his fault. Please don't blame him."

"He knew that I didn't want Didi to take Jenny, and he still allowed it. I don't know if I can ever forgive that. He went behind my back. And you're defending him? Do you and Michael condone what Patrick did by letting Didi take Jenny? You had something to do with this too, didn't you, Priscilla? What about Michael? Was he in on this too? You all went behind my back."

"Valerie, I know that you're angry with us. I wish that you would give us a chance to explain things," said Michael. "Let us tell you what happened last night. Please, Valerie."

"Valerie," said Patrick.

"What are you still doing here? I told you to leave."

"Please, let me talk to you, Val."

"Why? So you can tell me more lies? I will never trust you again, Patrick. And I will never forgive you."

"What are you saying, Valerie?"

"Valerie, Patrick didn't lie to you," said Priscilla.

"Patrick, I don't think that I can ever trust you again. I don't think that I can ever forgive you."

"Valerie, I'm sorry," cried Patrick.

"Leave me alone, Patrick! I'm very close to calling a divorce attorney."

"No, please. Don't do that. I made a mistake, Valerie, I'm sorry. Don't give up on us."

"Look, Valerie," said Michael, "this isn't Patrick's fault. It isn't anyone's fault. It's just a terrible, unfortunate thing that happened. You were being unreasonable for not letting Didi see Jenny. Don't forget, I still hold the cards concerning Jenny. All of these years, you and Patrick have only had temporary guardianship. None of us have ever taken the time to make it permanent. We've all been too comfortable with this arrangement, that it never crossed any of our minds to make things permanent with you and Patrick."

"What are you saying, Michael? Are you going to take Jenny away from us?"

"I'm sure that's not what he's saying, Valerie," said Patrick.

"Why are you still here?" asked Valerie. "Please leave!"

"I'm sorry, Valerie. I really am. I'll leave. I'll go check on the kids. Don't give up on us."

"Goodbye, Patrick. I don't want to see you anymore. Just go!"

"Don't give up on us."

"Go!"

"Valerie, you're being a little hard on Patrick. What happened was very unfortunate, it was an accident. Any one of us could be involved in a car accident. We don't know all the details, but certainly, you can't blame Patrick or Didi. After the party, Didi was about to leave the house, but Jenny wouldn't let her go; she just held onto her. That's why I suggested Didi take Jenny home with her. It wasn't Patrick, it was me. If you want to be mad at anyone, be mad at me."

"Alright, Michael, I'll be mad at you."

"That's fine. Now I'm going to tell you something that your father used to say to me when I would get angry at some of the lawyers at trial; he'd say, 'It's alright to be angry, Mike. But don't let that anger fester up inside you, because then it becomes hate.' That's great advice, Valerie, I hope you take it to heart."

"I will, Michael. Once, Dad gave me that same advice. Look, I'm sorry about how I've behaved. I'm really hungry. This baby wants me to eat, right now. Do you know how to get to the cafeteria?"

"Sure, we'll walk you to the elevator."

"I'm sorry, Priscilla. Maybe I'll feel better after I've had something to eat. When you see Patrick, will you ask him to give me a little time?"

"You bet," said Michael. "When your divorce becomes final, you'll have all the time in the world."

"What?"

"You said that you wanted a divorce from Patrick. I heard you say it."

"Obviously, I didn't mean it. But Priscilla may want to consider that option."

CHAPTER EIGHTEEN

Hello, It's Me

She didn't have to wait long for the next elevator to arrive. When the door opened, Valerie quickly boarded; impatiently waiting for the brief ride to begin. Without warning, grumbling noises could be heard by the five or six passengers in the elevator with Valerie. A horrified look appeared on her face as she hoped that the other riders would not figure out that the growling sounds escaped from her body. Her hunger pangs were becoming increasingly louder. As soon as the doors opened, she speedily exited the elevator, and wasted no time getting to the cafeteria.

Once she got to the serving line, she grabbed a tray, and began to load it up. She got a cheeseburger, french fries, a Caesar salad, an eggroll, a slice of chocolate cake, and a large diet soda. Then she looked around for the most secluded table that she could find, and sat down.

She removed her food from the tray, and arranged it on the table, then began to eat, starting with the Caesar salad. Next, she ate the chocolate cake, then she quickly devoured the eggroll. After eating a few bites of the cheeseburger, she found it to be unpalatable, with a texture that felt like rubber.

On the verge of feeling nauseated, she pushed the burger aside; then realizing that she was still hungry, she took another bite out of it. The burger wasn't as good as what she made at home, but she figured that it wouldn't kill her if she continued to eat it. When she made cheeseburgers at home, she mixed chopped onion into the meat for flavor, and added a slice of cheese while the burger was still on the stove, allowing the cheese to melt on the meat.

Looking around the cafeteria, she happened to notice an attractive young woman walking in her direction. As the young woman got closer; Valerie realized that she was actually heading towards her table. Within the next few seconds, the young woman stood before Valerie.

"Hi, do you mind if I sit here?" she asked.

With her mouth full, Valerie was unable to answer. She held out her hand, motioning for the young woman to wait. But, instead of waiting, the young woman pulled out a chair from across the table, and sat down.

"Thanks, Val," the young woman said, as she sat down.

"Excuse me, do I know you?" Valerie asked.

"Do you know me?" the young woman asked. "Hello, it's me."

"Excuse me? Who are you?"

"You don't recognize me, Valerie? Have I changed that much? Let me see your mirror."

"Who are you?" Valerie asked again, sounding a bit annoyed.

"Well, can I have the mirror, please? Then I'll tell you who I am."

"No, I don't have a mirror."

"Valerie, you have a mirror, you always keep a mirror in your purse. Check the small zippered pocket; that's usually where you keep it. You ought to keep your keys there too, then you wouldn't waste so much time in the morning looking for them. Why don't you do that?" the young woman asked.

Valerie, shocked by the young woman's statement, asked, "How do you know what's in my purse? And how do you know anything about when I can't find my keys?"

"Will you please give me the mirror? Then you can get back to your burger. How is it? It's probably not as good as the cheeseburgers that you make, right? I love how you put the chopped onion in the meat before you cook it. Mmm…. it's so delicious. But my favorite is your French toast."

"You need to tell me who are you?" Valerie insisted. "How do you know anything about the way I make hamburgers?"

"I thought that you would recognize me, Valerie. I guess I must look different. Can I please borrow your mirror? I want to see how I look. Why are you being so stingy with your mirror?"

"I'm sorry, here's my mirror. Something about you is very familiar, I don't know what it is," Valerie said, to her mysterious new friend.

"Wow," the young woman said, gazing at herself in the mirror. "I look so different. No wonder you don't recognize me, I don't look like me. I am very pretty! Not that I was unattractive before, but I just never paid attention to that kind of thing. You know what I mean? I never thought about it, it was never important to me. I've never been vain, like Didi. What do you think, Valerie? Do you like my new look? I think that I look a lot like Priscilla, although I do see a little bit of Didi around my eyes. Not the color of the eyes, just the shape. Don't you think so?"

"Okay, that's enough! How do you know me? How do you know my sisters? I gave you the mirror, now stop playing games, and tell me who you are."

"Alright, I'll tell you, since there is no way that you'll figure it out. But I'm sorry, I just can't get over how pretty I am. Hey, why are there so many empty plates here? Did you eat all of this food by yourself? That's a lot of food. You usually don't eat this much, unless…. Valerie, are you pregnant?"

"Tell me who you are," demanded Valerie.

"Okay, but are you pregnant? I have noticed that you've put on a little weight. I thought you were just getting fat, you know, because of the extra pizza that you eat when Patrick is not looking. It's pretty cool how you do that; 'No, Patrick, this is only my second slice. Why? How many have you had?' You're pretty slick, Valerie. Yup, you sure are. So… your baby… hoping for a girl this time?"

"I don't eat pizza behind Patrick's back. And how do you know about that? How do you know things about me? Would you please tell me? I'm dying to know."

"You're not dying, Valerie. You're always so dramatic. 'I'm dying to know, I'm dying to know'. Give it a rest, would you?"

"I am not dramatic!"

"No, Valerie, you're not dramatic. I'm sorry. I must be thinking of someone else, okay?"

"Would you please tell me who you are?"

"I'm sorry, Valerie. I guess I'm a little nervous about telling you, because I don't know how you will react. But I need to tell you. I'm just going to say it, I'm Jenny."

"Your name is Jenny?"

"Yes, my name is Jenny. It's not Jennifer, it's Jenny."

"That's my sister's name."

"I know that. You picked the name, remember? Didi was so mad, wasn't she? You did that to be spiteful, just to make her mad. But it was hilarious. And you called her the B-word! Valerie, I can't believe you did that. And you said it right in front of everyone, including Mom and Dad. And if calling her the B-word wasn't bad enough, you made fun of her because she was named after a prostitute. That was really mean, Valerie. Yeah, it was funny, but it was still mean."

"What? Wait. How? How... do you know that? Did Didi tell you? Do you know my sister, Didi? Why did you say Mom and Dad, as if they were your parents?"

"Of course, I know Didi. But I wish that I knew her a little better. I don't know her as well as I know Priscilla, or you. I said Mom and Dad as if they were my parents, because they were my parents."

"You're freaking me out. Who are you?"

"Well, you know my name, it's Jenny. How many girls named Jenny, besides me, do you know?"

"I don't know who you are, or how you know things about me. I don't know you. Okay?"

"Valerie, it doesn't matter how many times you say, 'I don't know you,' it's not going to change the fact that you do know me. I'm your sister. Look into my eyes, and look into your heart, then you'll know that I'm telling you the truth."

"Look, whoever you are, you're crazy!"

"No, Valerie, I'm not crazy! I don't know how this is happening, any more than you do. But I'm not crazy! If anyone is crazy, it's you!"

"I am not crazy!"

"Well, neither am I! I am not the one who told people that my father was a serial killer. I mean, really? How could you say that about Dad?"

"What?"

"You heard me. You wore a blue dress on your first date with Patrick. When you came downstairs, he was playing with me on the floor. He brought you flowers, and Mom put them in a vase for you. Before you left,

Dad whispered something in your ear. Then you got this petrified look on your face. It was so funny."

"What are you … How do you … I … I … What's going on? I must be dreaming."

"You're not dreaming. Valerie, look at me. I'm not deformed. Remember when you were worried that I would be born deformed? That's what you told Mom and Dad the day they told you that she was pregnant with me. You made mom cry. Did you know that?"

"I'm not believing this. I am dreaming. I don't understand what's going on, or how you can be who you say you are. There's no way. I must be losing my mind."

"There you go again, Valerie, being dramatic. Patrick is on his way down. He's worried about you. He'll be here any moment. You talk to him, I'll wait for you outside in the garden. It's a walk-out basement, just through those doors. When he gets here, don't tell him about me. I'm not here for Patrick, I'm here for you. Besides, he won't understand."

"That makes two of us."

"You may not understand now, Valerie, but you will, soon. It'll all come together, you'll see. Come out to the garden when Patrick leaves, alright?"

"Okay, I'll go out to the garden, whoever you are."

As Patrick approached Valerie, she braced herself for an unwanted conversation. She was still a bit incoherent about her mysterious new friend.

"Valerie, are you still angry with me?" asked Patrick.

Valerie answered his question with a question, "Did you happen to see the girl who was just here?"

"Yeah, who is she?"

"I don't know. I mean, I think I know. But it's impossible, so, I don't know. Maybe it is possible. In that case, then I know. But it can't be, so I don't know."

"Valerie, are you alright?"

"I don't know."

"Okay, Val, I hope that you'll be alright. I just wanted to tell you that I'm sorry. I didn't mean to go behind your back by letting Didi take Jenny. I really didn't mean to hurt you like that, and I'm sorry."

"I know, Patrick. I know that you didn't mean to do it, but you still did."

"I'm sorry. I want you to know that I will be sorry for the rest of my life. It's not looking good for Jenny, Didi either. I will never forgive myself. I'm sorry, Valerie. I'm so sorry," Patrick sobbed. "Please forgive me."

"What is going on, Patrick?"

"They're in surgery. They should be out by now."

"Patrick, we don't actually know anything yet, so let's not jump to conclusions. I'm still angry, I'm not ready to forgive you, just yet. Go back with the family. Please, I need time to be alone, so I can process everything. I'll be fine, I just want to be left alone."

"Alright. See you soon?"

"Yeah, I'll see you later."

Valerie went outside, and sat on a bench in the garden. She buried her face in her hands, and cried.

"Valerie, please don't cry. You're going to make me cry."

Valerie looked up to see her mysterious new friend.

"You need to tell me who you are, and why you're trying to make me believe that you're my sister."

"Valerie, I'm not trying to make you believe anything that isn't true. I am Jenny. I don't know what's going on. Really, I don't. I don't know how this is happening, but it is happening. Believe it or not, the choice is yours. You've taken care of me since I was three years old, when Mom and Dad died. Then you married Patrick. I was your flower girl, remember?"

Valerie reached into her purse, and took out her wallet. She opened her wallet to reveal a photograph of Jenny. "This is my baby sister, Jenny," she said. "As you can see, Jenny has Down syndrome, and right now she's in surgery."

"I know that, Valerie. Look, I don't know how to explain what's happening. God is mysterious, and He doesn't have to explain things to us. But what I do know is that I've been given this chance to, for lack of a better term, put the Down syndrome away. I don't know how this is happening, but I do know that it's temporary. Isn't this great? I have this chance now to talk to you. We can talk, Valerie, like real sisters and real friends. That's what you've always wanted, isn't it? For us to be able to talk to each other? Haven't there been many times when you've wanted me to be just like you? Haven't you wondered what goes on in my head? Haven't you wanted to reach into my mind to see what I might be thinking about? I know that you have, Valerie, because you've told me. You've said that to me many times."

"This is impossible."

"Valerie, do you remember the first time you saw me, when I was a baby? Priscilla was holding me in her lap. I was sleeping, but I remember waking up to an awful stench. It was horrible! I think Dad cut one."

"This is impossible!" Valerie cried.

"With God, anything is possible, Valerie. Don't you remember, Dad used to say that all the time? Valerie, if you're still not convinced, look at my hand. Do you see this scar?"

"What scar? You don't have a scar."

"My scar! It's gone! Valerie, I had a scar on my hand. It's not there anymore. Well, of course, it's not there anymore. Duh! I have this new body. But the scar is still there on my old body. You see, Valerie, I've had this scar since I was three years old. My sister was ironing her dress in her bedroom, she was getting ready for a date with her boyfriend. The phone rang, and she went to answer it, but she couldn't find it. Her room was always super messy. She couldn't see the phone because it was under a pile of clothes. But she found the cord, and she yanked it; accidentally knocking over the ironing board, causing the iron to fall on my hand. It only touched my skin for a second, but that caused a burn. I screamed at the top of my lungs! My sister picked me up, and ran to the bathroom; she stuck my hand under cold running water. My parents had already passed away, but my two uncles were there with their wives, my aunts; they were there to babysit me while my sister went out on her date. My sister yelled out to them, 'Jenny burned her hand!' Then they ran upstairs to see what was going on, and…"

"Is this happening? Is this really happening? It can't be! Is this true? Is this real? It can't be real. Are you real? I feel like I'm dreaming. I have to be dreaming."

"You're not dreaming, Valerie. Just like you weren't dreaming that day when Mom and Dad went to visit you, the day after Thanksgiving. Remember?"

"Jenny?"

"Yes, Valerie. It's me, I'm Jenny. I don't know what, or how this is happening, but it's happening. It's really happening. You've wanted this to happen for a long time. Well, here I am. I'm here, Valerie."

"I can't believe it."

"Believe it. I have a message for you, it's from Mom and Dad. I asked Dad if I could use a hand gesture when I delivered the message, and he said no."

"What's the message?"

"Let it go. You're still blaming Didi for something that she didn't do. She is not responsible for Mom and Dad's death."

"What's the gesture that you wanted to show me?"

"I want to smack you upside the head. Luckily for you, Dad said no."

"That's mean. You don't know all the facts."

"Neither do you. You have no idea what Didi has been through, and you hold her responsible for something that is not her fault. And now you're angry with Patrick too? You think he went behind your back?"

"He did go behind my back. They all did."

"Would you come off it already? Do you think that they all did something to you? Come on, Valerie! Knock it off! Patrick has kept his promises to you, and to Dad. He loves you, he's taken good care of you; he's a good provider. And he's taken good care of me, just like he promised Dad that he would. Valerie, look, he doesn't deserve to be treated the way that you are treating him. There are a lot of women who would jump at the chance to be with Patrick. Take a good look at him. He's very handsome. I mean, he is fine!"

"Jenny! He's my husband, your brother-in-law!"

"I know that. I'm just repeating what I've heard other women say about him."

"What women?"

"I don't know these women, Valerie. They're women in the hospital that I've overheard talking. There were some women in the cafeteria, there was a nurse in the E.R. By the way, she doesn't like you. She told another nurse to check you out, and they both agreed that Patrick can do much better than you. She told the other nurse that she hopes you follow through on your threat to divorce him. Then she would be ready to step in, to comfort him, and help him forget all about that nasty woman he was married to. She would show him how a real woman treats a man. She said some other things too, but I'd rather not repeat those words. Valerie, did you threaten to divorce Patrick?"

"I didn't mean it."

"Well, you'd better watch it. Believe me when I say that it's not only the E.R. nurse, there are lots of women who would be more than willing to offer comfort to Patrick should he have his heart broken."

"How do you know that?"

"That's the word on the street. Face it, Valerie, there are plenty of women who would jump at the opportunity to be with Patrick. And I would be amiss if I didn't mention Elaine."

"Who is Elaine?"

"Elaine, wow. She's my nurse right now, I'm in the PACU."

"What do you mean by PACU?"

"PACU, the post-anesthesia care unit. It's the recovery room, you dipwad. After patients have had anesthesia, they need to recover. That's if the family wants them to wake up, most of the time they do. Geez, Valerie, how dumb are you? Like I was saying, if I was going to worry about anyone, it would be Elaine, the PACU nurse. She's been flirting with Patrick."

"What? She was flirting with Patrick?"

"Yup. You got it, sister."

"How dare he?"

"Relax, Valerie. Patrick wasn't flirting back with her. She was flirting with him. Boy, was she flirting with him! I'm telling you, Val, you'd better worry about her. On a scale of one to ten, you're only a seven, maybe a six. But Elaine, she's a ten! She is really hot!"

"I am not a six or a seven," Valerie annoyingly said.

"I'm also factoring in your attitude."

"There's nothing wrong with my attitude."

"Valerie, first your ugliness was just towards Didi. I get it. You blame her for what happened to Mom and Dad. It's not right, but I get it. But now you're being so mean to Patrick. He doesn't deserve that. No one does, not even Didi. All my life, you've wanted me to be like you, so we could talk. I remember how you used to voice your frustrations to me. Which wouldn't have been so bad, except your frustrations were about me; about my having Downs syndrome. I couldn't help how I was born. Why were you taking your frustrations out on me?"

"I'm sorry, Jenny. I didn't think that you understood what I was saying."

"Valerie, ever since I was born, Dad used to tell you to watch what you said around me. Do you remember him telling you that?"

"Yes, I remember. I'm sorry, Jenny."

"You're sorry? I'll let you know if I forgive you, Valerie."

"What?"

"I said that I would let you know if I forgive you. Oh, wait a minute; you don't like it if people don't forgive you, but it's alright if you don't forgive others, huh? Hasn't Didi apologized to you? She has apologized to you for things that she didn't even do. And still, you won't forgive her? But you expect me to forgive you? Look, Valerie, I don't know how much time I have to be like this, with this new body. But let me tell you what I do know; if that big truck didn't run the red light, Didi and I wouldn't have been involved in the accident. My being here; like this, like you, is a result of that accident. Don't you understand that? Valerie, if I die tomorrow, then at least we've had this time together."

"Jenny, are you dying tomorrow?"

"I don't know, Valerie. A big decision will have to be made soon, about me and Didi. Will we stay in this world? Will we join Mom and Dad? That will be God's decision. Same as Mom and Dad's death, God's decision."

"Jenny, you've talked to Mom? Have you seen Mom and Dad?"

"Yes, Valerie. They're wonderful! Dad is hoping that Didi pulls through this so you can make things right with her. But he's not going to hold his breath about it. Right now, it's time that you go. You need to check on me. The family is very worried about you. You know, because of what happened; the car accident, you being pregnant, and acting like a sourpuss."

"I am not a sourpuss, Jenny. Is that what you think? Because it's not true. But I will admit that I've been a little moody lately, I guess."

"You listen to me, sourpuss, you need to get up there and see me. Let the family know that you're alright. I'm in the PACU, oh sorry, Val. I forgot that you don't know what that means. I'm in the recovery room, you know where people recover? I didn't think that I would have to dumb down my vocabulary to talk to you."

"You don't have to dumb down your vocabulary, Jenny."

"Oh, but, Valerie, I don't mind."

"You're mean, Jenny."

"I'm not any meaner to you than you are to Didi. Valerie, keep this in mind; if Didi doesn't make it, you will never be able to forgive yourself. I know that you're angry, but remember: don't let that anger fester, it'll turn into hate. Dad told me to tell you that."

"I know that you're right, Jenny. I know that Dad is right, I know that Michael is right."

"Why don't you go now, Val? Join the family, see me and see Didi. Okay?"

"Alright, Jenny. I'll see you. And about Didi, I'll try."

"Well, that's a start. Rome wasn't built in a day. Go on now, but remember, Valerie, I've been in an accident. You may not recognize me, I don't look the same."

"You don't look the same right now, either."

"No, I mean there are tubes all over the place. I'm hooked up to a machine. My head is swollen, and my face is bruised."

"Alright, thanks for the warning. Hey, Jenny, will I see you again? I mean, this way, how you are now?"

"Yes, Valerie, you will. I'll come to you when I can. But remember, I'm only here for you, so don't share our secret."

"Okay, Jenny. I'll see you later."

"I'll see you later, Val."

CHAPTER NINETEEN

The Rain, The Park, And Other Things

When Valerie walked into the PACU waiting room, Patrick was nowhere in sight. She let her imagination get the best of her, wondering if he was off somewhere with the hot nurse, Elaine.

"Valerie," Priscilla called, from behind her, "are you alright?"

"No, Priscilla, I am not alright. I know that this isn't anyone's fault, but I'm still angry with Patrick, and even more angry with Didi. And I don't know why, but I'm just a tiny bit angry with you and Michael."

"I know that you're angry with us. You feel like we went behind your back, but we didn't. Jenny is not only your sister, she's my sister too. She's also Didi's sister. You know that Didi has been wanting to be more involved in Jenny's life for a while now. It wasn't just all of a sudden. A few months ago, she asked you if she could spend a little time with Jenny; you refused to let her. Then she asked you a few days ago, and again, you refused. Alright, she hasn't always been there for us. I understand that. But she's trying, and you won't meet her half way."

"Well, I've tried to meet her halfway."

"Valerie, you have done no such thing. Didi called me a few months ago, after you refused to let her spend time with Jenny. She wanted me to intervene. I talked to Patrick about it, because we were together in my office when she called. I see him a lot more often than I see you, so I talked to him first. He said that he would discuss it with you. He's been trying to do that."

Michael entered the room, holding two cups of coffee.

"Are you alright, Dollface? Would you like a cup of coffee?"

"No, thanks, Michael."

"Good, because I only got two, and I'm sure that your sister isn't going to share hers. Let me explain what happened. After you went to bed, Didi was getting ready to leave. She went around the room to say her goodbyes to everyone. When she said goodbye to Jenny, Jenny held her tight, and wouldn't let her go. That's why I suggested that Didi take her home for the night."

"I know that I shouldn't be acting this way towards everyone. I don't know why I'm so angry."

"It's your hormones, Dollface. Every woman who is pregnant goes through it. You should have seen how Priscilla treated me the three times when she was pregnant. What a nightmare. She was a real nightmare."

"He's exaggerating, Valerie. Do you want me to go in with you to see Jenny?"

"No, thanks, Priscilla. I'll go in by myself."

"Well, Dollface, at least let us prepare you for what to expect when you see Jenny. She's got ...."

"I know, she's hooked up to a machine and there are tubes everywhere. Her head is swollen, her face is bruised, and she doesn't look the same. I probably won't recognize her."

"Yeah, that's right. How did you know?"

"I raised Jenny. I know everything about her, except what room she's in."

"Through those doors, then ask the nurse."

"Do you want me to go with you?"

"No, Priscilla. I'll be alright. Thanks."

Valerie walked away from Michael and Priscilla, heading towards the door leading to the PACU. She walked through the doors, then to the nurses' station, where she encountered a very attractive nurse. Saying that she was attractive would be an understatement; she was drop-dead gorgeous, stunning, captivatingly beautiful. She was young, probably in her mid-twenties. She was holding a compact mirror, and applying pressed powder to her face. Her left hand was bare; no wedding ring, though certainly with her looks, she must have had a steady boyfriend. Her light brown hair cascaded down her shoulders, concealing most of her name badge. A couple of letters peeked through strands of her shiny hair; a capital E and a lower-case L. Her name started with El. Valerie wondered what her name was. It could be Eleanor, or Elizabeth. It could also be Elaine, the hot nurse that Jenny warned her about. Valerie hoped it was not her, but it wouldn't matter if it was.

"Excuse me," Valerie said, interrupting the nurse's beauty session. "May I ask you what room Jenny Negron is in?"

"Sure," responded the beautiful nurse, who by this time, was applying lipstick. As she answered Valerie's question, she flipped her hair back, revealing her name badge, which to Valerie's dismay, displayed the name, Elaine.

"Jenny is down this hall, room eight. If you're here to see Jenny, then you're probably going to want to see her sister. She's further down in room twelve."

'She wasn't so bad,' Valerie thought to herself. 'Maybe Jenny was mistaken about Elaine flirting with Patrick.'

"Before you go down there to visit your friends, can I ask you for a favor?" asked Elaine.

"Sure, what is it?"

"If you happen to see a tall, very attractive man, he's an older man, around thirty; would you give him a message for me?"

"Do you, uh, do you know his name?" Valerie nervously asked.

"I sure do. I've called it out several times last night while I dreamed about him. His name is Patrick," Elaine said, with a slight giggle.

"Oh, um, what's, uh, what's the message?" Valerie asked, even though she did not really want to know.

"I'm Elaine, and I'm going on my coffee break. Let him know that I'll be in the cafeteria, and he can join me if he wants some; coffee, or anything else," Elaine said, seductively.

Valerie stood there with a lump in her throat, completely intimidated by Elaine's coquettish behavior. She had always managed to stick it to

Delores when she behaved badly, but this situation was different; this woman wanted her husband. She was absolutely unnerved by Elaine's come-hither manner, yet, she would not tolerate it. She was going to show this floozie who was boss.

"Elaine, I'm sorry," Valerie said, switching gears from her usual sweet, delightful, mild manner to a brutal, ferocious destroyer, "but my husband isn't interested in a dalliance with you. I know all about your flirtatious behavior. You'd better cut it out, if you know what's good for you."

Leaving Elaine standing with her mouth wide open, Valerie briskly made her way down the hall to room eight.

Having been forewarned regarding Jenny's injuries, when Valerie opened the door, she was aghast upon seeing her. Hesitantly, she went to Jenny's bedside, pulled a chair closer to the bed, and sat down next to her. She gently stroked Jenny's swollen face, then wiped away the tears that rolled off her cheek, and onto Jenny's arm. She wondered about the time she spent in the garden. Was she really with Jenny? She questioned her sanity, and raised doubts about whether her time spent with the new Jenny happened at all.

"Wait a minute," she said out loud, "it must have been true. How could I have possibly known about Elaine? It was Jenny. It had to have been you, Jenny."

"What do you mean by that? It had to have been Jenny?"

Valerie turned around to find Patrick standing behind her.

"Patrick, where have you been?"

"Home, checking on the kids, getting them ready for bed. All the kids are there. Lauren's been holding down the fort. What did you mean by that? It had to have been Jenny?"

"Nothing. Never mind. I forgot what I was going to say. How are the kids? Do they know what's going on?"

"They know a little, not a lot of details. Lauren has talked to them. She's been great, doing that for us. Once again, Valerie, I'm sorry."

"I'm trying to come to terms with everything, Patrick. Look at Jenny."

"I know, honey. I am truly sorry. I don't think that you will ever forgive me. I wish it had been me in the car accident. I would rather die than have you hate me."

"No, Patrick. I don't wish that. Bring that chair over here, come sit next to me. None of this is your fault, I know that. I just want Jenny to be alright."

"I want that too, Valerie. Look at her. I wonder if she can hear us. Jenny, can you hear us? I love you, sweetheart. You're my girl, and you always will be. Please don't leave us."

"Patrick, I think she can hear us. And she knows that you love her."

"I hope so. You know, when people from work found out that we are going to have another baby, they said, 'Hey, congratulations, Patrick. Are you hoping for a girl this time?' My answer was, 'it doesn't matter to me, as long as it's healthy.' Do you know why it doesn't matter to me, Valerie?"

"Well, no. I thought that you would want us to have a girl. We already have two boys."

"I already have a girl. Jenny's my girl. We raised her together, Valerie. She's not like a sister-in-law to me, Jenny's more like a daughter. She's my daughter, Val. And right now my heart is breaking because I might lose my daughter. And to make matters worse, it's killing me, knowing that my wife holds me responsible for what happened to our daughter."

Patrick took Jenny's hand, then put his head down on the side of the bed, and began to cry.

"Patrick, I'm sorry," Valerie said. "I'm sorry for how I've been treating you."

Valerie held her husband tightly, and they cried in each other's arms.

Valerie was in the state of being half awake, and half asleep. The sounds of the day were tapping into the layers of her consciousness, which slowly pushed her awareness towards waking up. She still hadn't opened her eyes, but she realized that her sleeping position was very uncomfortable. Then she remembered that she was not in her own bed. She was in the hospital, curled into a ball on a couch in the waiting room. At her insistence, Patrick went home to rest, shower, and tend to the kids. Valerie would do the same when he returned. She slowly opened her eyes as she moved around to get comfortable.

"Good morning, Valerie. No change in Jenny's or Didi's condition."

"Jessica, where's Jeff?"

"He's in there with Didi. He's not doing so well. He's taking all of this pretty hard. You know, Valerie, I haven't been in this family for very long; I'm actually not a part of it at all, but my heart hurts too. I hate what's happened to Jenny and Didi, and the pain that everyone is going through. I hurt for you. I love you all. I hope you know that."

"Thank you, Jessica. I know that Jenny really likes you, she drew a picture of you. And the kids adore you, Jeff's and mine. Has Didi given you a hard time about that?"

"No, not at all," said Jessica. "Didi and I have no ill feelings towards each other. I love her children. She knows that, and appreciates it."

"Really?"

"Really, Valerie. Didi and I get along pretty good. We had a great time, the last time we got together."

"At the graduation party?"

"We had a good time at the graduation party, but I was talking about dinner, two weeks ago. She invited Jeff and me to have dinner with her and Bill at their house. We had a great time."

"You've got to be kidding me, Jessica. Are you serious?"

"Yes, Valerie. I know that Bill looks a little intimidating, with the tattoos, and his long hair; but he is actually a very nice man."

"Okay, Jessica. Thank you for that commentary."

"Valerie, I've heard that you're blaming the accident on Didi. It was not her fault."

"I know, Jessica. I'm working on it."

"Excuse me, ladies." A man walked into the room, holding a folded piece of paper. "Are one of you, Valerie Cole?"

"I'm Valerie Cole."

"Ms. Cole, I volunteer here at the hospital, at the information desk. Someone asked me to give you this note. Sorry, I would have gotten it to you sooner, but I've been a little busy."

"Thank you," Valerie said. She took the note from the man, opened it, and read it silently. It read:

Valerie,

Meet me at the park. The same park that you and Dad used to take me to when I was a little girl. See you soon!

Jenny

"Jessica, I'm going to run an errand. Would you tell Patrick that I'll be back later?"

"Sure. Are you alright? Do you mind if I ask where you're going?"

"Um... I, uh... I have to meet Karen."

"Doesn't Karen know that Didi and Jenny are here, in the hospital, in critical condition?"

"Yes, she does, but I'm a little hungry, so we're going to grab a bite. After all, I'm eating for two."

"I'm sorry, Valerie. Of course, you need to eat. Do you mind if I ask where you are going?"

"Maybe DeMarco's."

"DeMarco's? Why did you have to say DeMarco's? I've had DeMarco's pizza on my mind since last Tuesday. Do you mind if I tag along? I am a little hungry, myself. I'm sure Karen won't mind."

"No, don't come! Karen, well, she wouldn't want you there. It's nothing personal, it's just that she's going through something right now, with her husband."

"Oh, I just saw her with her husband, at the party. They seemed fine."

"Yes, they seemed fine, but they're not. They are not fine, not at all. They've got all sorts of problems. It's a very unfortunate situation. Very unfortunate."

"Hi, Valerie. Hi, Jessica. How are Jenny and Didi? Any improvements?" asked Karen.

"Karen, how long have you been standing there? What are you doing here?" Valerie asked.

"I just got here, just now. I walked through that door, and here I am. I came by to see how your sisters are doing. Did I miss something?"

"You didn't miss anything, my sisters are terrible. Thanks for stopping by. I'll see you later," Valerie said, as she tried to push Karen towards the exit.

"Valerie, I just got here. I'd like to stay for a few minutes. Do you mind? It's raining outside."

"No, of course not."

"How are you, Karen?" asked Jessica.

"I'm fine. Guess what? John is taking me to Hawaii for our tenth anniversary! He just told me the news over breakfast. Isn't he the best? It seems like every day, we fall more in love with each other. Is it still that way for you and Patrick, Valerie?"

"Yes, it's just like that. Thank you for asking. Shouldn't you go now?"

"Valerie! What's wrong with you? You're acting strange," said Jessica.

"Yeah, you don't seem happy for me, about my trip to Hawaii. What's wrong?"

"Nothing is wrong," Valerie snapped.

"Valerie, who is that note from?" Jessica asked. "It's not from Karen."

"What note?" Karen asked.

"Valerie got a note, a few minutes ago. She said it was from you, now she wants to leave to meet someone."

"It's not that I want to leave, I have to leave."

"Valerie, who is more important than your sisters, right now?" asked Karen.

"Well …" stammered Valerie.

"Well?" Jessica asked.

"Well …"

"Well?" asked Karen.

"Well … I have to go now. You wouldn't understand."

"Valerie, yesterday you said that you wanted a divorce," said Jessica.

"Valerie, you can't divorce Patrick! Is there someone else?" Karen asked.

"I'm not going to divorce Patrick."

"But is there someone else?" asked Jessica.

"No. There's no one else," said Valerie.

"Valerie! You're having an affair? I can't believe it! You know what Cory did to me, or have you forgotten?"

"No, Karen, I haven't forgotten."

"He was sleeping around, behind my back. Now you're doing that to Patrick?"

"Valerie, are you sleeping around?" Jessica asked.

"Valerie, you know that you're my best friend, you can tell me anything. So, tell me, are you sleeping around? Well? You're not answering me, so it must be true! You're sleeping around!"

"Can we keep our voices down?" asked Valerie.

"Valerie, you're a married woman," said Karen. "The time to sleep around was before you got married. But no. You wanted to be a virgin. Didn't you?"

"I'm not sleeping around."

"Who are you meeting?" Karen asked.

"Well …"

"Valerie, you don't have to answer," said Jessica. "It's not our business if you're having an affair. I don't condone your behavior, but I'm not going to judge you. Or at least, I'll try not to. Karen and I will try our best to keep your adulterous secret to ourselves. Right, Karen?"

"Alright," Karen said, tearfully.

"Okay, thanks," said Valerie. "Bye."

"Valerie, wait," Karen said, between sobs, "it's raining outside; take my umbrella. You're my best friend, and I want you to have it. Keep it for as long as you need to, and don't forget about all these years that we've been best friends."

"Okay, thanks. Bye now."

"Valerie, wait, before you leave; does Debra know?"

"No, Karen, she doesn't. Bye, now. See you later."

"Val, please use protection," said Jessica.

"Don't worry, I have Karen's umbrella."

Valerie was thrilled at the thought of seeing Jenny at the park. Because she took extra precautions while driving in the rain, it took her a little longer than usual to get there. She considered an alternate place for her and Jenny to hang out if the rain didn't let up. When she arrived at the park, she saw Jenny on the playground, swinging fast and high. She didn't seem to care that she was getting wet; she has always enjoyed the rain. One of Jenny's favorite things to do on rainy days was to look out the window. Sometimes, to get a better look at the raindrops as they fell, she would open the front door; allowing the foyer to get the full gully wash experience. Valerie never took such incidents too kindly. Patrick, on the other hand, never seemed to tire of such adventures.

Jenny was wearing a blue rain jacket, which she wore by hanging the hood on her head, causing it to flap in the wind as she swayed back and forth on the swing. Valerie got out of her car, and suddenly, the sun broke through. She made her way to the spot where Jenny was swinging. Mud gathered on her shoes, forcing her to walk slower than she would normally walk.

"Hey, big sister!" yelled Jenny.

"I never thought I'd hear you call me your big sister. It's nice."

Jenny jumped off the swing while it was in mid-air.

"I've always wanted to do that; jump off the swing like that. It was fun. I've had a nice morning, Valerie. I met a woman who had an eight-year-old autistic child, he was non-verbal. She was a very nice lady, and her son was a very sweet boy. I was able to communicate with him. His mother was quite surprised."

"That's amazing, Jenny. What did you talk about?"

"He was non-verbal, we didn't really talk, but we communicated through gestures and feelings, mostly feelings. He asked me to give his mother a message. He wanted her to know that he loved her. When I gave her that message, she smiled. She just went along with it, you know, to be nice. But when I gave her the other part of the message, she was in a bit of a shock, and then she cried."

"What was the other part of the message?"

"He wanted to let his mother know that she shouldn't worry about what happened."

"What happened, Jenny?"

"They were at the top of the staircase, she tripped, and fell into him, causing him to tumble down the stairs. He broke his arm. She felt terrible about it, but it wasn't her fault. It was an accident. But that didn't matter, she felt guilty anyway. This happened over a year ago, and she's felt guilty since then."

"That's terrible, Jenny."

"Yeah, her son wanted her to know that he loved her, and didn't want her to feel bad anymore. It was time that she moved on. She cried, and hugged me before they left."

"Jenny, that's incredible."

"I've had quite a morning, Valerie. Guess what else happened? This is crazy. Guess where I got this rain jacket from?"

"I don't know, Jenny. Where did you get it from?"

"A boy."

"What boy?"

"A cute boy, he liked me. He was twenty-four years old. He said I was pretty, and he asked me out on a date."

"Jenny, a guy asked you out? What did you say?"

"I said no, of course. First, I asked him if going on a date means kissing. He said yes. Then I told him that there was no way I would go out with him if I had to kiss him, because that was gross. Then he laughed."

"Oh, Jenny, I'm sorry. Did he hurt your feelings?"

"No, Valerie. Why would my feelings be hurt? I don't care about some dumb boy, he probably has couties. Who cares? But while he was laughing, it started to rain, so he gave me his jacket. He said I could keep it. Do you know what that reminded me of?"

"What did it remind you of, Jenny?"

"It reminded me of when you met Patrick. Remember, the first time that Mom took us to Andy's Handy Pharmacy? Remember how she needed to buy some ointment for my diaper rash, and then she asked you if you wanted to get some lunch? Do you remember, Valerie? Patrick said hello to you, but you just stood there, with your mouth open. Do you remember what a dork you were?"

"I wasn't a dork. I was shy."

"Same thing, Valerie. Those were fun times, weren't they?"

"Yes, they were, Jenny. And I already told you, I wasn't a dork, I..."

"Yeah, yeah, yeah. You were shy. Whatever."

"I really was shy, Jenny."

"You were a shy dork. Ask anyone, they'll tell you."

"Jenny, do you have a point?"

"No, not really."

"Jenny, can I ask you something? How do you remember things that happened when you were a baby? I'm amazed by that."

"It's all amazing, Valerie. I'm in the hospital, in a coma; at the same time, I'm sitting here talking to you. It's all amazing, don't you think so?"

"Yes, Jenny. It all amazes me! But especially, how is it that you can remember things that happened when you were ten months old? Even when you were first born, how do remember that?"

"I don't know, Valerie. I just do. I don't have a good answer for you, but I do have a couple of theories. One theory is that there's a difference between people like me, and people like you. Every day that passes, people like you constantly learn new things, and meet new people. The information stored in your brain will at some point become old, and is replaced by all these new things in your life, recent events. But for people like me, we're not learning new things every day. God made us to be content with what we know. So, things that may be irrelevant to you, stay in the forefront of our minds."

"Wow, that's profound," Valerie responded.

"Yeah, it's really deep, isn't it? I got another theory; I think this one is better. Certainly, it's more believable. You see, Valerie, I believe that people like you, highly intellectual people, you are all just dumb."

"I like your first theory better. But, let me ask you; do you think that people like you, wish that they could be people like me, you know, intellectually?"

"Speaking for myself only, I would have to say no. I don't see you, or people like you, superior in an intellectual way. I love my life just the way it is. Have you ever wished that you had someone who would do everything for you? Someone who would cook all of your meals, and wash the dishes, and clean up afterwards? Someone who would do your laundry? Someone who would drive you around anywhere you needed to go? Well, I have that. Sure, I do little things, like make my bed, and pick up my clothes from the floor; you know, things like that. But you do everything else for me. You're like my servant. People like you, serve people like me."

"I never thought of it that way, I guess that's true," Valerie said.

"And another thing, I never have to worry; about money, about paying bills, about keeping up with the Joneses. I have no responsibilities, and no obligations. People like me, we don't have a care in the world. We're happy. We get excited when it's lunch time. Give me an extra big slice of chocolate cake, it would be the equivalent of you winning the lottery. I had so much fun at my graduation party! Thank you for doing that for me, Valerie. It was the best day of my life. Everybody came; I got so many gifts, I danced all night. And it didn't cost me one ounce of worry. But you, on the other hand, you worked really hard to make sure everything ran smoothly. You had to call everybody, you had to buy a lot of food, and beverages, and the decorations. It cost you a lot of money, I'm sure. Do you see what I'm saying? I would never trade being a person like me, for being a person like you, for anything in the world. But I'm glad that Didi and I were in the car accident. I'm so glad that it happened, even if I die as a result. Because if I were not in the physical state of being so close to death right now, then I wouldn't be here, in this physical state that I am in, where I'm able to talk to you."

"But, Jenny, if you wouldn't want to be a person like me, and you are close to death right now; why are you glad that this happened?"

"Because, Valerie, this is what you wanted. This is what you've always wanted, for me to be like you. But it's alright; there's nothing wrong with you wanting that. You're good to me, you and Patrick have always been good to me; you've given me everything. Even though I just said that I wouldn't trade being a person like me for being a person like you, I have wanted to be like this, temporarily. I've always wanted to give you a special gift. Something that no one else could ever give you. The one thing that you've always wanted, was for me to be like you. You used to tell me that all the time while I was growing up. That's why I've wanted to be this way, for you. Being like this is my gift to you. I may pay for it with my life, but it's worth it; because I've made you happy by giving you what you've always wanted."

"Jenny, I don't know what to say."

"Say that you'll take me to DeMarco's. I'm hungry. Then maybe I'll tell you about another special gift for you. You're going to love it."

"What is it, Jenny?"

"I'm going to show you where it is tomorrow, but I guess it would be alright if I told you about it now. You've never found your engagement ring, have you?"

"My engagement ring? You know where it is?"

"It's buried somewhere in the backyard. I don't exactly know where. Trixie buried it. I sure do miss her."

"Jenny, did Trixie tell you that she buried it?"

"Valerie, Trixie was a dog. Dogs don't speak, they bark."

"Well, then how do know that she buried it?"

"I saw her bury it under a tree. She buried it, then dug it up. Then she buried it in another spot, then dug it up again. I saw the last time she dug it up, and the last spot where she buried it. I don't know if I can remember which tree, but we'll figure it out tomorrow. We'll spend the whole afternoon together, just like today. Me and you; two sisters, two friends. Can we come back here tomorrow?"

"Sure, Jenny. We can come back to the park again, tomorrow."

"Can we leave now to DeMarco's?"

"Sure, let's go. I'm starving."

"You're not starving, Valerie. You're just hungry. There you go again, being dramatic."

CHAPTER TWENTY

Cherish

After filling up on pizza, Valerie left Jenny to return home. When she arrived, she was greeted by Mrs. Ladson, the next-door neighbor. For many years, Mrs. Ladson and her husband, had been neighbors and great friends with Frank and Anna. Now a widow, she frequently served as the neighborhood's emergency babysitter.

"Mrs. Ladson, thank you for coming over, and taking care of the kids. Not only mine, but my sisters' as well. They didn't give you much trouble, did they?"

"Everything is fine. But last night, Matty couldn't breathe out of his left nostril. It seems that it was clogged up by some kind of puffy cereal."

"I'm sorry."

"That's alright, dear. I just thought he was a little old to be sticking things up his nose, but then I remembered that you were about the same age when you got a wad of chewing gum stuck in your ear. How are Jenny and Delores? Any improvements?"

"No, not yet. Priscilla said that Didi woke up for a few seconds, but Jenny has not woken up at all."

"It just breaks my heart. Jenny is the sweetest little girl, and Delores has always had a heart of gold. They're both angels."

"My sister, Delores?"

"Yes, Valerie, your sister, Delores. I know that she has always been a little, what's the word? Well, let's just say that she's got the looks, and she knows it, okay? But I know the other side to her. I know that she can be a loving woman, like your mother. Do you still have that scar under your chin?"

"Yes, I do. Do you know about that?"

"Yes, I know all about it, Valerie. I remember the day it happened. Do you remember how it happened?"

"No, I don't. Anytime that I asked my mother about it, she'd change the subject."

"She never wanted to talk about it. You were about two or three years old; your mother was carrying you while she was watering the lawn. Delores was about eight or nine years old, she was riding her bicycle up and down the street, doing pop-a-wheelies. I went over to say hello to your mother; then we got to talking. You started wiggling, so she put you down. At first, you stayed right by her side. Then before we knew it, you weren't there. I turned my head, and I screamed, 'Anna, look!' You were in the middle of the street, and a car was coming up, pretty fast. We both ran towards you, but we weren't fast enough. And there, in the opposite direction of the car, comes Delores. She was riding her bicycle as fast as she could, straight up in the middle of the street; I guess in hopes that the driver of the car would see her, and stop. But he didn't seem to slow down. When Delores caught up to you, she jumped off her bike, grabbed you, and tried to pull you out of the way. The driver of the car slammed on his brakes, just in time. Delores wouldn't have made it, getting you and herself, out of the way. When the car screeched to a stop, she fell to the ground while holding you in her arms. You landed on the fender of Delores' bike, and a sharp edge cut you under your chin. Your mother was terrified. By the grace of God, neither one of you were seriously injured."

"I never knew that, Mrs. Ladson. I wonder why my mother never wanted me to know."

"Your mother never wanted your father to know. She felt so guilty about what happened, we both did. We cried about it, long after it was over; we both blamed ourselves. I felt that it was my fault because I distracted your mother. But, of course, your mother blamed herself. She said that she nearly lost two daughters that day."

"I wonder why Didi has never told me about that. She couldn't have forgotten."

"Valerie, let me tell you something; about fifteen years ago, when my husband was still alive, we went on our very first plane ride. We went to the vineyards in California. I saw Delores at the airport in San Antonio. She was there waiting for someone; I think a boyfriend. I hadn't seen her for a couple of years, since your parents died. We talked for a while, and I told her that if she ever needed anything, I wanted her to call me. I've always had a special place in my heart for Delores, I think because she is about the same age as my daughter would be. And I know she's been hurting since your parents died. She blames herself for the accident, and she shouldn't. I cherish Delores, very much."

"I didn't know that you felt so strongly about Didi, and I didn't know that you had a daughter."

"She died before you were born. Her name was Janet, she was our only child."

"Mrs. Ladson, I'm sorry."

"It was a long time ago. Anyway, Delores gave me something that day at the airport. Now I want her to have it back. Will you give it to her for me?"

Mrs. Ladson retrieved her purse from the coat tree. She pulled out a small sandwich bag, which had a necklace in it. She removed the necklace to reveal a pendant hanging from a sterling silver chain. The pendant was oval shaped, with an angel on one side, and an inscription on the other. The inscription read, *For He shall give His angels charge over thee, to keep thee in all thy ways.* Below the script, it read Psalms 91:11.

"That day at the airport, I told Delores how deathly afraid I was to get on that airplane. She told me that she would let me have her guardian angel, to protect me on my flight. She pulled out this pendant, and placed in my hand. I thanked her. I told her it was beautiful, and asked where she got it. She said she found it on the street, close to the railroad tracks, the day that the two of you almost got hit by that car. Valerie, I want you to give this back to her so her guardian angel can get back to work, and protect her. I just bought this chain for it, Delores never had a chain. She kept it in her wallet."

"Mrs. Ladson, thank you for telling me that story. I'll make sure that Didi gets this."

"Thank you, Valerie. Now I want you to get something to eat, get some rest, visit with the kids, then you get yourself back to the hospital. Your sisters need you. I'll be here if the kids need me. They're all good kids. You girls have done a great job at raising them. They're so well behaved. Your parents would be proud of their grandchildren."

"Thank you, Mrs. Ladson."

"You're welcome."

Valerie slept for about ten hours. When she woke up, she lay in bed, wondering if the last few days actually happened, or if it had been a dream. Maybe she would walk down the hall, and find Jenny, fast asleep in her bed. Maybe it was still Sunday morning, and Delores had not taken Jenny with her, and there had been no car accident. Maybe Patrick was downstairs on the couch, where he had fallen asleep. That's what made sense.

She decided to check on Patrick's whereabouts, but first, she'd take a look in Jenny's room. If Jenny was there, then Valerie would know that these past few days didn't really happen; it would have been a dream. If Jenny was not in her room, it would confirm that she really had visited Valerie in a different state of being. Apprehensive about opening the door to Jenny's bedroom, she took a deep breath before turning the doorknob. The room was empty. It looked exactly as it did on the afternoon of Jenny's graduation party. Valerie was comforted to know that the past few days, had indeed, been the real thing.

She was lured to the kitchen by the smell of bacon. Seeing Patrick fix breakfast was a key moment for Valerie. In a split second, she was faced with a number of realizations about her husband. For one thing, he was incredibly handsome. That was not only her opinion; according to Jenny, several nurses at the hospital shared the same point of view, especially Elaine. Other attributes she was reminded of were Patrick's sense of humor, sensitivity, cooking skills, the fact that he was an awesome father to his children, a great lawyer and provider, a wonderful uncle, an excellent brother-in-law, a God-fearing man, and he loved her. He loved her enough to put up with the terrible way she had been treating him over the past few days.

At this crucial moment, Valerie knew she had to stop taking Patrick for granted, and give him the same respect, devotion, and appreciation that he gave her.

Once again, Lauren would be in charge of her sister and cousins, while the adults were at the hospital. Lauren did not take her newfound responsibility lightly. She ran a tight ship, but did not let the power go to her head.

"Lauren, call Mrs. Ladson if you need her. She'll come over to give you a hand with the kids if you need help."

"That's alright, Uncle Patrick. I've got everything under control. I'm going to call Mrs. Ladson, and give her the day off. I got this, really, I do."

"Lauren, are you sure that you can handle everything by yourself?"

"I've got this, Aunt Valerie. Don't worry. If I need Mrs. Ladson, I'll call her. Tell my aunts to get better soon so they can come home. I miss them."

"You got it, boss lady," Patrick said.

"Thank you, Lauren," said Valerie.

For Valerie, thinking about Jenny in this new physical state of being was surreal. It was frightening, yet, at the same time, it was beautiful. It was something that she could never have imagined to happen, yet, it did. She wanted to tell Priscilla and Patrick about Jenny's incarnation, so they might also enjoy getting to know this new Jenny. Then she remembered that Jenny told her not to reveal her identity, which was good, because she got to keep this new Jenny all to herself.

Patrick and Valerie arrived at the hospital to find Priscilla, Michael, Jessica, and her two uncles, sitting with Bill in the waiting room. Delores and Bill had been married for less than a year; during which time, he had made numerous attempts to initiate some kind of common ground between Valerie and him. Unfortunately, he hadn't had any success at developing even the slightest friendship with her. Everyone else got along great with Bill. It was Valerie's incessant resentment towards Delores which would not allow her to return even the slightest bit of friendship to her new brother-in-law. Offering him a half-hearted greeting, she took a seat a few chairs away from him and the others.

It took her a few minutes before she remembered the new commitment that she made to herself about not taking Patrick for granted, so she moved to sit next to him. Just as she sat down, Bill stood up, and left the room.

"Did everyone see that?" Valerie asked.

"See what?" asked Patrick.

"See what Bill did, just now? He walked out, just because I came over to sit with everyone."

"Valerie, he did no such thing," said Patrick.

"He had someplace to go," said Priscilla.

"What's more important than being at the hospital with your wife who is in the intensive care unit?" asked Valerie.

"Come on, Valerie," said Jessica, while glaring at her, "you're not being fair. He had somewhere to go. Just like you did yesterday, remember?"

"I'm sorry. I have to go in there and see Didi, and I'm nervous."

"Do you want me to go in with you?" asked Priscilla. "Kevin and Jeff are in with her now. Aunt Gina and Aunt Nancy are in with Jenny."

"Yes, please go in with me, Priscilla. I don't want to go by myself."

A steady stream of friends dropped by to offer comfort, support, and prayers to the family. Some of those included; Kim Bell, Jenny's high school teacher; also Mr. Principal and his wife, Mrs. Principal. Delores' friend, Jennifer, stopped by with her husband, Bob. She and Jeff shared an enjoyable reunion. Pastor Craig had long since retired, but he passed the torch on to his son, Mark. Both pastors dropped by to offer prayers, and words of encouragement.

Valerie took a deep breath before entering Delores' room. She was taken aback at the sight of her; she had never seen Delores look so dreadful. She pulled up a chair, and sat down at her bedside, Priscilla sat down on the other side of the bed. Valerie took out the pendant that Mrs. Ladson gave her.

"Priscilla, have you ever seen this pendant before?" she asked, as she dangled the chain in front of her.

"It looks familiar. It's beautiful, I like the verse inscribed. Where did you get it? Wait a minute. Is this Didi's?"

"Yes, Mrs. Ladson wanted me to give it back to her. Didi gave it to her a few years ago. Do you know the story behind this pendant?"

"I think so. Didi told me about it, how she had it in her pocket the day that she saved your life. Do you remember that?"

"No, I don't. But Mrs. Ladson told me about it. I was two or three years old when Didi saved my life."

"You were not two or three years old, Valerie. You were six or seven years old when Didi saved you from drowning."

"What?"

"You don't remember? Dad took us camping. Mom didn't go because she went to be with Aunt Teresa. Remember, Aunt Teresa was recovering from surgery? So, Mom spent a few weeks in El Paso to be with her. Remember how Dad loved taking us camping?"

"Yeah, that's why I love it so much."

"That's why I love it too. But Didi hated it. Remember? She always wanted to stay home by herself, but Mom and Dad never let her. They thought that she would invite guys over, and she probably would have."

"That's right, she did hate to go camping. So, what happened, Priscilla?"

"Well, Didi always spent her time flipping through the magazines that she brought along with her. Dad rented a canoe, so he could take the four of us out on the water. He asked me to help him carry one end of it; from where he parked the truck, to our camping site near the lake, which was probably about one tenth of a mile or so. Before we left to get the canoe, Dad scolded you about going into the water by yourself; but you didn't listen, and you went into the water anyway. Didi was too engrossed with her magazines, so she didn't notice that you wandered off into the lake, by yourself. When she looked up to see where you were, you were not where you were supposed to be. She looked onto the lake, she saw you bobbing up and down in the water. She ran to the water, and jumped in after you. Then she pulled you out. But you know something?"

"What's that?"

"Didi couldn't swim. The water must have been about ten or twelve feet deep, but she went in anyway; because if you were going to drown, so was she. She managed to pull you out of the water, and when she got closer to the shore, she passed out. There was a group of people who saw what happened, they were probably in their mid-twenties. A guy grabbed you, and pumped the water out of you. Another one grabbed Didi, and performed mouth-to-mouth on her. By that time, Dad and I saw what was going on, and we dropped the canoe, and ran to you and Didi."

"I sort of remember this. I thought it was a recurring dream, but I guess I was remembering what actually happened. Why didn't she ever tell me? You never told me about this before, either. And neither did Mom or Dad. Why?"

"Dad never wanted Mom to know about it. He felt so guilty. He blamed himself for being negligent. He said that he almost lost two daughters that day."

"Priscilla, I never knew any of this."

"Didi's not a perfect sister, but she does cherish you, Valerie. You don't know how much it hurts her that she no longer has a close relationship with you. You used to share sister-things with her, remember? You used to ask her advice on boys, and makeup, and hair; everything about life in general. But you stopped doing that. I'm the oldest, Didi came to me about those things, and she still does. You used to go to Didi about those things, and if Jenny were able to, she would go to you about those things."

"I just don't understand why she had to ruin everything."

"What do you think she has ruined?"

"Everything."

"What's everything, Valerie?"

"Well, for one thing, she ruined her marriage."

"That was between her and Jeff. Whatever happened between them had nothing to do with us. I love Jeff, he will always be one of my best friends, but he's no saint either. He and Didi were the same, they were both big flirts, and their flirting may have gone too far. I care about my sister's happiness, and for the first time in her life, she's happy. Bill makes her happy. She and Jeff will always be good friends; it just wasn't meant to be for them."

"Did Jeff ever cheat on her?"

"Valerie, that's not for me to say. What happened between Didi and Jeff was their business, not ours. I do know this, Didi didn't ever want you, or me, to know about Jeff's flaws. She didn't want to influence the way we feel about him. He's the father of our nieces and nephew, he's always going to be a part of our family. We both love him, but Didi is our sister, and you shouldn't judge her because she and Jeff didn't make it. They're both finally happy now. Live and let live. And as far as Mom and Dad go, you have no idea the impact their death had on Didi. It's way past the time for you to let that go."

Valerie lost her emotions as she wept over Delores. She and Priscilla carefully placed the chain and pendant around Delores' neck, then Priscilla left the room; giving Valerie a few moments alone with Delores. As she looked at her sister, lying on the bed, close to death; she saw a different Delores. Although her appearance was a far cry from the attractive, sexy, alluring semblance of what everyone perceived Delores to be; for the first time, in possibly her whole life, Valerie saw an unfamiliar beauty within her sister; an unselfishness that she didn't even know existed. She saw an angel, a guardian angel who looked after her, and kept her safe from harm. A guardian angel who saved her life, on at least two occasions. She wondered why it was unknown to her before; was it because Delores had always hidden this attribute, or was it because this characteristic emerged on very few, and far between occasions? Either way, Valerie came to realize that she did cherish Delores.

CHAPTER TWENTY-ONE

Undercover Angel

"How was it seeing Didi," asked Patrick. "Are you alright?"

"I'm alright. Do you mind if I leave? I want to take a drive."

"Do you want me to drive you somewhere, Val?"

"No, thank you. I want to be by myself. I have a lot of things to think about, you know, I just want to clear my head."

"Sure, Val. Will you come back here? Should I catch a ride home with someone?"

"Yeah, catch a ride. I'll see you at home, later."

"Do you really have to go, Valerie?" asked Jessica.

"Yes, Jessica. As I told Patrick, I just need to clear my head. Everything will be fine, I promise."

"Okay," Jessica said.

"Alright. I'll see everyone later. Bye, Patrick."

"Bye, honey."

Valerie was eager to meet Jenny at the park. Hoping to catch the next elevator, she walked down the hallway at a faster pace than usual. Still several yards away, she heard the ding, indicating that the elevator door was on the verge of opening. She decided to wait for the next one, rather than run to catch it.

Once the elevator door opened, a few people exited. Some headed towards her direction, others went down a different hallway. Of those headed her way were an elderly couple, a man bringing flowers to someone, a couple of doctors, and the very attractive nurse, Elaine. Passing each other in the hallway, an acrimonious glare was cast by Valerie towards Elaine's direction, while Elaine went to great lengths to avoid eye contact. In some measure, running into Elaine wasn't all that bad. It prompted Valerie to re-evaluate how, just moments earlier, she said goodbye to Patrick. She didn't embrace him, nor kiss him goodbye. The commitment she made to herself just hours before, about not taking Patrick for granted, had already gone out the window. Before meeting Jenny, she wanted to return to Patrick to bid him a proper farewell.

She waited a few minutes, hoping to gather a little boldness, then she turned around, and made her way back down the hall. She walked into the waiting room, Patrick was standing by the window, looking out. Jennifer and Bob were still there, as well as Pastor Craig and Pastor Mark. Elaine was also there, speaking to a family about their loved one. Patrick happened to turn around at the same moment Valerie walked through the door. Even though it had only been a few minutes since he last saw her, he was delighted to see her again.

"Valerie, you're back. Did you forget something?" he asked.

Knowing that she had an audience, which included Elaine, Valerie unmasked a provocative side of herself; a side that shocked Patrick, as well as everyone else, to the core. Even Valerie was quite surprised by her demeanor. She didn't know that her voice was able to convey a message in such an erotic tone.

"Hi, Mr. Lawyer," she said, running her fingers through her hair, then gently shaking her head, and repeating the motion. As she sashayed across the room towards Patrick, she captured the attention of everyone.

After managing to pick his jaw up off the floor, it took a few attempts for Patrick to find his voice, "Valerie ... honey.... hi."

"Hi, baby. I just came back because I forgot to give you something."

"What... what... what did you forget to give me? Baby."

"I forgot to give you a kiss goodbye."

In that very moment, Valerie pressed her lips against Patrick's, initiating a long, steamy, passionate kiss. While pressing her body hard against his, she lifted her knee to the side of his waist, and wrapped her leg around him, while her foot gently rubbed against the backside of his leg. Her aim was to grab Elaine's attention, and deliver a message: Patrick is off limits! Elaine got the message, loud and clear. While some seemed to enjoy the show, the pastors covered their eyes with their hands, peeking through their open fingers, perhaps unknowingly. After an ample amount of time, Valerie, lovingly and tenderly, pulled away from Patrick to bring their make-out session to an end.

"I'll see you later, at home," she said, still using her new erotic voice. "Give Jenny a kiss for me, and give Didi my best."

Without delay, she was gone.

"What was that all about?" asked Jeff.

"Yay, Valerie! You go, girl," said Jessica.

"Mr. Lawyer?" asked Michael.

"She's her mother's daughter," said Jim.

"Wow," said Patrick. "I don't know what's gotten into her, but I'm not complaining. I hope it lasts for a long time."

"I liked it better when she was mad at all of us," said Priscilla.

Jenny was sitting at a picnic table, talking and laughing with a married couple who were there having a picnic as their baby slept in a stroller. They were a handsome couple, about Valerie's age. The man was very attractive; he wore a muscle shirt, which accentuated his toned physique. The woman, though very slightly overweight, was also extremely attractive. Despite a few extra pounds around her abdomen, her arms and legs were toned, and her complexion was smooth and rosy. Jenny waved Valerie over to join them.

"This is my big sister, Valerie."

"Valerie? Valerie Negron?" the man asked, excitedly.

"Valerie Negron?" the woman asked, wearing a scowl on her face.

"Have we met?" Valerie asked the couple.

"Valerie, it's me, Jason Clark."

"Jason Clark? I'm sorry, I didn't recognize you. You look great, Jason."

"Thanks, I started working out during college, to build up this bod. I had to do something to win the hand of the prettiest girl at Jefferson

High. Of course, Amy didn't give me the time of day when we were in high school."

"Amy? Do you mean Amy Lopez?" Valerie asked, expressing disdain at the thought of her old high school classmate. "I haven't seen Amy Lopez in years. I wonder if her push-up bra is still holding up. Even better, I wonder if she's fat. I would love it if she were fat; I'd pay money to see that."

"Valerie, Amy didn't give me the time of day in high school, but when we got to college, we spent a lot of time together. We became great friends, and that led to romance. We've been married for over twelve years."

"I just had a baby, Valerie," Amy sneered.

"Well, it was great seeing you, Valerie. Take care," said Jason. "And it was nice meeting you, Jenny."

Before leaving, Jason gathered his and Amy's belongings, and put them in the stroller's basket. Valerie was taken aback by seeing Amy. She didn't recognize her with the extra weight, and Amy's hair color was also different; fat Amy was now a blonde. Subsequently, realizing that she had insulted her, Valerie was embarrassed by her blunder. Amy, however, was not about to take Valerie's flippant remarks lying down; she had a few choice words for her former rival. She patiently waited for Jason to leave with the baby, then she laid it down on the line.

"Well, Valerie, I heard that you were married to Patrick; you can thank me for that. If I hadn't turned him down the many, many, many times that he wanted me, and I mean he really wanted me; well, who knows? I could very well be Amy Cole. There were so many times, Valerie, before and even during the time that he dated you in high school, when he came really close to taking my virginity. But much to his disappointment, I said no; each and every time. By the way, that money you'd pay to see me fat; I'll give you a break on that. When my doctor gives me the okay to start working out again, it'll take me a week to drop these *ten* extra pounds. But you, on the other hand, you will always look like that. You will always be inferior to me, second-best, mediocre. Face it, Valerie, you were a cute kid; but as a woman, you're inadequate. Well, Jenny, it was a real pleasure meeting you. I think you're an angel, a real beauty."

"I'm a real beauty? Thank you, Amy! That's a great compliment, coming from you," said Jenny.

"Maybe you'd like to hang out sometime, Jen."

"Oh, I think that would be so much fun! But as much as I'd love to hang out with you, Amy, I really can't. I'm actually here for Valerie."

"Well, Jen, call me if you change your mind. And Valerie," Amy said, changing her tone to emphasize the sultry charisma she was known for, "tell Patrick to call me if he changes his mind too. Listen to me, what am I saying? I didn't mean to say *if* he changes his mind; I mean *when* he changes his mind."

At that moment, Valerie was wishing that, for Amy's benefit, she could do an encore performance of the erotic kiss she gave to Patrick earlier that morning. She would have loved to put Amy in her place, the same as she did to Elaine, but Amy had already walked away. She hadn't gone too far; though the span of terrain between the two rivals was growing wider, the closer Amy got to her car. If Valerie was going to get back at her, she had to do it quick, while Amy was still within shouting distance.

"You're just jealous!" Valerie shouted. "Patrick chose me over you! And your own husband, would rather be with me!"

Although Amy may have heard the shouts aimed at her, she continued on her way.

"So, that's Amy Lopez?" asked Jenny.

Valerie, continued to shout, "And Patrick never came close to taking your virginity! You've never said no to anyone! You lost it in junior high, to your Snoopy toothbrush!"

"Valerie, there are kids around."

"Oh, sorry, Jenny."

"Do you realize how dumb you sound?"

"I know, it was dumb. But she is so annoying! She's infuriating! Even after all of these years, she is just so UGH! Not only that, Jenny, but she provoked me. Did you hear what she said to me?"

"Yes, Valerie, I did. I'm standing right here."

"She said that Patrick wanted her? While we were dating? I don't think so! I DON'T THINK SO, AMY!"

"Valerie, Amy left. She's not here."

"I'm inferior to her? Second-best? Inadequate? I don't think so!"

"Don't forget mediocre. She also said that you were mediocre."

"I don't think so, Jenny!"

"I didn't say it, Val. Amy said it."

"I DON'T THINK SO, AMY!"

"Valerie, Amy's gone. She got in her car, and drove away with her hunky husband."

"And do know what else, Jenny?"

"No, Valerie. I don't know what else, and I don't care. Why are you letting her get your panties in a bunch? It's over. She's gone. You have Patrick, he's your husband. He chose you. He married you."

"You're right, Jenny."

"Of course, I'm right. Now can we move on?"

"Yes, I'm sorry."

"It's alright, Val. So, that's Amy Lopez? I've heard you and Karen talk about her before, and have always wondered what she looked like. Wow, even with ten extra pounds on her body, she sure is hot! She's right up there with Elaine, the hot nurse. Don't you agree? Who do you think is prettier, Elaine or Amy? I think it's a tie. Certainly, Elaine is younger; but Amy doesn't show her age at all. Not like you do, Valerie. I didn't know that she was as old as you. Can you imagine how shocked I was finding out that the two of you went to high school together? I mean, look at her! She looks much younger than you, Valerie. You definitely show your age, I mean that in a good way. But Amy looks so young, and hot! I wonder who Patrick would pick? If he had to choose between Elaine or Amy. I know that he has you, but let's say you weren't in the picture; maybe you fell off a cliff or something. Or maybe you were eaten by sharks while swimming in the ocean, and now Patrick was alone, and he had to choose; would it be Elaine or Amy? He has a history with Amy, that's got to count for something. But on the other hand, Elaine is … wow! I mean, they're both, wow! Poor Patrick, I wouldn't envy him. That would be a tough call for him to make."

"JENNY! DO YOU MIND?"

"Sorry, Valerie. Listen, you need to try to forget about the hot women in Patrick's life. Let me tell you what happened to me earlier today, before I met Jason and hot Amy. It was another great day at the park for me. I met another boy! I like this one much better."

"You met another guy, Jenny? Aren't you popular? Did he have couties?"

"Well, he's a boy, isn't he? Don't all boys have cooties? But I like this one. I could hang out with him, he seems like he'd be a lot of fun. He's an entomologist."

"An antomologist? What's an antomologist?"

"An *en*tomologist, Valerie. He's a scientist, he studies insects. Have you ever opened a dictionary, in your life?"

"Have you?"

"Yes, Valerie, all the time. I like reading Patrick's dictionary. That must be why I'm so smart. Hey, how about lunch? I'm hungry."

Valerie bought a couple of hot dogs from a hot dog vendor, and the two sisters enjoyed lunch in the park. Jenny told Valerie all about the entomologist, then they reminisced about their parents; which eventually led to the topic of Delores.

"Did you see her, Valerie?"

"Yes, I did."

"And?"

"And what? She looks awful."

"Well, how do you expect her to look? You're not very nice, Valerie. I don't know why Dad used to call you Cupcake. Cupcakes are supposed to be sweet, right?"

"Yes, Jenny, cupcakes are sweet."

"Well, if you're a cupcake, I don't think you're very sweet. I think you're bitter, you're more like a carton of milk that went bad."

"A carton of milk that went bad? That would be sour or spoiled, not bitter."

"Well, that's what you are, Valerie. You're a spoiled, bitter sourpuss. Why haven't you tried to make things right with Didi? And don't say because she's unconscious; that's not an excuse, she can hear you. What in the world are you waiting for, Valerie? After everything that we've talked about?"

"I know, Jenny. I realize that I was wrong, and I'm sorry for that. I'm going to make things right by her. I found out some things about Didi; now I have a whole new perspective about her."

"What did you find out?"

"I found out that Didi saved my life. She risked her own life to save mine. That's mind-boggling, it's unbelievable. Don't you think it's unbelievable, Jenny?"

"No, I can believe it. Are you talking about the time when you almost got run over by a car, or other time when you almost drowned?"

"How did you know, Jenny?"

"Lucky guess."

"Lucky guess?"

"Valerie, doesn't that tell you something about Didi? All these years you've blamed her for Mom and Dad's death. She had nothing to do with it. Dad made the decision to go out that night. And Mom made the decision to go with him. Mom and Dad had guardian angels to protect them, and many times, they did. There were many times when they were in situations that they might have died."

"When was that, Jenny? I don't remember that."

"You don't know about those times, Valerie. You weren't even born during some of those times. Their guardian angels did their job, they saved them. And the night of the car accident, the angels were there, and they did their job. But their job wasn't to save them that night, their job was to take them home; to their new home in heaven. We all have angels, Valerie. But their job may not be what you think it should be. And sometimes they rely on people to help them do their job; like the two times when they relied on Didi to save you. Didi thought that her guardian angel saved both you and her during those times. But that wasn't how it happened. She didn't have a guardian angel during those times, because she didn't need one; you did. You're the one whose life was in danger. You're the one who wandered into the street when a car was coming down the road too fast. You're the one who almost drowned at the lake that day. You're the one who needed a guardian angel, Valerie, not Didi. But there are only so many guardian angels, not enough to save the world. That's why sometimes angels have to rely on people to help them out, people like Didi."

"Is Didi my guardian angel?"

"She was during those times that you needed her to be."

"Wow. I'm amazed. Didi was my angel. I never knew that."

"That's because she was on an undercover assignment. Shh, don't blow her cover, Valerie."

"I won't, Jenny. I'm blown away by these revelations about Didi, my undercover angel."

"Yeah, she was, Valerie. Don't be too angry with her, you never know when you'll need her to save your life again. Right?"

"Yeah, I guess so, Jenny."

"So, do you want your ring back?"

"The engagement ring that Patrick gave me? Yes! I do! Where is it?"

"It's at home. Do you have a shovel?"

"A shovel? Do I need one?"

"It would be a good idea if you had a shovel. Remember, I told you that Trixie buried your ring?"

"Yes, right. All this time my ring has been in the backyard."

"Yup, the entire time. So, let's get going, Val."

"Let's go. We'll need to stop by the hardware store to pick up an extra shovel. We only have one."

"An extra shovel? Do you think that I'm going to help you dig? I just had surgery, I'm not taking any chances with my recovery."

"Alright, I'll do it by myself. After all, it's my fault that we lost the ring."

"Can we stop at the cemetery before we go home? Please?"

"Of course, Jenny. Of course, we can."

CHAPTER TWENTY-TWO

Yesterday Once More

The drive to the cemetery was somber. Valerie felt a little guilty for not visiting more often. She hadn't visited her parents' graves in over a year. As she pulled the car over to the side of the road, closest to where her parents were buried, Jenny instructed her to keep driving a little further.

"Why don't you want me to stop, Jenny?"

"I do want you to stop, just not here. Keep going, all the way to the back."

"The back? Isn't that the children's cemetery?"

"Yes, it is. I'll tell you when to pull over."

Valerie drove all the way to the very last section of the children's cemetery. Confusion led to questions which she resisted from asking. Following Jenny's direction, she pulled over, and they got out of the car.

"Come on, Valerie."

Jenny walked up to a grave. She looked at the name on the headstone, before moving on to the next, continuing until she found the headstone she was looking for.

"Who's buried out here, Jenny?"

"She is," Jenny said, as she pointed to a headstone.

Our Sweet Angel
Hannah Eloise Parker
January 26, 1976 - February 28, 1983

"Jenny, this is sad. She was only six years old."

"She was seven years old."

"Did you know her? Oh, what am I asking? Of course, you didn't know her."

"No, Valerie, I don't really know her, per se, but we have met once."

"How could you have possibly met her? When did you meet her?"

"I met her a few days ago."

"Jenny, do you realize how crazy you sound? You're saying that only a few days ago, you met a little girl who has been dead for eight years."

"She's been dead for ten years, Valerie, learn math. Now let me ask you something; do you know how crazy that you would sound if you told someone that you were hanging out with your little sister who has Down syndrome, but the Down syndrome is put on 'hold' temporarily?"

"Alright, alright, I get what you're saying. I'm sorry. So, who is Hannah? Tell me about her."

"Hannah had Down syndrome too. She was about the same as me, intellectually. And like me, she liked to sing and dance. She loved strawberries. She had long hair; it was brown, and she wore bangs. Her mother always had her hair fixed in braids. She had this monkey; it was a toy, and the monkey had a banana in his hand. She used to pretend to eat the banana; then call herself Hannah banana. She was the cutest thing, Valerie. Would you like to get to know her father? He's a wonderful man. He and Patrick would be great friends, and you and his wife could get to know each other. I mean, really get to know each other. I'm sure Hannah's father would like to get to know me better too, if I live through this."

"Jenny, you will live through this. I'll bet he'd love to get to know you too. You would probably remind him of Hannah. Jenny, can I ask you something?"

"Sure."

"How is it that you could meet Hannah, and talk to Mom and Dad? I don't get it."

"Well, people like me, with a severe case of Down syndrome, and those who have severe autism, and dementia, and of course, babies; we're special. We have an insight to heaven. We see angels all the time. Sometimes they talk to us."

"I've seen you talking to someone, Jenny. I thought you had an imaginary friend."

"There's nothing imaginary about angels, Valerie. Have you ever seen when a baby smiles, and you wonder why they are smiling?"

"Angels?"

"Yes, they're looking at the angels. Do you remember Grandma Sandra, before she died? I wasn't born yet."

"Yes, I do remember Grandma Sandra. She had dementia. Sometimes it was as if she was talking to someone, but no one was there. Dad used to say it was her invisible friend. Mom was very sad. Was Grandma Sandra talking to angels, Jenny?"

"Yeah, Valerie, she was."

"That's amazing, Jenny. It's beautiful and amazing."

"It is, Val. Beautiful and amazing."

"Jenny, can you see angels?"

"I haven't seen any in the last few days, since I've been like this, in this physical state. Maybe I'm not able to see them while I'm like this. Valerie, we should go now. But before we go home to find your ring, can we make one more stop? I'd like to go to a thrift store or maybe an antique shop?"

"Sure, Jenny. Is there anything in particular that you're looking for?"

"Yes, I know exactly what I'm looking for. Will you buy it for me, if I find it?"

"Of course, I will."

"Thanks, Val."

"We're looking for a jewelry box," said Jenny. "It's porcelain, and has a ballerina on top. The color is ivory with light pink tones, and it plays music."

"Alright, Jenny. But we don't have to go to a thrift store, we can go to the mall, and I'll buy you something brand new."

"No, Valerie. It has to be that one, nothing else will do. It's not for me, it's for Hannah's dad. It was Hannah's music box, she wants him to have it."

"Okay, what song does it play?"

"Well, don't they all just play Swan Lake? Hey, Valerie, wouldn't it be cool if we found a music box that played the theme from Rocky? If you ever find one like that, you get it for me, okay?"

"That's right, Jenny! Patrick used to take you with him to the theater whenever a new Rocky movie came out. I forgot about that."

"Not only Patrick, but all three of my brothers-in-law love Rocky, and because of them, so do I. I remember when the first one came out, it was a year after Mom and Dad died. I loved how Patrick would buy me popcorn and candy, then he'd say, 'Here you go, Jenny, we won't tell Valerie. It'll be our little secret.' And I loved how Jeff would let me sit on his lap, and he'd tap my shoulder, and turn his head so I would think that a stranger tapped my shoulder, and not him; I always knew it was him. And I loved how Mike would raise my hands above my head, then using his Rocky voice, he'd say, 'Yo, Jenny, we did it.' I loved those times, Valerie. And I miss those days, they weren't too long ago; those days were last week. Don't get me wrong, I am enjoying this time with you. I am absolutely loving it. We are true sisters, and true friends. But I wish it were yesterday again; I miss those days so much. What about you, Valerie? Do you ever wish it were yesterday once more?"

"Sometimes. I love my life; being married to Patrick, having kids, having you in my life, it's all so wonderful. But sometimes I do wish it were yesterday once more. Life was different; Mom and Dad were alive, Didi and I were closer. It seems like a lifetime ago."

"You can never go back to yesterday, Valerie; but I can. I love how my being here, like this, has made you so happy. But I'm starting to miss me. The 'me' that's the little girl, the 'me' that will be a little girl forever. It won't be much longer, Val."

"Jenny, are you leaving already? I'm enjoying this time with you. We're having so much fun, and I love our talks. I've always wanted that with you."

"Valerie, please remember that my time like this is temporary."

"Yes, Jenny. I know that our time together is only temporary. And besides, I miss my other Jenny too. I miss my pictures; every day you draw a new picture for me. I miss watching you dance, and hearing you sing. The boys miss you too. They want you to come home."

"I miss them, Valerie. I don't know how much time I have to be here like this, so let's make every minute count. Let's look for the ballerina. We may not find it, but I really hope that we do."

"Okay, Jenny. We'll start here. There are a few other thrift stores that we can check out too."

After searching a few thrift stores, Valerie finally came upon a beautiful ballerina jewelry box. The ballerina was standing on one leg, while the other leg was bent at the knee, croisé, with pointed toes. Her arms were stretched out, slightly bent at the elbow, while her hands hovered above her head.

"Jenny, could this be it?"

"I think so, Valerie," Jenny said, excitedly. "This is great! We found it! Now let's go find your ring."

CHAPTER TWENTY-THREE

I Got a Name

"Jenny, are you sure that Trixie buried it here, this spot, underneath this tree?"

"I'm pretty sure, Valerie. Oh, I miss Trixie. Where did Patrick bury her, anyway?"

"I don't remember where he buried her; I think I'd better stop digging until I find out where she is. I wouldn't want to find her," Valerie said.

"Mommy," said Matthew, running outside to greet his mother. "Lauren said that Daddy called, and he's coming home now. Who's that girl? She looks like Aunt Jenny. Hey, girl, you look like Aunt Jenny."

"What?" Valerie asked.

"He knows who I am," Jenny whispered.

"Matthew, why do you think she looks like Aunt Jenny?"

"Because, she is Aunt Jenny! Aunt Jenny, you can talk English! Bobby! Bobby! Come and see Aunt Jenny! She can talk English, instead of that other language that she talks!"

"Matty, this isn't Aunt Jenny. This is Mommy's friend."

"Aunt Jenny, I missed you!" Matthew threw himself into Jenny's arms. "I'm glad you're not sick at the hospital no more."

"Where's Aunt Jenny?" shouted Bobby, as he went outside to join his brother. Behind him, were his father, his uncle Jeff and Jessica, his aunt Priscilla and uncle Mike, and his aunt Susan and uncle Steve.

"Hi, Val." Patrick gave Valerie a tight hug, then whispered in her ear, "I've missed you."

"Are you feeling alright, Dollface?" Michael asked.

"I'm fine, Michael. Really, I am. I just needed to get away."

"Who is your pretty friend?" asked Jeff.

"Uncle Jeff, don't be so silly. That's Aunt Jenny," said Matthew.

"That ain't Aunt Jenny," said Bobby. "Aunt Jenny is in the hospital. I'm gonna go inside and make Aunt Jenny and Aunt Didi a get-well card, cuz I want them to hurry up and get well so Aunt Jenny can come home."

"But Aunt Jenny is right here," said Matthew.

"Boys, why don't you both go inside the house," said Valerie. "Bobby, you make a get-well card for Aunt Jenny. And Matty, you make a get-well card for Aunt Didi."

"Okay," the boys said. They ran back into the house to start on their projects. Just before entering the house, Matthew turned to Jenny, and said, "Aunt Jenny, I love you. I'm happy that you're home."

"I love you too, Matty," Jenny yelled back. Turning to the family, she said, "It takes so little to make kids happy. I hope that's alright with you, Valerie, that I let him think I'm his aunt Jenny. I didn't want to spoil his fun."

"That's fine. It's no problem at all," said Valerie.

"It's fine with me too. I'm Patrick, Valerie's husband. Honey, why haven't you introduced us to your friend?"

"Oh, where are my manners? Well, um, this is my husband, Patrick."

"And?" asked Patrick.

"And what?" asked Valerie.

"And what about everybody else? Never mind. This is my sister, Susan, and her husband, Steve."

"Howdy-do. I'm Michael. I'm married to Valerie's sister, Priscilla."

"Hi, I'm Priscilla. This is Jeff and his girlfriend, Jessica."

"It's nice to meet you all," said Jenny, as she proceeded to shake everyone's hand.

"Well, that takes care of that," said Valerie.

"Valerie," said Michael, "your friend knows all of us, but who is she?"

"Oh, well ... She's um... well... she's a very sweet girl."

"Should we just call her Sweetie Pie, or does she have a name?"

"I got a name," said Jenny. "My name is…."

"Michael, of course, she has a name," Valerie said, quickly, deliberately interrupting Jenny. "Why would you ask that? I mean, everybody has a name, right?"

"Well, Valerie, what's hers?" asked Jeff.

"Her name? Sure, I can tell you her name. It's not a big deal. Why does everybody always make a big deal out of nothing? Her name is Je … Je … Her name is Je… Je… ahem, there must be something in the air, ahem. Does anyone have a cough drop?"

"Her name is Je… Je…?" asked Michael.

Valerie let out a couple of hard hacks, stalling for enough time to contemplate what she would say next.

"I don't think that we have any cough drops, but would you like a glass of water, Val?" asked Patrick.

"She doesn't need a glass of water; I can turn on the water hose for her," said Jeff.

"I'm not drinking from a dirty water hose," Valerie said.

"Valerie, you're not coughing anymore; I guess you're alright, now," said Priscilla

"I've never heard of anyone having the name Je Je." Michael said. "What kind of name is that?"

"My name is Jenna," Jenny said. "Valerie is alright. She's just coughing from all this dust created from the dirt. Isn't that right, Valerie? You're just fine, huh?"

"Yeah, I'm fine."

"Valerie has told me so much about everyone. I feel like I've known you all my whole life."

"Forgive me for staring, Jenna. It's just that you look so much like my mother when she was young," said Priscilla.

"I do?"

"Yes, you do. You really do."

"Well, thank you, Priscilla. I'll take that as a compliment."

"Stop staring at her," said Michael.

"Jenna, I'm sorry," Priscilla said. "It's just that your resemblance to my mother is uncanny. I'll try not to stare, but if I do, please forgive me."

"No forgiveness is necessary. I'm truly flattered."

"Valerie, don't you see the resemblance?"

"No, not really. I don't see it."

"She must be Anna's doppelganger," said Michael. "Jenna, Anna was their mother. She's been gone many years."

"Yes, I know. I'm sorry for what happened to your parents, Priscilla. Valerie has told me all about them."

"What's a doppelganger?" asked Valerie.

"It's someone who bears a strong resemblance to another person of whom they are not related. Often, they look exactly the same, almost ghostly," said Jenny.

"I've never heard of that word before. Have you, Patrick?" asked Valerie.

"Sure, I've heard of a doppelganger," said Patrick. "There was an episode about it on the Twilight Zone. You should have watched it with me."

"Yeah, Valerie. You should have watched it with him," said Jenny.

"I don't like scary movies."

"Twilight Zone is not a movie," said Patrick.

"Yeah, Valerie. It's not a movie," said Jenny. "And it's not scary, either. But if you don't want to watch the Twilight Zone, then at least pick up a dictionary every once in a while. That way you'll know about words like doppelganger and entomologist."

"And habeas corpus, you don't know what that means, either," said Patrick.

"And marshmallow. Remember, you used to say marchmellow?" said Priscilla.

"I know what a marshmallow is, Priscilla. I was five years old when I said marchmellow. When are you and Didi going to move on from that?"

"Valerie, is Jenna the friend that you met up with yesterday and earlier today?" Jessica asked.

"Yes, we had lunch together, yesterday and today."

"Oh, I'm so happy to hear that! It's wonderful meeting you, Jenna. I'm so relieved."

"Why are you relieved?" Jeff asked.

"No reason, just forget it," said Jessica.

"Priscilla," said Jenny, "Valerie has told me all about your uncles, Danny and Jim; and your aunts, Gina and Nancy. I'd love to meet them."

"Well, as a matter of fact, they'll be here soon. I'll be fixing supper for the whole family. Jenna, can you join us?" asked Priscilla.

"I'd love to join you! Thank you."

"Well, we're missing our baby sister, Jenny. But maybe you can substitute for her, if you'd like."

"I can do that."

"Valerie, can I ask you why you're digging?" asked Patrick.

"Well, Patrick, I'm just digging, that's all," Valerie nervously said.

"I know that, honey, but why?"

"Well, I was just digging a hole."

"Are you digging to China? What's going on?" asked Michael.

"I'm curious about that too," said Jessica.

"Well, uh, I was just digging, so I got this shovel from the garage, because I needed it to dig."

"But why do you need to dig, Valerie?" asked Patrick.

"Well, honey, uh," an uneasy Valerie stammered.

"Maybe I can clear things up," said Jenny. "Valerie told me that she finds it therapeutic to dig. With everything that's happened to her sisters, she's been sad and gloomy. And then being pregnant on top of that, she's been emotional. And cranky, she's also been very cranky."

"I have not been cranky!"

"Valerie, it's alright. We understand," said Jenny. "You're going through a lot right now. You've been a real sourpuss."

"You sure are, Dollface. A real sourpuss."

"Oh, Doll, I'm sorry. I guess I've been neglecting you, and that's why you've been such a sourpuss. But why dig? I remember when you were a little girl, you used to write down your feelings in a diary. You were so cute. You should have seen her, Patrick. She had this diary, and it had a little lock on it with a tiny, little key. Didi used to open it with a bobby pin and read it."

"What?" exclaimed Valerie.

"I didn't read it. Didi read it, and Dad did too."

"What? I can't believe Daddy would do that to me! I just can't believe it!"

"Lighten up, Dollface."

"Yeah, Valerie. Don't be so dramatic," said Jenny.

"So, Valerie, back to the question; why dig?" asked Susan. "There are so many other things to do to release your feelings. It seems to me that there is no purpose for digging."

"Well….." said Valerie.

"Valerie said that she wanted to plant a garden," said Jenny.

"Valerie, you don't plant a garden next to a tree," Michael said.

"Yeah, I told her that," said Jenny.

"And you don't need to dig a hole very deep," said Jeff.

"I told you, Valerie, don't dig too deep," said Jenny.

"What kind of garden? Flowers or vegetables? What kind of seeds did you get? You don't even have seeds, do you?" Michael asked.

"Honey, you need seeds to plant a garden," said Patrick.

"Yeah, I told her that too," said Jenny.

"Well, Valerie, can you finish your digging another time? Let's get supper going so it'll be ready when our aunts and uncles get here. Jenna, are you handy in the kitchen? Would you like to help us with the cooking?" asked Priscilla.

"I would love to, Priscilla, but I am not handy in the kitchen," said Jenny.

"You don't know how to cook?" asked Priscilla.

"I don't know how to do anything. I've never even turned on a stove before, not in my whole life."

"In your whole life, you've never turned on a stove? Really?" asked Steve.

"Do you know how to use a can opener?" asked Jeff.

"A can opener? Nooo," answered a confused Jenny.

"Do you know what a can opener is?" asked Jeff.

"Nooo," answered Jenny. "Wait, a minute; is it that thing that's kind of long, and you put in on a can, and twist the knob, and then it opens, and then tuna fish comes out?"

"Yeah, and it opens all kinds of cans, not just tuna," said Jeff.

"Well, that makes sense. I've never used one before, but it looks easy enough. I'll bet I could learn," said Jenny.

"How is it that you've never used a can opener before?" asked Michael.

"I've never had to use a can opener, or do anything else, for that matter. I've had someone do things for me, all my life."

"Really, you've had servants?" asked Susan.

"Yeah, you could say that."

"You've never done anything?" Steve asked.

"No."

"How about laundry? Have you ever done your laundry?" asked Jeff.

"No, I've never done laundry."

"So, you've never done anything? Ever?" Patrick asked.

"Well, I make my own bed. Not very well, but I do it anyway. And I can pick things up off the floor, like toys and clothes. I can take my plate to the kitchen counter when I'm done eating. And I can help bring groceries into the house, but I've been told not to put them away, because I usually put things in the wrong place. Once, I got yelled at for putting a pound of hamburger meat in the pantry. I won't make that mistake again," said Jenny.

"You didn't know that hamburger meat needs to be refrigerated?" Michael asked.

"No, I guess not. I've never given it much thought. I was just trying to be helpful. But I guess that I wasn't."

"That's okay, Jenny. Don't feel bad. At least you tried," said Valerie.

"Valerie, her name is not Jenny," said Priscilla.

"That's alright," said Jenny. "I know that she has her sister on her mind, and our names are similar."

"What kind of car do you drive, Jenna?" asked Jeff.

"I don't have a car. In fact, I don't even know how to drive. I get driven everywhere I go."

"You have a chauffeur?" asked Steve.

"I guess I do."

"That must be nice, to not have to do anything; and to have your own servant and chauffeur," Jeff said.

"It is nice," said Jenny. "I wouldn't want my life to be any other way."

"Your parents must be well-off," said Priscilla.

"My parents have an abundance of riches and treasures. They live in a huge mansion with many rooms. Yup, they sure do. I wouldn't tell you that if it wasn't true."

"I'd love to see the house sometime. Is it close by?" asked Susan.

"It's not close by. And someday, you will see it. You will all have the chance to see it. But that won't be for a very long time. Hey, while you're fixing supper, does anyone mind if I stay out here and work in the yard? I can finish what you started, Valerie."

"Really, Jenny?" asked Valerie.

"Valerie, she's not Jenny, she's Jenna," said Priscilla.

"I mean Jenna. You would do that for me, Jenna?"

"Of course, Valerie. You're like a sister to me. I would do anything for you."

"You're a very sweet girl, Jenna," said Priscilla.

"Thank you, Priscilla. Before everyone goes into the house; can I ask you a question, Patrick?"

"Sure, Jenna. What is it?"

"Well, you see this hole where Valerie was digging?"

"Yeah."

"That's not where you buried Trixie, is it?"

"No. Trixie is over there, to the left, beneath that big tree."

"Thanks. That's good to know."

CHAPTER TWENTY-FOUR

This Diamond Ring

Spaghetti is always a good choice for feeding a large group of people; it's economical, easy and quick to prepare, and most importantly, it's delicious. Despite the meal preparation requiring minimal effort, eight people were bumping into each other in the kitchen, in an attempt to have food on the table by the time the aunts and uncles arrived. Such togetherness made it easier to probe Valerie about her new friend. There was much about Jenna that intrigued everyone. Valerie was hit up with assorted questions, making her feel ill at ease about Jenny being at the house. But inquiring minds wanted to know, so she had to come up with some answers.

"Valerie, how long have you known Jenna? I've never heard you mention her before?" asked Patrick.

"Well, that's because I haven't known her for very long."

"You've never brought her to the house before, have you, Val? I've never seen her here, and it doesn't seem like the boys have seen her before."

"No, Patrick. Today is the first time that I've brought her here. As a matter of fact, when we got here, we just went directly to the backyard. The kids were watching TV, so I didn't want to disturb them. We didn't come into the house."

"She seems to know a lot about your parents. And Trixie's been dead for a long time, she knows about Trixie too," said Michael.

"We've grown very close, very fast," said Valerie.

"There's something about her that's odd, but in a wonderful way," Priscilla said. "I find myself drawn to her. I don't know if it's because she looks so much like Mom, or what it is. I wonder if she's a distant relative to us. She could, somehow, be related to Mom's family. I wish Aunt Teresa were here, so that she could meet Jenna."

"Valerie, is Jenna the girl from the hospital cafeteria that you met the other day?" asked Patrick.

"The girl from the hospital that I met the other day?"

"Excuse me, everyone," said Jenny.

"Jenna! Look at you! Your arms are covered in dirt, all the way up to your elbows!" exclaimed Priscilla.

"Well, I was putting the dirt back in the hole, then I saw something shiny. I was a little curious about what it could be, but it turned out to be nothing. Since I was having so much fun in the dirt, I thought I would dig a little deeper."

"Did you find anything, Jenna?" asked Valerie.

"I found a lot of bugs. I wish my friend were here, he's an entomologist. He would love all these bugs that I found."

"Is that all you found?" asked Valerie. "Bugs? Did you find anything else?"

"Did you lose something, Valerie?" asked Susan.

"No, I was just wondering if she found anything else. It's a big yard, who knows; there may be a buried treasure out there."

"Don't worry, Dollface. If she struck oil, you got first dibs. I know the law."

"I didn't strike oil, but my digging did lead me to find this."

Jenny held up a tiny, black, dirty, velvet ring box.

"My ring!" exclaimed Valerie.

"I don't believe it. May I?" asked Patrick. He took the dirty box from Jenny, and opened it. "I don't believe it. I just don't believe it. This diamond ring, it has been lost for seventeen years. How in the world did you find this, Jenna?"

"I just saw the box in the dirt. I picked it up, and opened it, and inside was this diamond ring. This beautiful diamond ring. I figured it must belong to Valerie."

"Valerie, do you remember the night of our senior prom, when I tried to propose to you?"

"Yes, Patrick. I made you drop the ring."

"Well, I'll be a monkey's uncle," Michael said.

"Your dog, Trixie, she must have found it and buried it," Jenny said.

With the ring box opened, Patrick knelt down on one knee, next to Valerie.

"Valerie, after all these years, with you now knowing how our lives are together as a married couple, and knowing all of the mistakes I've made, especially concerning Jenny, would you still marry me?"

"Patrick, you haven't made any mistakes as far as Jenny is concerned. You've taken wonderful care of her, just like you promised my father you would. And you've been a wonderful husband to me, and a fantastic father to our children. I would marry you over, and over again, every day, for the rest of my life."

"Come on, Dollface, let's not get so mushy," Michael said, as he dabbed away a few tears from his eyes.

"This is incredible," Susan said. She smudged her mascara while wiping away a few tears.

"Congratulations, Valerie! I wasn't here for the first time around, but I'm so happy to be a part of it now," said Jessica.

"Valerie, I'm so happy that you have your ring back," said Priscilla.

"Are you alright, Jenna?" asked Jeff.

"Yes, I'm fine. Michael's right, Valerie can get her point across without getting mushy. I think I'll go wash up. I'll be right back."

Without difficulty, Jenny went directly to the restroom upstairs.

"Did Jenna just go to the bathroom? She's never been here before, how does she know where it is?" asked Jeff.

"Well, Jeff, how hard could it be for her to find the bathroom? She lives in a mansion; if she can find the bathroom in a mansion, with all those rooms, then I'm pretty sure that she can find the bathroom in Patrick and Valerie's house," Jessica said.

"That was strange," said Steve. "She didn't ask where the bathroom is; she went there directly, as if she knew exactly where she was going. There's something about that girl."

"Does anyone else find it strange that she got all of our names right, the first time?" asked Jeff.

"I still can't get over that she knew where the bathroom is," said Steve.

"I think you guys are jealous because she's rich, and she has her own servants and chauffeurs. She seems to be a very sweet girl," said Jessica.

"What are you all trying to say?" Valerie asked. "Jenny is my friend. I mean Jenna. Jenna is my friend. Her name is Jenna and she's my friend."

"No one is trying to say anything, Valerie. She's a very sweet girl. She does remind me of your mother. Not just the way she looks, but her mannerism is just like Anna's," said Michael.

"I agree with you, Mike. Somehow, in many ways, she's just like Mom," said Priscilla.

"Excuse me, I hope you all won't think I'm rude," Jenny said, as she rejoined the family. "I don't know much about cooking, but whatever you're making, I don't think it's supposed to smell like that."

"The spaghetti! You burned it, Michael!"

"You did, Priscilla! I was in charge of the sauce."

"Well, look at the sauce!" Patrick said, "It's boiled over! What a mess!"

"The aunts and uncles will be here any minute. Let's get this cleaned up," Priscilla said.

"Aunt Jenny," said Matthew, "can you color with me?"

"Sure, Matty. Let's sit down at the table. Emily, Nicole, Monica, would you girls like to sit with us? You can draw pictures."

"Yeah, I like to draw pictures," said Nicole.

"You're good at that, aren't you?" asked Jenny.

"Pretty good."

"I'll bet that you like to draw funny pictures of people?"

"Yes," said Nicole.

"Those are called caricatures, and you do a great job."

"I like to draw too, Miss Jenna," said Monica.

"I know, Monica. You're good at drawing animals, right?"

"Yeah," said Monica.

"I don't know how to draw, but I want to hang out with you too," said Lauren.

"That's okay, Lauren. You're pretty good at supervising. Why don't you supervise this art session?"

"Yay! I get to be the boss!"

"You seem to know a lot about the kids, Jenna," said Steve.

"Valerie's told me a lot about the kids; not to mention that I have a sixth sense. It's a gift."

"Mom," Lauren hollered, "Uncle Jim just drove up. I'll open the door for them."

"Great," Priscilla scoffed. "That's just great."

"Why don't we just go to a restaurant, honey?"

"Well, Mike, I guess we'll have to."

Priscilla and Valerie welcomed their aunts and uncles into the house. Jenny remained seated at the table. Gina provided an update on both Jenny and Delores. Delores had greatly improved; she regained some consciousness, and was able to breathe on her own. She was also able to move her arms and legs, although very slightly. Jenny remained unconscious, however, it was the opinion of the doctors that she should have awakened by now. The surgeries were successful, and at times, she had responded positively to various tests performed. Because of her intellectual level of having Down syndrome, it would be difficult to determine whether she has suffered brain damage.

Gina was not happy about having to eat at a restaurant.

"I don't understand how anyone can ruin spaghetti. It's the easiest thing to make. You boil water, it's not that hard. Eight adults couldn't do that?"

"I'm sorry, Aunt Gina," said Priscilla.

"Me too," Valerie said.

"That's alright," Gina said. "I know you girls are not the best cooks."

"Well, let's get going. I'm so hungry, I could eat a horse," said Jim.

"Dad, can we go to DeMarco's?" asked Lauren.

"Yeah! DeMarco's!" echoed the kids.

"Come on, Jenna," said Patrick. "You can ride with us."

Jenny slowly rose up from the chair; apprehensively, she emerged to the living room. Now that she realized how much she resembled her mother, she wondered if Gina, Danny, or Jim would see the similarities.

"Sure, Patrick. Thank you," she said. She walked straight to Gina, with her arm extended for a handshake. "You must be Valerie's aunts and uncles. It's a pleasure to meet you all."

"Oh, my heavens! Anna! You came back from the dead!" Gina shrieked.

"Aunt Gina, this is Jenna, Valerie's friend," said Priscilla.

"Anna. You're Anna, my sister-in-law and best friend. I'd know you anywhere," Gina said.

She took Jenny's hands into her own, then gently touched her face.

"I'm Jenna, but you know what they say, 'we've all got a twin somewhere,' I guess I'm Anna's twin."

"Aunt Gina, she's grandma's doppelganger," said Lauren.

"Do you know what that word means, Lauren?" asked Valerie.

"Of course, I do, Aunt Valerie. I have a dictionary."

"Jenna? Is that your name?" asked Jim.

"Yes, sir. If my presence makes anyone uncomfortable, I can leave. I don't want to make anyone uncomfortable."

"No, Jenna, no one wants you to leave," Jim said. "You're a lovely young lady, and you happen to bear a striking resemblance to my sister-in-law, who is deceased."

"Pardon us, Miss Jenna," said Danny. "As my kid brother just mentioned, you look an awful lot like our sister-in-law. My brother, my wife and I, are in a little bit of shock right now. Please forgive us."

"Yes, dear," Gina said. "Please forgive me. I'm being very rude to you, and I'm sorry."

"I just called DeMarco's, and let them know that we're a large party, and we're on our way," said Jeff. "So, let's be on our way."

"Yeah! DeMarco's!" yelled the kids.

CHAPTER TWENTY-FIVE

Ma Belle Amie

As usual, when the whole family gets together for a meal, they need two tables; one for the kids, and one for the adults. DeMarco's was very accommodating by rearranging tables to meet their needs. Without giving it any thought, Jenny sat at the kids' table.

"Yay, Miss Jenna's sitting with us," Bobby said, as he clapped his hands.

"She's Aunt Jenny," said Matthew.

"Matty, this is Miss Jenna," said Lauren. "Aunt Jenny is in the hospital with Aunt Didi, they'll be home soon. Miss Jenna, I'm glad you're sitting with us."

"Me too, Miss Jenna," Emily said. "Me and my sister like you a lot."

"Yup, I do," said Nicole.

"You're pretty, Miss Jenna," said Monica.

"You are pretty, Miss Jenna. I know they said that you look like my grandma. I never met my grandma; I was born a few months after my grandma and grandpa died, so I never got the chance to meet them. But I do think that you look a lot like my mom," said Frankie. "Our mom is pretty too."

"Thank you, Frankie."

"Hold it, Jenna," said Jim. "We want you to sit with us at the adult table."

"Yeah, Jenna," said Michael. "Come sit with us. We want you here, at the head of our table. You're our guest of honor."

"Oh, I've never sat at the grown-ups' table before. Sorry, kids. I've waited for this day my whole life," said Jenny.

"Awe..." the kids said.

"I'll make it up to you," said Jenny. "I'll order five great big desserts, and you all can split it."

"Thanks, Miss Jenna!" the kids shouted. "We love you!"

"I love all of you. You're great kids."

Michael pulled the chair out for Jenny. The men waited until she was seated before sitting down. The waiter took their order, and the food was served shortly after. At a later time, he would bring the kids five big servings of chocolate brownie, topped with an ice cream sundae.

"You've never sat at the adult table before at your house?" Jessica asked.

"Well, when it's just the immediate family, sure. But when the whole extended family comes over; my sisters, their husbands, their kids, my aunts and uncles, then no. I always sit at the kids' table. This is the first time that I've sat at the grown-ups' table. It's nice, I like it."

"Are you the baby of the family?" asked Danny. "How old are you, Jenna?"

"Daniel Negron! Shame on you. You never ask a woman her age. Don't answer him, Jenna. It's none of his business," said Gina.

"It's alright, Gina. I really don't mind."

"I'm sorry, Jenna. Since you're young, I didn't think it was a big deal. When you're old like my wife, then it's a big deal," said Danny.

"Uncle Danny! That's not nice," said Priscilla.

"Can you please shut up, dear, so Jenna can speak? I'll deal with you later, at home," said Gina.

"Danny boy, you're in so much trouble," said Jim.

"I don't really know how old I am," said Jenny.

"Typical woman," said Jim.

"What I meant was, I've never really thought about my age. But if I do the math, let's see, I was born on December 20, 1972. That would make me...."

"December 20, 1972? That's the day Jenny was born!" exclaimed Priscilla.

"Oh," said Jenny. "Yeah, that's right. Valerie told me."

"What a coincidence," said Jeff.

"Yeah, it sure is," said Jenny.

"My birthday is March 26, 1958!" Valerie shouted out.

"Yes, Dollface. Every year you make it a point to remind everyone. You usually don't start doing that until February. But thanks for the early reminder."

"Your welcome," said Valerie.

"Valerie, it's still too early to shop for your birthday gift," said Nancy. "Priscilla's birthday comes before yours, dear."

"Yes, Aunt Nancy. I'm sorry about that."

"It's wonderful about Didi, that she's shown improvement. I can't wait to see her," said Priscilla.

"It is wonderful about Didi," said Nancy, "but we still need to keep praying for Jenny. She's not out of the woods yet."

"I may have misunderstood, Aunt Nancy. I thought Aunt Gina said that the doctors expected her to regain consciousness," said Priscilla.

"They do, dear," Gina said, "but it's hard for them to determine what's going on. She responds to the tests that they give her, but she's still not coming out of it. It's like she's in another place that she doesn't want to leave."

"I'm sure she'll come around," said Jenny.

"How can you be sure?" asked Gina.

"Because, look at this wonderful family. This is a loving family. Who wouldn't want to come back to this? Anybody would," said Jenny.

"You're a very sweet young lady," said Nancy.

"Thank you."

"Jenna, dear, what is your last name?" asked Gina. "I wonder if you're not related somehow to Anna's family."

"Anna?" asked Valerie.

"Your mother, Anna," Michael said.

"Oh, well, there's Mom, and then there's Anna, the lawyer from your office, the one with the long hair."

"That's my cousin, Angie, and she quit working there two years ago."

"Valerie, honey. Are you alright? You've been acting strange all day," said Patrick.

"No, I haven't."

"Yes, you have," said Priscilla. "What's with the digging in your backyard? And shouting out your birthday a few minutes ago? And this afternoon? What in the world was that all about?"

"What was all what about?"

"You, coming back into the room to kiss Patrick."

"He is my husband. I didn't know it was a crime to kiss your husband."

"It's not a crime to kiss your husband, Valerie. But it's the way that you kissed him, in front of everybody. It was like a scene from the movie, Body Heat."

"Really? Do you think that I'm as sexy as Kathleen Turner?"

"No," said Patrick.

"Thanks a lot, Patrick," said Valerie, a bit disappointed.

"But you don't have to be. What I mean is, let's do another take on that scene, just to be sure. How about tonight, in our bedroom?"

"I don't know what's going on here, Valerie. But you and Patrick are beginning to sound a lot like Mom and Dad. Can you both please put a sock in it?"

"I just asked a simple question. I asked Jenna about her last name. And the poor dear didn't even have a chance to answer. Instead, I get all this porno talk. It's like listening to Frank and Anna on a Tuesday. Or any day of the week, for that matter," said Gina. "May they continue to rest in peace, until I get up there."

"See, Aunt Gina agrees with me," said Priscilla.

"Jenna, do you mind telling us your last name?" asked Jim.

"Her last name?" asked Valerie.

"Her last name, Valerie. Mine is Negron, yours is Cole. We were wondering about Jenna's," said Jim.

"Mine used to be Negron too. And then I got married to Patrick, now it's Cole," Valerie said, exhibiting nervous behavior.

"Interesting, Valerie," said Jenny. "Tell us more. We're dying to know."

"Yes, Valerie. Tell us more." laughed Priscilla. "We're dying to know. We're literally dying."

Priscilla continued to mock Valerie, for a few minutes, as the others joined in.

"Jim, you asked me about my last name," said Jenny. "It's …"

"It's Wade," Valerie blurted out.

"Jenna Wade?" asked Priscilla. "I've heard that name before."

"I have too," said Nancy. "Are you related to the Wade family in Fort Worth?"

"No, I'm not," said Jenny.

"Well, I don't think there are any Wades in Anna's family," said Gina. "Where are you from, Jenna? Are you from Crystal Springs?"

"No, she's from Dallas," said Valerie.

"Jenna Wade from Dallas?" asked Michael.

"Do you have family, besides your parents, Jenna?" asked Steve.

"I have three older sisters, they're married."

"I knew a girl with the last name of Wade when I lived in Dallas. What are your sisters' names?" Jeff asked.

"Mmm, this pizza is so delicious! It's good! It's really, really good! Has everyone tried the pizza? It's really, really good," Valerie said, disrupting the flow of the conversation, while taking another slice off the pizza pan.

"Yeah, we've all had DeMarco's pizza before, Valerie," said Jeff. "At least once a week for the past 25 years."

"Well, how many slices have you had, Dollface? That's got to be your third slice."

"No, it's just my second."

"No, Valerie, it's your fourth," said Jenny.

"That's alright, dear. You're eating for two," said Gina.

"Jenna, I hope that you'll be able to meet Delores and Jenny," said Nancy.

"Jenny has Down syndrome, right?" Jenny asked.

"My baby niece has Down syndrome. She might be a little lower functioning that a lot of others who also have Downs. But I see Jenny just as I see my other nieces; beautiful, smart, fun, silly, she's no different," said Jim.

"Yeah, we all love Jenny very much," said Danny.

"Well, I'm sure that Jenny loves you all right back," said Jenny.

"Yes," said Priscilla. "We all adore Jenny. I wish Mom and Dad would have had the chance to raise Jenny, themselves. But Valerie and Patrick have done an excellent job. Thank you, Valerie and Patrick, for stepping up to the plate. I must admit, at first, I had doubts about Valerie being able to care for Jenny, but I changed my tune pretty early on."

"I had faith in you the whole time," said Michael.

"You and Didi," said Jeff.

"Didi?" asked Valerie.

"Yeah, Didi," said Jeff. "She had faith in you, Valerie. She knew that you and Patrick would be better than anyone else to raise Jenny."

"When did she say this, Jeff? Didi wasn't involved with the family back then. Remember?"

"Didi has never stopped being a part of this family; I'm the outsider. When we broke up a hundred times, she always told me that no matter what, she wanted me to know that I was welcome to continue being part of this family, her family. And now she welcomed my new girlfriend into her family. Didi and I didn't work out, but that's life. She's happy now, and I'm happy for her. We've both moved on, Bill is a great guy, and a great stepfather to my children."

"I never knew Didi had faith in me to raise Jenny. She never told me."

"She reached out to me the day before your wedding," said Jeff. "Her friend, Jennifer, told her that you were getting married. She was so happy for you. She asked me how I'd feel about her going to the wedding. I told her that it didn't matter, she should go. Her presence would be the best wedding gift that you would get. But she thought that you wouldn't want her there. I guess that's why she decided not to go. I never told you about it, Val, because I didn't want you to feel disappointed that she didn't go. And I never asked Didi why she didn't go, either. I never brought it up. We were both hurting so much at that time."

"Well, it was probably best not to bring it up," said Michael, subtly glancing in Valerie's direction.

"Valerie, we have a confession," said Susan. "Didi was at your wedding. Please don't be mad at us, but Steve saw her outside, about to drive away. She was in tears; she really wanted to see you and Patrick exchange your vows. So, Steve decided to hide her during the ceremony. Valerie, we love you and we love your family, they're our family too."

"I'm sorry, Valerie. We should have told you, but you've been at odds with Delores off and on, for some time," said Steve. "She's our friend."

"I'm not mad at either one of you. I promise," said Valerie.

"Well, I'm sorry that I won't have the chance to meet her. I really should be getting back to my family now," said Jenny.

"Oh no," the family bemoaned.

"You don't have to leave yet, dear, do you?" asked Gina.

"Please, stay a little longer, Jenna," said Danny.

"Yeah. Can't you stay a while longer?" asked Nancy.

"Jenna, I'd like for you stay a little longer too, if you can," said Priscilla. "I've enjoyed today, spending time with you. I know that I just met you, but I feel like you're part of the family. I feel like I've known you for a long time. Maybe it's because you remind me of my mother; but you feel like a sister to me. Doesn't she feel that way to you, Valerie?"

"Yes, Priscilla. She feels like a sister."

"Thank you, Priscilla," Jenny said. "You don't know how much it means to me to hear you say that. I know so much about you, from Valerie, of course. You're a wonderful sister, and I'll bet Jenny would tell you that herself, if she could."

"I've always wondered if Jenny knows how much I love her. I know that Didi and Valerie know how much I love them, but I've always wondered if Jenny knows."

"I'll bet that she knows."

"Thank you, Jenna. That's very nice of you to say."

"I would love to stay, and spend more time with all of you, but I have to get back. It's time for me to go," said Jenny.

"Do you have to get back to Dallas tonight, Jenna?" asked Michael. "That's a long way."

"Yes, I will travel a long way to get back to my life, the life that I know. I want you all to know that as I travel back, I will try to always remember this day. I don't know if I'll be able to remember it forever, but I will cherish it for as long as I can."

"You sound like you're saying goodbye forever. Let's not say goodbye forever. Let's plan your next visit," said Priscilla.

"It's not goodbye forever. But I don't think that I'll have another opportunity to visit again, like this." said Jenny.

"How are you getting home, Jenna?" asked Jeff. "I know that you don't drive."

"Well, I thought maybe Valerie could drop me off at the train station. Would you mind, Valerie?"

"Of course, I wouldn't mind. But do you really have to go now?"

"Yes, Valerie. It's time. I've enjoyed hanging out with you, I've loved it. But it's time for me to go."

"Alright, Jenna. I'll take you to the train station."

"Thank you, Valerie."

"Valerie, I can go with you to drop off Jenna, if you'd like."

"I appreciate that, Patrick. But I think I'd like to go by myself. We might do some girl talk. You should get the kids to bed."

"Well, Jenna, I've enjoyed meeting you."

"Likewise, Patrick."

"Thanks for finding Valerie's ring. I still can't believe that you found it. It's a miracle."

"Miracles happen every day."

"If only you could meet Delores and Jenny before you leave," said Nancy. "Are you sure that you can't stay a little longer, Jenna?"

"It would be nice if I could stay a little longer, but I can't. I must get back to my life."

"Maybe another time, dear," said Nancy."

"Maybe. I sure have enjoyed meeting you aunts and uncles. Thank you for the stories."

"We've enjoyed meeting you, dear," said Gina.

"Yes, we have," said Nancy.

"I hope you can come back again, soon," said Danny.

"I hope so too," said Jim.

"Thank you. I'm very grateful for this time that I got to spend with you. Valerie is very fortunate to have you as her aunts and uncles."

"Jenna, I've enjoyed meeting you too," said Michael.

"Thank you, Mike. I'm glad that I got to see you, and Jeff, and Patrick."

"See us? Do you mean that you're glad that you got to meet us?"

"Oh yeah, I mean that I'm glad that I got to meet you."

"You're so sweet. Jenna, ma belle amie."

"Merci beaucoup," said Jenny.

"What did you say, Mike?" asked Jeff.

"He said 'my beautiful friend.' It's French."

"That's right, Jenna. I took French in college; I used to speak French to Jenny, all the time, while she was growing up."

"Do you speak French, Jenna?" asked Patrick.

"No, I don't. I only know a few words and phrases that I picked up from my brother-in-law. He used to speak French to me all the time while I was growing up. Priscilla, thank you for letting me be your sister for the day."

"It was my pleasure, Jenna. You can come back to visit anytime. Bring your parents next time, I'd love to meet them."

"My parents would love you, Priscilla. They would adore you."

"So, bring them by."

"It's impossible."

"Why is it impossible?"

"It just is."

Jenny threw herself into Priscilla's arms, and held her tightly, not wanting to let her go.

"The last train to Dallas will probably be leaving soon. We should go now, Jenna," said Valerie.

Jenny slowly pulled herself away from the long embrace she and Priscilla shared. Priscilla gently swept the hair away from Jenny's eyes before they shared a gaze.

"You even have the same eyes as my mother. I feel like you're going to take a part of my heart with you when you leave."

"I just might do that. Goodbye, Priscilla."

"Goodbye, Jenna."

"Goodbye, everyone. Goodbye, kids."

"Bye, Miss Jenna," said the kids.

"Don't go, Aunt Jenny," said Matthew.

"This Aunt Jenny has to go home now, Matty. But your other Aunt Jenny will still be here," said Priscilla, as she gave a wink to Jenny.

"Oh, Aunt Priscilla. I didn't know I had two Aunt Jennies."

"Hey, Matty," said Jenny, "your other Aunt Jenny is getting better; soon she'll be leaving the hospital and going home."

"Okay, well, bye, Aunt Jenny number two," said Matthew.

"Bye, Matty," said Jenny. "Before I leave, I'd like to thank you all for the most wonderful day that I've ever had. Take care, everyone. Goodbye."

CHAPTER TWENTY-SIX

Reflections Of My Life

Valerie drove aimlessly around town. She didn't know Jenny's destination, and didn't want to break the stillness, which surrounded her and Jenny, by asking where she needed to go. The tranquility allowed her to mull over the latest revelations about Delores. She never knew that, all those years ago, Delores had championed for her to be given the chance to take care of Jenny.

"Turn by the high school," Jenny said. "Then go north."

"Is there somewhere in particular that you need to go? I don't understand how, or where you will be going back to your life. You know, your life with me?"

"I don't understand either. I don't know how I got here, and I don't know how I'm leaving. But I know that you need to drive north. I'll let you know as more information becomes available. Wasn't that crazy that Matty knew who I was?"

"Yes, it sure was. Why do you suppose he knew, and the other kids didn't?"

"Matty is still little, he's young. He only recently lost his insight to heaven, but he still has his innocence about certain things. Kind of like me, Valerie; the other me, the real me. Do you remember when the boys were really little, and Patrick used to camp out with us on the living room floor?"

"Yeah. He used to tell me that he loved listening to y'all. He said that it sounded like the three of you were having actual conversations."

"We were having actual conversations."

"Really, Jenny?"

"Yes, Valerie. We had actual conversations. On your end, you and Patrick heard us babbling. You know my vocabulary is limited to a few words here and there. When Matty was a year old, he had no real vocabulary, either. Bobby had the largest vocabulary between the three of us, but he was very much a child; 100 percent innocence intact, and he still had his insight to heaven. Even though he knew a few actual words, he was still able to understand the babel that a one-year-old child communicates; also, the babel that I communicate."

"Do you mean baby talk?"

"Yeah, you can call it that. I miss our talks; Bobby, Matty, and I, we had some good talks. Oh, Valerie, those were sure some fun times. But those days are gone, forever. Bobby no longer remembers, and soon Matty will forget too. But you have this new baby coming. I can't wait to meet her. I'll have someone to talk to, and laugh with."

"Her? Am I having a girl? Do you know that?"

"I don't know, Valerie. Sorry, I misspoke."

"No, you didn't. You know that I'm having a girl, don't you?"

"I don't know, Valerie. Forget what I said."

"Wow, I'm having a girl!"

"Congratulations, Valerie."

"Thank you, Jenny. I'm having a girl! I'm so excited!"

"Well, pay attention to your driving."

"Oh, I am. I remember this road, Jenny. In a few miles, we'll be out in the country, and there will be a fork in the road. Are you sure this is where we need to go?"

"I'm not sure about anything. Keep driving."

"It's getting dark, Jenny."

"Yeah, Valerie. It's called nighttime. It happens when the earth rotates, and the sun is on the other side of the world."

"You're such a smarty pants."

"That's my job, Valerie. You were a smarty pants to Didi, and she was a smarty pants to Priscilla. You said you wanted us to be real sisters. Well, you got it, sister. I think that fork in the road will be coming up soon. You'll need to stay left."

"Got it."

"Val, look at some of these houses, they're pretty old."

"Jenny, these houses look familiar. I came here once with Dad."

"Do you remember that, Valerie? He brought you out here to get Trixie from Mr. Gonzales. We're going to see Mr. Gonzales."

"We are? Why? Is he still alive?"

"Not for very long, Val. He's dying. He needs someone, so, he won't be alone when he dies."

"Oh, Jenny, I'm sorry."

"Don't be sorry. It's his time. He wants to go, he misses his family. Even so, he still needs someone to be with him. We can't let him die alone. Dad wants us to be there for his friend."

Valerie turned into the familiar driveway that was still unpaved. She wasn't at all concerned about her shoes getting dirty in the dried mud puddles that covered the ground. In the twilight, she could see a large pecan tree in the yard between the driveway and the house. This was the twig that her father planted for his friend in the summer of 1972. She couldn't imagine how old Mr. Gonzales would look; he looked ancient when she met him that day her father surprised her with Trixie.

As Valerie walked with Jenny towards the front door, she felt the calmness, but anticipated the storm; that storm being her own fear of the unknown. She certainly had never spent any time with anyone who was on their deathbed. In spite of her uneasiness, she didn't take this mission lightly. She sensed it was a great responsibility that she needed to fulfill for Mr. Gonzales, her father, and herself.

When they reached the front door, they discovered it was locked. Valerie walked around the house, checking for open windows, while Jenny looked around the porch, hoping to find a spare key. Through a window, Valerie saw Mr. Gonzales lying on the living room floor. He was lying on his side, skewed across the floor, with his feet next to the couch; seemingly as if he had fallen after standing up from a sitting position. Seeing him on the floor, not knowing if he was dead or alive, sparked an adrenaline rush surging through her body. She ran to the back of the house, hoping to find the back door unlocked. Jenny immediately followed.

After an unsuccessful attempt at prying open the back door with a crowbar she found lying on the ground, Valerie used it to smash through a window. She broke enough glass to allow her to squeeze through, but some glass was stuck in the frame, exposing jagged edges. Being extra careful not to touch any part of the broken glass with her body as she crawled through, somehow, a piece of the jagged edge managed to work its way into her inner thigh, resulting in a gash. When she stepped into the house, she opened the back door for Jenny, leaving a sporadic blood trail from the window to the door.

Together, the sisters ran to Mr. Gonzales to determine if he was alive. His eyes were open, but they were heavy; he seemed to be cognizant. The girls tried to lift him up off the floor, but his body was weak. He did not have the strength to raise himself up.

"Valerie! You're bleeding!" Jenny exclaimed.

"I'll be alright. Let's turn him over on his back."

Valerie and Jenny got down on the floor next to him, and flipped his body over to his back. Valerie stayed on the floor with him, and held his hand, while Jenny searched his house; looking for a pillow to place under his head, to make him comfortable.

"Look for the telephone too, Jenny. Call 9-1-1," Valerie yelled out.

"Young lady, ya cain't call the ambelince. I ain't got no phone. I ain't got one in years. I ain't got nobudy ta call so I told 'em people at the phone compnee ta come an pick her up. I ain't got no need fer a phone."

"Mr. Gonzales, how can I call for help? I'll have to drive away to get help, but I don't want to leave you."

"Naw, ya ain't gotta do that. It almost time fer me ta go. I sur do thank ya. It mighty kind of ya ta stop by an help a old man. How'd ya know I needed ya?"

"Here are some pillows for Mr. Gonzales. And here's something for your leg, Valerie. Did a piece of glass get stuck in your leg?"

"No, Jenny. I just got cut."

"Okay, that's good. I need to apply pressure, and tie this tightly, around your leg."

"I'm alright, Jenny."

"Valerie, don't argue with me."

"Okay."

"Then I'm going to make Mr. Gonzales comfortable with these pillows."

"Annie Negron! Boy, that a good sign. Now I know fer sur I'm goin' ta heaven. The good Lord sent me my own personal angel, straight from heaven ta take me home. Praise the Lord! How's Frankie my boy doin? I sur do miss him."

"Mr. Gonzales," said Valerie. "This isn't Anna."

"What's that?" asked Mr. Gonzales.

"Nothing, Max," said Jenny. "She didn't say anything. Frank is fine. He's waiting for you to join him."

"That mighty nice. Annie, ya look so young an purdy. Like ya always do."

"Thank you, Max," said Jenny.

"How ya girls? Ya got one, she a lawyer. She always been real smart. An ya got that one, she always been real purdy, she always got a lot fellers fightin' o'er her. My boys used ta say that they was gonna win her hand someday. But they never come back from fightin' in the war."

"I know, Max," Jenny said. "I'm sorry that happened."

"Ya had another girl, no, two of 'em. I give one girl a puppy, long time ago. She was the sweetest, little girl, just sweet as can be. She was so happy I give her that puppy."

"Max, that was Valerie. She's right here."

"Mr. Gonzales, I'm Valerie. I'm here. I'll stay with you. See, I have your hand, and I'm not letting go."

"Yur Valrie? Ya all grown up."

"Yes, sir."

"Yur as purdy as yur mama. Ain't that right, Annie?"

"Yes, Max. Valerie is very pretty."

"Annie, ya got one more young un. The lil' girl, she got a handicap. I 'member Frankie brung her over few times. She sur was a cute lil' thing, she was same like my granddaughter. Ya know, she got the same handicap."

"I didn't know it at the time, Max, I realized it later. I wish the girls had a chance to play together."

"Annie, I wanna thank ya, fer lettin' Frankie help me all 'em years, ya know, wit the money."

"What do you mean?" asked Jenny.

"Ya know, the nuity. E'ry month the check come in the mail."

"Oh, right. The annuity. Frank loved you, Max."

"Ya tell Jimmy an Danny not ta visit no more, K?"

"Don't worry, we'll let them know."

"This house ain't much. I done already sold the land, all but this lot the house sits on. I'm gonna give it ta my son-in-law. I done already make my will. He gonna git the money that left over from when I done sold this land too. He deserve it. He always been good ta me, even after my Annette passed on. He always take care a me, real good. He sure a good man. I sure do love him, just like he was my own boy. Now he got himself a new wife, so guess he ain't my son-in-law no more. I ain't met her, but I reckon she real purdy. He still comes ta see me, an take care a me, best he can. He come by this mornin' ta see me. He sur did. He say he want me ta move wit him an his new wife, but I ain't gonna do that. It ain't right. I ain't gonna be a burden ta him an his wife. Its better if I go live in heaven. Its time fer me ta go, anyway. Hey, Annie? How can ya be here wit me? Ya done already go ta heaven wit Frankie, ain't that right?"

"Yes, Max. Valerie and I just came to comfort you until the angels come."

"I'm ready ta see Norma. Ya 'member my wife, Norma?"

"Yes, I do," said Jenny. "She was always good to us."

"I been missing her fer lotta years. Miss my boys an my girl, an my Hannah too."

"Valerie, I think they're here." said Jenny.

"Who's here?"

"The angels. I think they're here for Max, to take him."

"Jenny, where are they? I don't see anything."

"I can't see them either, but I feel their presence. Look at Max's face. He looks very serene. He's looking at something towards the ceiling."

"They're beautiful."

"Who is beautiful, Max?" Jenny asked.

"They're going to take me now. I'll be face to face with the Lord in a few minutes. I can't wait to meet Him."

"Mr. Gonzales, don't go. Let me take you to the hospital," Valerie cried.

"It's alright, Val. There is nothing you or anyone can do. It's his time. The angels are doing the job they came here to do. They're going to take him. Remember, we talked about that?"

"I know we did, Jenny. But I feel like I should do something."

"There's nothing that you can do, Valerie, it's his time."

"I feel helpless."

"He's gone, Valerie."

"Mr. Gonzales," Valerie cried, "thank you for giving me Trixie, my puppy. I'm sorry if I was rude that day. I was a dumb kid. I'm sorry for not coming to visit you when I said that I would. I'm so sorry."

Valerie buried her face in one of the extra pillows that Jenny brought from the bedroom, and continued to cry.

"It's alright, Valerie. He didn't realize that you were a little rude that day. He found you to be a sweet girl. Every time he saw Mom, he told her how sweet you were to him. He didn't really expect you to visit. His daughter was still living at that time, she was good to her father. She spent time with him. Even after she got married, she and her husband were very much involved in his life. Valerie, are you alright? We'll have to go now. You'll have to call the authorities."

"I'll be alright."

Valerie and Jenny said goodbye, one last time, to Mr. Gonzales. They walked out the front door, leaving it ajar so that when the paramedics arrived, they could get inside the house easily.

"Now what, Jenny?"

"I guess it's time to say goodbye. Let's sit for a few minutes. Come on, let's sit on the car. I've always wanted to do that."

"You've wanted to sit on the car?"

"Yeah, it looked like fun whenever Didi did it. Of course, she did it so boys would notice her."

Assisting each other, the girls hopped on the trunk of the car. Although she was not very comfortable, Valerie didn't mind sitting there. She knew her time with Jenny would soon be over, so she wanted to enjoy whatever time remained. Sitting on the cool steel of the car, they were surrounded by the blackness of the sky. There were a few stars which shone down, but not enough to produce sufficient light. Headlight beams of a passing car whisked by, casting a short-term illumination, which Valerie used to her advantage; to look at the face of her sister for the last time.

"How is your leg, Val?"

"It's really not as bad as it looks. I'll be alright."

"Yeah, you'll be alright."

"Jenny, I'm glad that I was here for Mr. Gonzales. I can't imagine how lonely it would be to die alone. I think about Mom and Dad; I'm glad that they went together, and were not alone. They had each other."

"No, they weren't alone, Valerie. You don't know the details of what happened that night. Didi has never told anyone."

"Didi? What does she know about it?"

"She was there, Valerie."

"What? How do you know?"

"How do I know anything, Valerie?"

"Mom and Dad?"

"Yes. It's really not my story to tell, but I'll tell you anyway, because I don't want you to ask Didi about it. It's still traumatic for her."

"Okay."

"That night, after Mom and Dad left to look for Didi; they found her at a hospital as she was leaving. They had a good talk, Dad and Didi made up, like they always did. Didi followed them home, driving her own car. But as you know, they didn't make it. Out of nowhere, a herd of deer crossed the road. Dad was driving about 55 or 60 miles per hour. He had a lead foot. He always did, remember?"

"Yeah, I remember."

"He swerved to avoid hitting the deer, but there were too many. He lost control of the vehicle. Somehow the truck went airborne, and ended up hitting a tree. Mom was ejected. She went through the windshield. She had fallen asleep on the ride home, so she never knew what happened. One minute she was sleeping in the truck, the next minute she woke up in heaven. Dad lived about forty minutes longer than Mom. His legs were severed from his torso."

"No," Valerie cried, quietly.

"Yes! Valerie! That is how it happened! Remember, Didi was following them, she saw when Dad lost control of the vehicle, and when it flipped upside-down. She ran over to them, and along the way, she fell down.

Valerie, she landed on top of Mom. I won't tell you what condition Mom was in."

"I can handle it."

"No! You can't! And neither could Didi. After she was able to pick herself up from the ground, she had to leave Mom's side to find Dad. She hoped, against all odds, that Dad would survive. She held his bloody body in her arms until he died."

"I never knew."

"No one knew. Didi never told anyone. She's kept this to herself all these years. Can you finally understand the horrific trauma that Didi has experienced? That's not easy to get over. You didn't have to know these details to open your heart, and know that your sister was having a hard time."

"I'm sorry," Valerie tearfully said.

"Don't tell me. I'm not the one that you've been mean and nasty to."

"I know. I've treated Didi horribly, for such a long time. Thank you for telling me about how Mom and Dad died, Jenny. All these years, I've blamed her for their death, when actually, she played such an important role. Just as I did tonight, for Mr. Gonzales."

"That's true, Valerie."

"Thank you for sharing that with me, and thank you for these past few days. I'm a different person because of you. I've learned so much from you, Jenny."

"Have you? I didn't do anything. Whatever you've learned, it wasn't from me. I might have helped you a little, but those lessons that you've learned have always been within yourself."

"Maybe that's true. A week ago, I had so much bitterness. It's gone now."

"I'm glad it's gone. After I leave, I know that you and Didi will be better, right?"

"Yes, we will. I'm going to miss you, Jenny. I mean, I miss my other Jenny. But it's still hard to let you go."

"I know, Val. I didn't think that it would be this hard for me to leave, either. I didn't expect to see the whole family, but I'm glad that I did."

"So much has happened, Jenny. It was a privilege for me to be with Mr. Gonzales during his last moments. I'm glad that I was able to be here, and that he wasn't alone when he died. And I can't believe I'm going to say this, but I'm glad that Didi had the car accident."

"Why is that, Val?"

"It took that car accident to happen in order for me to see the error of my ways. Now I'm forced to look at my shortcomings. I have to look at my life, and everything in my life, differently. I would have never known that Didi saved my life, twice. Or that I needed to quit blaming her for what happened to Mom and Dad. I would have never known you, the way you are now. It's funny how things can change in a moment. Jenny, now when I look into a mirror, I'm not only going to see my reflection, I'm going to see the reflections of my life. I'm going to see Patrick and the kids. Mom and Dad, Priscilla, Michael, and Didi; they'll be staring back at me, because not only are they a part of my life, they're a part of me. Jenny, you will also be staring back at me. The way you are now, this new Jenny, and my Jenny that I've taken care of since you were three years old. Also, Jenny, the baby. The baby who used to frustrate me because you couldn't learn to walk or talk as fast as other babies who were the same age. The baby that I was jealous of, because you required so much attention from Mom and Dad. I was the baby, then you stole the attention that Mom and Dad used to give me. Jenny, maybe that's why I was frustrated with you, maybe that's why I had a little resentment towards you. Not because you were imperfect, because I now realize that you've always been perfect, but because I was jealous. When Mom and Dad died, I wasn't jealous any more. When I started raising you, I never had any frustrations with you. All these years, not one frustration. You have never given me one single disappointment. Not one."

"Oh really? Then why did you yell at me when I put the hamburger meat in the pantry? Huh, Valerie?"

"I'm sorry, Jenny. I love you."

"I love you too, Valerie. Don't ever forget that. And don't assume that I don't understand or know what's going on when you're talking to me, or when we're just hanging out with family. No, I don't always understand everything, but sometimes I do. Like that day at school when those ladies came by, and you got mad at them. The only thing that I really understood was that you were fighting for me. I didn't understand exactly what it was about; but I knew it was because you were willing, as you always are, to do anything for me."

"Yes, Jenny. I would do anything for you."

"I know that. Thank you, Valerie. And thank Didi for me too. That was a pretty dress she bought me for my graduation party."

"The dress with the flowers? Didi bought that for you?"

"Yes, she did. I know that you thought Priscilla bought it for me, but she didn't. Delores bought it for me. Delores has bought me lots of things over the years. You've always assumed it was Priscilla who splurged on me, and sometimes it was; but sometimes it was my sister, Delores."

"I never knew that."

"No, you didn't. But now you do."

"Thanks for telling me, Jenny."

"You're welcome. Oh, and I'd like to apologize to you about something. Those times that we went grocery shopping; I'm sorry that I used to ram the shopping cart into you. I was just having fun. I know that's why you won't let me push the shopping cart anymore. If I promise to never do it again, will you trust me with the cart?"

"I don't know, Jenny. We'll see."

"Okay, Val. That's fair."

"Jenny..."

"Valerie, you have to go now."

"Are you sure?"

"Yeah, I'm sure. It's time."

"Jenny, I can't leave you here alone. You're afraid of the dark, remember?"

"Not anymore. Well, I'm not afraid right now. Valerie, I hope this was everything that you wanted it to be; that I lived up to your expectations as a little sister."

"Jenny, you've exceeded my expectations. Did I live up to yours?"

"You always have, Valerie. Oh, I almost forgot to tell you something; take the ballerina with you when you go to the hospital. You'll meet Hannah's dad there."

"Oh, Hannah's dad? How will I know who he is or where to meet him?"

"You'll know, Valerie. Just keep the ballerina with you, don't put it in your purse or in a bag. Carry it around with you in your hand. Hannah's dad will see it, and he'll approach you. And one more thing, I wrote you a letter. The first night I was here, I didn't know how much time we would have together; I wrote it then, after you left me in the garden. A couple of the women who made complimentary remarks about Patrick, were nice enough to give me some stationery. That's how I was able to write the letter."

"Where is it, Jenny?"

"When we were at home this afternoon, I went upstairs to wash my hands, and I went into your bedroom. I put it in Dad's Bible. But don't read it yet, wait a little bit. Let our lives get back to normal, maybe in a few months. You'll be pretty busy nursing me back to health, and then the baby will be here before you know it. Maybe sometime after that, if you're not too busy, and you happen to think about this time that we had together, then you can read the letter."

"Alright, Jenny. I'll do that."

"You'd better go now, Valerie. I love you."

"I love you, Jenny. Are you sure that I should leave you here?"

"Yes, Valerie. That's what you're supposed to do."

"Okay, can I hug you one last time this way? Then I'm going to hug you as my other Jenny, every single day, forever."

"Yes, Valerie. Goodbye."

"Goodbye, Jenny."

CHAPTER TWENTY-SEVEN

Traces Of Love

Before heading home, Valerie stopped at a convenience store to use a payphone, so she could inform the authorities about Max. She dug through her purse, searching for loose change to make the phone call. She dropped the coins into the coin slot of the payphone, and dialed 9-1-1. She gave the operator the needed information regarding Max, and was assured that someone would be on the way promptly. Hanging up the receiver, she was quite surprised to get her money back from her phone call; she forgot that emergency calls were free.

Patrick was backing his car out of the driveway, just as Valerie drove up. He hollered at her through his car window, telling her to park her car and join him.

"Are you on your way to the hospital, Patrick? I'd like to see the kids before I leave again."

"There's no time, Val. You have two sisters that are asking for you. Where have you been? Did Jenna get off alright?"

"Did you say I have two sisters that are asking for me?"

"Jenny's awake! She's asking for us. Come on, Valerie. Get in, I'll bring you up to speed."

"Wait, Patrick. Let me just run inside for a minute."

"Be fast."

"I will."

Valerie dashed into the house, up the stairs, then into her bedroom. She snatched up a small shopping bag which was on the floor next to her bed. Inside the bag, was the ballerina music box. Then she opened the wooden chest that sat on the floor, at the foot of the bed. She removed several items before finding a satchel.

"I'll pick this mess up later," she said to herself, knowing that she wouldn't. After a few hugs and kisses to the kids, she went back outside to join Patrick, who had grown impatient, and was blasting the horn on his Mustang. Instantly, he became alarmed when he noticed Valerie's blood-soaked blue jeans.

"Valerie! What happened? Are you alright?"

"I'm fine, don't worry. It's not as bad as it looks. It's a long story, I'll tell you later. Let's go see my sisters."

Steering the car with his left hand, freed Patrick's right hand; allowing him to take Valerie's hand into his own, and give it a tight squeeze. Valerie, cherishing the moment of closeness with her husband, basked in the exhilarating sensations emitted from Patrick's touch. With the exception of her erotica performance at the hospital, the daily exchanges of affection between her and Patrick, seemed to have been so far in the past.

When Valerie and Patrick arrived at the hospital, they went in to see Jenny first. As soon as they walked through the door, Jenny exclaimed,

"Pak, Pak!"

Patrick ran to her side.

"Jenny! I've missed you too."

"What about me, Jenny?" asked Valerie.

"Val!"

"Valerie," said Patrick, "I don't think I've ever heard Jenny say your name before."

"No, she hasn't. She's always called me Ree. She's never been able to say the V, the vuh sound. That's why she's always skipped the first part of my name."

"Jenny, can you say Valerie's name again? Say her name again, honey."

"Val," Jenny said, as she pointed to Valerie. Then she pointed to Patrick. "Pak."

"Jenny, you're my smart girl," said Patrick.

"Yeah, true," said Jenny.

"Aunt Valerie, Uncle Patrick, my mom is asking for you," Kevin said, as he entered the room. "I'll visit with Aunt Jenny while you visit with my mom."

"Kev!"

"Hi, Aunt Jenny! I've missed you."

"She's missed you too, Kevin," said Valerie.

"Aunt Valerie, what happened to your leg?"

"It's a long story, Kevin. I'll tell you later, but I'm alright. Would you two mind giving me a few minutes alone with Jenny?"

"Sure, Val. We'll be out in the hall. Bye, Jenny. I'll see you later," said Patrick.

"Bye bye, Pak."

"Jenny," said Valerie, "how are you? I'm glad that you're going to be alright. Do you remember what's happened these last few days? Do you remember that we went to DeMarco's, and ate pizza with the family? Do you remember that we went to the park? Do you remember seeing Mr. Gonzales? Do you remember that you found my ring? Do you remember this ring?"

Valerie showed Jenny the ring on her finger. Jenny looked at the ring, and touched it. Valerie removed it from her finger, and gave it to Jenny so that she could thoroughly examine it. Her examination resulted in a huge, bright grin. Jenny returned the ring to Valerie by slipping it on her finger. Seeing the look on Jenny's face, Valerie came to a conclusion.

"I think that you do remember, Jenny. I'm going to help you get better, then you're going to help me when the baby comes. I know that you want me to see Didi, so I'm going to see her now. I'll see you soon."

"Bye bye, Val."

"See you later, Jenny. Sleep tight, my sweet girl."

Valerie and Patrick stood outside the door to Delores' room. She was nervous, so she held Patrick's hand tightly. She took a deep breath as Patrick reached for the door to open it. Someone on the other side pulled it open, and abruptly exited the room, bumping into Valerie and Patrick.

"Oops, I'm so sorry. I didn't know you were there. Delores sent me to look for you, Valerie. Are you alright?" asked Bill.

"We're okay," said Patrick.

"I'm fine, Bill. Thank you. How is Didi?"

"She's going to be fine. She can't wait to see you."

"Let's go in," Valerie said. She linked her arm with Bill's, and he ushered her into the room.

"Hey, Dipwad. Thanks for coming by, I've been wanting to see you. What happened to leg? Are you alright?"

"Hi, Didi. It's a long story, I'm alright. I'll tell you about it later. How are you? You look beautiful. How is it possible for you to look so beautiful after everything that you've been through?"

"I guess I'm just a natural beauty."

"Yeah, you are," Valerie said.

She walked to her sister's side, and stooped down to give her a long, tight hug.

"I'm sorry that I took Jenny without asking you."

"No, Didi, don't be sorry. You had every right to take her, she's your baby sister too. I'm sorry that I've been so mean. And I'm sorry that I blamed you for what happened to Mom and Dad. All these years, Didi, I've blamed you. It wasn't your fault. I know that now. I've been taking my anger out on you. I was also angry because you divorced Jeff. I was a kid when he came into my life. I didn't want you to take him away from me."

"Valerie, it was wrong how Jeff and I started our relationship. I've always felt guilty about that; about what I did to Jennifer. That's why we couldn't make it, I never trusted him. If he cheated on Jennifer, I thought he would cheat on me too. You can't build a relationship if there's no trust. Yeah, I know that I cheated on him. It was wrong for me to do that. It was wrong for Jeff and me to start a relationship when he was already involved with someone else. And not just anyone, but my best friend. It was wrong."

"Didi, did Jeff cheat on you?"

"That's not important. We have a better relationship now than when we were married. He loves you, Valerie, and he will always be there for you; but Bill is my husband now. He's a good man, Val. And I'm a better person because of him."

"Bill, I'm sorry. I've never given you a chance. Please forgive me."

"You and Didi have had your issues. But we can move on. I hope this means that you will let us take Jenny sometime. Jenny and me, we get along great. She's a treasure to me."

"Valerie, Bill is really good with Jenny," said Delores.

"I trust you, Bill. Didi loves and trusts you. Patrick trusts you, and I trust you too."

"Valerie," said Delores, "I've missed you so much over the years. We've had our moments when we got close, then something always seemed to rip us apart."

"I've missed you too, Didi. There's something that I have to apologize for; my wedding. You came to see me get married, and I told you to leave. I'm sorry for that."

"Valerie, I was there. I saw you get married."

"I know, Susan told me. But you shouldn't have had to sneak in. I should have let you stay when you came in to see me. I should have asked you to stand up for me, like I asked Priscilla. I'm sorry, Didi."

"Don't apologize. I wasn't exactly there for you the way I should have been. We were both hurting over Mom and Dad. But I did get to see you get married. You looked so beautiful in that dress you wore."

"As beautiful as you are?"

"Pretty close, Valerie."

"Just pretty close?"

"Maybe for that one day, your beauty surpassed mine."

"I'll accept that," said Valerie. "Just for that one day."

"I also went to your graduations, Valerie; high school and college. I'm very proud of you."

"Really? I didn't know that. Well, I think you owe me some gifts; a wedding, and two graduations gifts."

"Well, you owe me a get well soon gift. What's in the shopping bag? Is that for me? What do you have in the satchel? Is that for me too?"

"Oh, you wouldn't want this. It's a ballerina music box. I found it at a thrift store."

"Let me see it."

Valerie took the ballerina music box out of the shopping bag, and held it up for Delores to see.

"Can I see it, please?" asked Bill.

"Sure," Valerie said.

"Where did you get this?"

"At a thrift store, downtown."

Bill's eyes welled with tears as he stared at the ballerina music box that he held in his hands. Turning it over, he carefully examined the small statue. "H," he whispered. He wiped the tears from his eyes before repeating himself in a louder tone as he pointed to the letter H, which was written on the bottom of the music box, with a permanent marker.

"Look at this H, do you know who wrote that H?"

"Looks like a child wrote it," Valerie said.

"Yes, a child wrote it. My child. My wife got this for her birthday from her parents when she was eight years old. Her mother died after she graduated from high school, so this became very special to her. One day, Hannah saw it sitting on the dresser, she liked it so much that my wife gave it to her."

"Did you say, Hannah?" asked Valerie.

"Yes, Hannah was my daughter."

"Is your last name Parker?"

"Valerie," Delores said, "My last name is also, Parker. I would think that you should know that by now. Bill's first wife and daughter, Hannah, were killed in a car accident when they were on vacation in Arizona."

"In 1983?" asked Valerie.

"How did you know that?" Bill asked.

"I must have read it in the newspaper, or maybe heard it on TV, on the news."

"I wonder how this ballerina found its way to a thrift store?" Patrick asked.

"My sister, she meant well. She thought it was time to get rid of stuff at the house before Didi moved in. She wanted Didi to feel comfortable in her new home, and not have my deceased wife's belongings around. She felt terrible when she realized that she got rid of some of Hannah's things too. Hannah loved this very much, so did my wife. Do you mind if I keep it? How much did you pay for it? I'll give you the money. I'd like to have it. It's sentimental to me."

"It's yours. You keep it, Bill. You don't owe me anything for it. It belongs to you."

"Thank you, Valerie."

"You're welcome. Can I ask you something about Hannah?"

"Sure, what is it?"

"Did she have Down syndrome?"

"Yes, she did. How did you know that? Was that in the news story?" asked Bill.

"It must have been. Is that why you've taken such a liking to Jenny? Does she remind you of Hannah?"

"I miss Hannah. And I always will, every single day, until the day that I die. She will always be my baby girl. Jenny is not Hannah. Jenny is my wife's baby sister; and so are you. I can never take Jeff's place in Didi's heart, nor in yours. And I wouldn't want to, either. Just like Didi can't replace my first wife."

"Valerie, you can't replace people that you love. They'll stay in your heart forever. But it's alright to love new people, and there's plenty of room in your heart for them too," said Delores.

"Jeff is an alright guy, you know? Me and him are pretty good friends, now."

"Bill, I'm sorry for how I've acted towards you."

"I don't want you to be sorry, Valerie. I want you to be nice to my wife."

"That's a great idea. How about being nice to me too?" Michael said, lightheartedly, as he and Priscilla entered the room.

"Valerie, what happened to your leg?" Priscilla asked.

"It's a long story, I'll tell you later. I'm alright. It's really not that bad."

"I'm glad it's not serious, Dollface."

"Valerie, that's a beautiful ring. Did you buy that for her, Patrick?" Delores asked

"Yeah, Didi, I did. I got it a long time ago, but never had the chance to give it to her. Bill found his miracle, and we've found ours. It's a crazy story; on the night of our senior prom, I wanted to ask Valerie to marry me. I even got down on one knee, but before I could take the ring out of the box to pop the question, she swiped it out of my hand, and it fell to the ground. It's been lost since then."

"Patrick dropped it, and it got lost," said Valerie.

"Anyway," Patrick continued, "after Valerie lost it, we looked for it, for several weeks. We were never able to find it."

"Now you've found it after all these years?" asked Delores.

"They didn't find it," Priscilla said. "Jenna found it. Remember the girl that I told you about earlier this evening?"

"The girl that looks like Mom? I wish I could have met her."

"You would have loved her, Didi," Priscilla remarked with delight. "There was something about her, something familiar, and special. I can't explain it, but I wish you would have met her."

"Valerie, will Jenna ever come visit again? I'd like to meet her," Delores asked.

"I don't know, Didi. I don't think so."

"Ugh. I wish I hadn't had this car accident. Then I would have had the chance to meet her too."

"Oh no, Didi," Valerie said, "you had to have had the car accident. If you didn't, then there was no way that Jenny, I mean Jenna, could have come. She was able to come only because of the car accident."

"What?" asked Delores.

"What do you mean, Valerie?" asked Priscilla.

"Oh nothing. I don't know what I'm saying. I'm talking crazy, I'm not myself right now."

"Oh, Valerie, not another erotic dance," said Priscilla.

"It wasn't a dance!" Valerie declared.

"But it was erotic," said Patrick.

"What's this about an erotic dance?" asked Delores. "What have I missed?"

"You haven't missed anything, Didi. Don't listen to Priscilla. But there is something else that I wanted to say to you."

"What is it?" asked Delores.

"Do you want us to leave the room?" asked Priscilla.

"No, please stay. Everyone can stay."

"Bill, your pager is ringing. It could be your father-in-law, you'd better call him," said Delores.

"I'll use the phone in the waiting room, honey."

"Please tell him I said hello, and I hope to meet him soon."

"His father-in-law?" asked Valerie.

"His first wife's father. I haven't met him yet. He's been having a hard time accepting the fact that Bill remarried. We understand his feelings. Bill is all he has left since his daughter died. Bill finally made him understand that they will always be family, but now, I'm part of the family too. Just because we're married, it doesn't change anything. Bill goes over to check on him every day. On the morning of the accident, he told Bill that he was ready to meet me. That's where I was going with Jenny, to meet Bill at his father-in-law's house. We had the accident on the way over."

"I'm sorry about that, Didi," Valerie said. "I hope you get to meet him soon."

"I will. We're planning to have him move in with us. Bill says he shouldn't be living alone anymore, and I agree."

Bill walked back into the room; his face was grieved, and his hands were shaking.

"He's gone, Delores. Max is dead. He had a heart attack earlier this evening. He's gone. I wish I had been there."

"No, honey, I'm sorry. I know how much you loved him. I'm sorry that I didn't get a chance to meet him. I wish you had been there too, Bill. I am terribly sorry. I'm glad you had the chance to see him this morning."

"This morning? Is that where you went to when you left the hospital this morning?" Valerie asked.

"Yes, I went to see Max, not knowing it would be the last time I would ever see him. He seemed fine. He was looking forward to meeting you, Delores. He wanted to come to the hospital to see you, but I felt that would be too hard on him. I told him to rest up, and he could meet you another time."

"Who called you, honey? How did you find out?"

"That was a deputy. They found the laminated card that I gave to Max to carry in his wallet. It had my name, and pager number on it. I wrote instructions for whoever finds the card in an emergency, to page me."

"I wish that he hadn't been alone when he died. Who found him?" asked Delores.

"He wasn't alone. I don't know who was with him, but he wasn't alone. The deputy said that a very kind lady stopped by, and stayed with him during his final moments. Then she called the authorities to let them know what happened."

"Bill, he had a guardian angel," Priscilla said.

"Bill, do you mean, Mr. Gonzales?" asked Valerie.

"Yes, Max Gonzales, my father-in-law. How do you know?"

"Because I was there. I was with him when he passed on."

"What? How do you know him? Why were you there?" asked Bill.

"Mr. Gonzales had been Dad's friend for years. He's the man who gave me Trixie when she was a puppy."

"So, what made you go see him tonight, Val?" asked Patrick.

"Dad."

"Dad?" asked Priscilla.

"I had Dad on my mind, and I remembered how much he cared for Mr. Gonzales. I thought I'd drive by, just to say hello, and see how he was doing. He didn't answer the door when I knocked, so I went to the window to peek in, and I saw him on the floor."

"Valerie, then what happened?" asked Priscilla.

"The front door was locked, so I went around to the back of the house to see if the back door was unlocked, but it was locked too. Then I looked around for something to try to break the door open. I found a crowbar, and I tried to pry it open, but I couldn't. I kept trying, but I just couldn't do it. That's when I used the crowbar to smash the window. I thought I was careful when I crawled through, but that's how I cut my leg."

"Valerie, you could have been seriously hurt." said Patrick.

"You did that for Max?" Bill asked.

"I didn't know him as Max. I knew him as Mr. Gonzales, the man who gave me my puppy, Trixie, when I was fourteen years old."

"Thank you for being there for him. Was he already gone when you got inside the house?" asked Bill.

"No, he was barely hanging on. I tried to get him up off the floor, but I wasn't able to. He didn't have a telephone so I couldn't call for an ambulance. I told him that I wanted to go for help, but he didn't want me to leave him, so I didn't. He said it was his time. I'm sorry, Bill. I should have left to get help."

"No, it was his time. I'm glad you stayed with him so he wasn't alone when he died. Did he have any last words?"

"He did. He said he was ready to go. He wanted to see his wife, and his boys, and his girl, and granddaughter."

"He had two sons that died in Vietnam. I've never met them. His girl was Annette, my wife. And you know Hannah was our daughter."

"Bill, he also said that he loved you. He didn't mention you by name, he referred to you as his son-in-law. He said he loved you like you were his own, and that you've always been good to him."

"Did he say anything else?"

"He got quiet. He had this serene look on his face, and he was looking up, towards the ceiling. He was looking at something, but I don't know what. I didn't see anything. Then he said, 'They're beautiful.' I asked him, 'Who is beautiful?' He didn't answer me, he may not have heard me, because he didn't even acknowledge my question. Then he said that they were going to take him, and in a few minutes, he would be face to face with the Lord. He couldn't wait to meet Him, Bill."

Bill's heart grew heavy, and he was obviously overcome with sorrow as he wept openly. He thanked Valerie for her virtuous act of compassion, then he left the room.

"Valerie, I can't believe you did that. You're very brave, I wish I had been there with you," said Priscilla.

"I'm not brave, Didi is the one who's brave. Didi, I want to tell you something. I want you to know that I see you differently now."

"How so?" asked Delores.

"Well, I found out some things about you that I had never known before. I found out that you saved my life, at least twice. Thank you for doing that. Tonight, I was with Mr. Gonzales when he died. That's not easy to be with someone when they take their last breath. I imagine it's even more difficult if it's someone you love, am I right?"

"What are you talking about, Valerie?"

"I think you know what I'm talking about, Didi."

Delores, a bit shaken up, wept quietly.

"No, Valerie. There's no way that you could know. I've never told a soul."

"What's going on, Valerie?" Priscilla asked.

"I know something about the night that Mom and Dad died."

"There's no way that you could know anything, Valerie. There's no way. It's not possible," Delores cried.

"What's not possible?" asked Priscilla. "Will someone please tell me what is going on?"

"Didi has gone through a lot since Mom and Dad died. I realize that now. Didi, I'm sorry that it's taken me this long to realize everything that you've gone through, and everything that you have done for me. But now I know. I honestly do. I know everything. And I want to thank you for being there for me. You've always been there for me. When I think about all that you've done for me when I was a little girl, and things that you've done for me during these years that I've treated you so badly, I now see how much you love me. What makes me sad is that I didn't return that love. I'll always hate myself for that."

"Don't hate yourself, Valerie. During those times that you say that you treated me badly, you still loved me. I know you did."

"I didn't show it, Didi. I didn't even see it, myself."

"I saw it, Val. You may not have shown me that you loved me, or you may not have seen it yourself, but the love was there. I saw it, I saw traces of it. Hidden behind your harsh words, were traces of love."

"Thank you for seeing it, Didi."

"Dollface, is that the satchel I gave you when you started high school? Don't tell me you haven't turned in your homework. It's a little late for that now."

"Yes, Michael, this is the satchel you gave me. I brought it because I have something for Didi. Here, it's all yours."

"What's in it?"

"Open it and find out."

Delores took the satchel from Valerie, and without hesitation, she opened it. She removed bundle after bundle of letters tied together with ribbons, which, at one time, were a bright, vibrant shade of purple. The years had faded the brilliant sharp tone, leaving the ribbons with a slight lavender tinge.

"Are these what I think they are?" asked Delores.

"If you think they are dirty limericks written by one, Mr. Francis Robert Negron, then you would be correct."

"Valerie, where did you get these?"

"Mom gave them to me, they were in the shoebox she had for me, filled with things she wanted me to have for my wedding. But these letters, she wanted you to have them. So here you are, Didi. They're yours. I'm sorry that I took so long to give them to you."

"Thank you, Valerie. I'm going to read each and every one. Because between the dirty limericks, and the erotica that our father expressed to our mother on a daily basis, are his sweet words that reveal an undying love between a husband and his wife. I will cherish these letters forever," Delores said.

"I've wanted to read them myself, but I've been afraid to. Knowing Dad, I'll bet his words are a little X-rated. But also, knowing Dad, I'll bet his words are sweet. I'm very curious, are the letters X-rated or sweet? Please let me know, Didi. I'm dying to know."

"You're not dying, Dipwad. But I'll tell you about it after I read them."

"Dollface, you're always so dramatic."

"Dad used to say that about you too, Val. All the time," Delores said.

"Valerie, it's time that we all let go of the past, and move on. Mom and Dad would want that," Priscilla said.

"You're right," said Valerie. "I'm ready to move forward."

"Me too," said Delores. "Let's do it, let's do this together."

Echoing the previous statement made to her by Jenny, Valerie said, "Two sisters, two friends."

"What about me?" asked Priscilla.

"You're the glue that holds us together," said Delores.

"We can't leave out Jenny, either," Priscilla said.

"No," Delores said, "we can't leave out Jenny."

"It's the three of us, and Jenny," said Valerie. "Max said that Priscilla is the smart one, Delores is the pretty one, I am the sweet one, and Jenny is the cute one. I guess that's true of us individually. But together, we're Frank and Anna's girls."

CHAPTER TWENTY-EIGHT

The Letter

The highly anticipated birth of Valerie and Patrick's baby had finally arrived; it was a girl, just as Jenny predicted. Valerie wanted to name her Patricia, after Patrick, but he liked the name Victoria, with Valerie's middle name of Lynne.

Victoria's homecoming would mark the first official social event of her life. Patrick and Valerie arrived home with their newborn a little before noon. The house was quiet. Bobby and Matthew were staying with Jeff, while Valerie was in the hospital giving birth to Victoria. Jenny was with Delores and Bill. Since recovering from the accident, Delores had been spending a lot of time with Jenny and Valerie.

"You just relax, Val. I'll get things ready for the party. Aunt Gina and Aunt Nancy will be here soon to give me a hand."

"What about my uncles?"

"Of course, they'll be here too. Uncle Danny's got a great surprise for you. Your cousin, Mario, and his wife, are moving back to Crystal Springs. Now that they've sent their youngest off to college, they want to be closer to the family."

"Great. I can't wait to see them. I haven't seen Mario in such a long time. When I was a little girl, he played tea party with me. He also taught me how to ride a bike, and how to make a telephone with two cans and a piece of string. Will everyone else be here too?"

"Let's see, Steve is still at work, but he and my sister will be here a little later. The boys are having too much fun with their uncle Jeff and aunt Jessica right now, but they'll be over later. Priscilla and Michael left about thirty minutes ago."

"And the kids?"

"Frankie has been hanging out with Kevin at his new apartment. They'll be over later, I think they'll be bringing girlfriends with them. Lauren and Monica are still hanging out with Emily and Nicole, over at Didi's. Jenny's having a blast with her nieces."

"That's great, Patrick."

"Everybody will be here for the party, Val. Even Aunt Teresa and Uncle George are coming; they're on their way now. And guess what? I just got off the phone with Brando. He and Debra just flew in, they're in San Antonio right now. Karen and John are picking them up from the airport."

"Really? I'm so excited! Patrick, this is wonderful! It's going to be a wonderful day! I want to take a quick nap before everyone gets here. I'll take Victoria upstairs with me. Would you please make sure that I'm not bothered, for about an hour?"

"Sure, holler if you need anything."

"Thanks, Patrick."

Valerie went upstairs to their bedroom, and gently laid her sleeping, newborn daughter on her and Patrick's bed. She had no intention of resting up before everyone arrived for Victoria's homecoming party. For some time now, she had wanted to read the letter that Jenny had written to her during their time together. Jenny's instructions to Valerie were to read the letter after their lives resumed to normal. During the several months since the accident, Valerie's life had not quite returned to the routine it was before everything happened. Her life had reached a new level of normalcy, which included a renewed relationship with Delores. The bond that developed between the two sisters had far surpassed the sibling rivalry once shared during their childhood. It was a sisterhood which Valerie shared with Priscilla, and even temporarily with Jenny; now after years of turmoil, she shared such a friendship with Delores.

Jenny's letter was exactly where she said it would be; in safekeeping, between the pages of the Bible once belonging to their father. The pages were yellow and fragile, but the leather cover was still in good condition.

Frank had always taken great care of it, and so did Valerie. She gently removed Jenny's letter from between the pages. It was not in an envelope, instead it was folded into an origami rectangle, with a pull tab to open it. It reminded her of Debra and Karen, and the many notes that they wrote to each other during high school. After pulling the tab to open the letter, she began to read it.

Dear Valerie,

I'm in the garden at the hospital, looking up at the window of the room where I lie, hooked up to a machine. You're sitting next to me, holding my hand, while stroking my cheek with your other hand. I can't see your eyes, but I imagine they are filled with tears, because I feel teardrops hitting my arm.

Patrick just came into the room, he's a mess. He's distraught, not only about what's happened to me and Didi, but also about how much he's disappointed you. I wish that I could say something to him, to comfort him in some way, but I can't. I didn't come here, in this physical state that I'm now in, for Patrick; I came here for you.

I know that you love me with all of your heart and soul, and you always have. But I also know that a small part of your heart has longed to be a big sister. Not just an older sister, but a big sister. The kind of big sister that gives advice to her little sister; about boys, and make-up, and things like that. You've wanted to be the kind of big sister that a little sister could look up to; but I'm not that kind of little sister to you, so you are not able to be that kind of a big sister to me. Instead, you've been more like a mother; and a very good one too. Even Mom said that if she'd had the chance to raise me, she couldn't have done a better job at it than you.

Sometimes life isn't easy for people with disabilities. Some have to deal with struggles as part of their daily lives. They may experience ongoing situations that are difficult to manage. I know some of those people. They are beautiful, loving people; some have Down syndrome, and are friends of mine, some have other disabilities. My life, as someone with Down syndrome, has been wonderful. No, I'm not verbal, which, at times is frustrating for both of us. I wish there was a better way for us to communicate, but there's not. However, I have been very fortunate that my ailments associated with having Down syndrome, have always been under control. I'm mobile, I'm well cared for, and I'm loved. Thank you for loving me, and caring for me, for all these years. You didn't have to do it, you wanted to do it. I can't tell you how much that means to me.

I hope that you find these next few days to be an exciting adventure for us, and that it brings you the big sister fulfillment that you've long for, because I love you, Valerie. You're the best big sister that any little sister could ever hope for. This mysterious, incredible journey into the depths of your imagination is a gift, resulting from your desire for us to be real sisters, and real friends. It's a special gift; a special experience that only you and I could share. I hope that you will enjoy this gift, and are able to have fond memories of the time that we're about to have. I only wish that I could wrap it up in a box with pretty paper, and a big fluffy bow, along with a nice pretty card that would read:

To Valerie, With love, Jenny

THE END

ABOUT THE AUTHOR

Debbie Parker grew up and lives in San Antonio, Texas. She is the guardian of her younger sister, who has Down syndrome. She is a mother, grandmother of four, and a real estate broker. When she is not selling real estate or writing, you'll find her kayaking, shopping, or road tripping around Texas.

www.ingramcontent.com/pod-product-compliance
Lightning Source LLC
Chambersburg PA
CBHW030321100526
44592CB00010B/510